skinnytaste
ONE & DONE

140 NO-FUSS DINNERS

For Your **Instant Pot®**, **Slow Cooker, Air Fryer, Sheet Pan, Skillet, Dutch Oven** & More

skinnytaste®
ONE & DONE

GINA HOMOLKA
with Heather K. Jones, R.D.

CLARKSON POTTER/PUBLISHERS
NEW YORK

CONTENTS

Introduction

*B*usy doesn't even begin to cover it. From balancing a career and keeping up with kids—and their after-school activities and homework—to hitting the gym, seeing family and friends, and managing all kinds of other obligations, it's a wonder any of us has time to even *think* about dinner. On the busiest days, it's too easy to overlook it entirely! Often, my days feel like a whirlwind. And yet, it is so important to me to find time to feed my family (and myself, of course) nutritious meals that are not just healthy, but also tasty.

Efficiency is key when it comes to weeknight dinners, and nothing is more streamlined than making a whole meal, start to finish, in a single pot. I wrote *Skinnytaste One & Done* to make cooking dinner a cinch, while maximizing both the health and flavor factors of your suppers. Each of the 140 recipes in these pages depends on a single cooking vessel, and the chapters are divided accordingly: Skillet (page 20), Sheet Pan & Baking Dish (page 72), Pressure Cooker (page 120), Air Fryer (page 168), Dutch Oven (page 212), Slow Cooker (page 244), and Grill Pan & Grill (page 274). All of the dishes here are designed for dinner (but you can certainly enjoy them for lunch) and have my signature Skinnytaste touch, meaning they're deeply satisfying and delicious, yet low in calories and fat. Hearty meatloaf (see page 97), cheesy pizza (see page 209), juicy burgers (see page 71), crispy pork chops (see page 190)—yes, these are all in here! As are fresh salads, fish, lean meats, and lots of veggies. My skinny tweaks make comforting, indulgent foods fair game for anyone watching his or her eating. And every one of them has been "field tested" by my very own picky family! A winning recipe has to be approved by my young daughter, my adult daughter, *and* my husband, so you can be sure the vetting is comprehensive.

I love one-pot cooking for two big reasons: One, the cooking steps are few and simple; and two, there aren't many dishes to clean! At the end of a long workday, few people have the bandwidth or patience to work through multiple tasks to finish a recipe. The less to do, the better! Plus, as much as I *really* enjoy cooking, I absolutely hate the cleanup, especially tackling dirty pots and pans. I develop and test recipes all day, most every day, for my Skinnytaste books and blog, then cook dinner on top of that, so those dishes stack up quickly. When it comes to weeknight meals, I'm always looking for the easiest way to get dinner on the table without using everything in my kitchen cabinets and drawers. Quicker cleanup means more time for family or—get ready for this crazy idea—for yourself. The "less is more" strategy of one-pot cooking means you can still end up with fantastic dinners—such as Southwestern Beef and Black Bean Soup (page 264), Dijon-Maple Chicken with Brussels and Butternut (page 79), and Creamy Butternut Pasta with Spicy Sausage and Spinach (page 215)—with hardly any fuss at all.

There are seven types of cookware used in this book, ones that I use in my home on a nightly basis: a skillet, slow cooker, electric pressure cooker (I love my Instant Pot!), sheet pan, Dutch oven (or a big pot), grill pan or grill, and air fryer. Each has a purpose and a place in my kitchen, and I built the recipes in this book around their strengths. The skillet, sheet pan, Dutch oven, and grill need no introduction—these workhorses are probably already well loved in your own kitchen. I've long been a big fan of pressure cookers, but my adoration reached a new level with the Instant Pot; I know I'm not alone! Electric pressure cookers make quick work of tough cuts of meat and other long-cooking ingredients like dried beans, while concentrating their great flavors. Then, for nights when I know I have zero time to cook, I turn to my slow cooker: I set it up in the morning, let it cook all day, and come home to a ready-to-eat meal. And the air fryer is my new favorite toy. This mini convection oven allows me to achieve deep-fryer results with very little oil and less cooking time, too. And it's more versatile than its name implies! It can even roast meats and bake breads. With this arsenal of tools, I've developed go-to recipes for all your no-time-to-cook kind of days. I like having a reliable list of dishes that I can turn to for new ideas, too, and that was my goal with this book: to serve as both your cooking inspiration and the ultimate guide to get it all done. Check out One-Pot Cooking 101 on page 10 for a more in-depth look at how to maximize each vessel or appliance and my tips for getting the best results.

Whether you love to cook or fear stepping into the kitchen, this book is for you! No dish requires difficult technical skills, nor do any call for hard-to-find ingredients. Though many of the recipes utilize my favorite appliances—pressure cooker, slow cooker, air fryer—for a lot of those instances, I've included notes on how to cook the dish using regular cookware. For example, if you don't own an air fryer, I've provided instructions on how to bake the dish in the oven instead. The results may be slightly different, but you'll still be able to get the most

out of this book. Scattered throughout, you'll also find Skinny Scoop sidebars where I share helpful tips, from how to work with certain ingredients and favorite products I recommend to how to store any leftovers. I've also included information on the health benefits of various ingredients in Food Facts boxes, so you can up your game when it comes to food knowledge.

Each and every recipe includes nutrition information right on the page. I know from my own experience of trying to live healthfully that you really need to know what's in the food you eat to feel confident that you're putting good things into your body. So, I've done this work for you! And, every dish has icons that indicate if it is quick (ready in 30 minutes or less), vegetarian, gluten-free, dairy-free, and freezer-friendly, so you can navigate the recipes with ease.

Skinnytaste One & Done grew out of my own experience of wanting easy weeknight dinner solutions, as well as hearing from so many fans of my blog and books that there's an endless need for super simple, really delicious meals that please an entire family—and are healthy! I hope that the one-pot-style recipes in this book truly fulfill that need and help make dinnertime easier and more enjoyable. Gathering around the dinner table is one of my favorite times of the day, and relieving the stress of getting a meal on that table is very important to me. With this book, you can spend less time thinking about, planning, and cooking supper, and enjoy more time with your loved ones instead!

Okay, so now I have to ask: Who's ready to get cooking? Great, I thought so! Let's get started.

RECIPE KEY

Look for these helpful icons throughout the book:

- (Q) QUICK (ready in 30 minutes or less)
- (V) VEGETARIAN
- (GF) GLUTEN-FREE
- (DF) DAIRY-FREE
- (FF) FREEZER-FRIENDLY

WEIGHT WATCHERS POINTS

For those of you on Weight Watchers, all of the up-to-date Weight Watcher Points are conveniently located on my website under the cookbook tab: www.skinnytaste.com/cookbook.

One-Pot Cooking 101

However simple the concept, cooking a whole meal in one "pot" will work the best if you follow a few simple tips. I can't begin to tell you all that I learned while putting this book together and figuring out how to make a meal in one vessel! My experiments ranged far and wide, and I'm delighted to have discovered unexpected techniques that are fun and delicious (by far, my favorite is baking bread in the air fryer!). In this chapter, I'll talk through the tricks I learned and tips to set yourself up for success, especially if you're new to any of these cooking methods or appliances. First things first though: It's important to start with good equipment! If you're preparing to dive into the recipes and going out to purchase any of the cookware, I've also shared key factors to look for as you consider your options.

Let's get started! Here's the skinny on all of the key players in this book.

Tools for Success

THE SHEET PAN

Baking sheet, cookie sheet, sheet pan—whatever you call it, this rectangular metal pan is a classic kitchen essential. I prefer to use the rimmed ones, since the raised edges prevent anything from rolling off and into my oven. Some brands make nonstick sheet pans, but I like to use a regular uncoated pan that I just spray with oil or line with foil, parchment paper, or a silicone baking mat to keep ingredients from getting stuck. Lighter colored pans are better than dark ones, since the latter heats quickly and can result in food that is burned on the outside and not cooked all the way through. This piece of equipment is inexpensive and versatile, so you'll use it again and again. Dinners such as Spicy Peanut Chicken and Vegetables (page 76), Crab-Stuffed Shrimp (page 113), Carne Asada Fries (page 102), and Caprese Portobello Pizzas (page 83) can be cooked all together on one pan, at the same time. It couldn't be easier!

Sheet Pan Basics

- All the meals here are made in the larger 13 x 18-inch size (also known as a half sheet pan), which is perfect for a dinner for four. For a larger family, you can double the recipes and use two sheet pans. For a family of two, you can halve the recipes and use a quarter sheet pan, which is 9½ x 13 inches.

- Line the sheet pans with heavy-duty foil or parchment paper (not wax paper) for easy cleanup. You might have to do some light washing later, but if they're lined well, cleanup will be a breeze.

- Look for pans made of heavy aluminum, which are built to keep their shape after repeated use without buckling.

- To prevent vegetables from drying out while they cook, make sure to completely coat them with oil. In most cases, the best way to do this is to put the ingredients in a large bowl, add the oil and any seasonings in the recipe, stir with a spoon or your hands, then transfer the veggies to the sheet pan. That said, if you're feeling lazy or extra tight on time, tossing everything together on the sheet pan itself works well and saves you from cleaning a bowl.

- Cut vegetables into roughly the same size pieces so they cook evenly.

- In general, the middle of the oven is best for even baking. Many recipes, including those on Bakepedia, will direct you to position the rack in the middle. If no direction is given, assume that your items should be baked here.

- If you have more than one pan that you'd like to bake at once and both pans won't fit on one rack, you can use two racks: one in the lower third and one in the upper third of the oven. Then switch the pans halfway through cooking, if needed, to prevent one from browning faster.

- Like grilling, broiling is cooking food a few inches away from intense heat—though in broiling it's directly above rather than below the food. You can use the broiler to cook something from start to finish, but it's also great for finishing a dish where you want to brown the top at the end.

THE SKILLET

From sautéing, searing, and stir-frying, to scrambling eggs and even roasting or baking, the skillet is an essential piece of cookware in any kitchen. They come in a variety of sizes, from small 8-inch ones to the larger 12-inch. They often come with lids, though not always, and you'll find nonstick versions as well as steel and ceramic-coated. In this book, you can test this workhorse pan's versatility in many ways: stir-frying (Spicy Stir-Fried Chicken and Shredded Brussels Bowls, page 29), baking (Mom's Skillet Chicken Pot Pie, page 37), searing (Cheesy Pork Chops with Mushrooms and Wilted Spinach, page 45), and quickly sautéing (Summer Veggie Zucchini Noodles with Burrata, page 49).

Skillet Basics

- I recommend a 10- or 12-inch skillet, which is the perfect size if you're cooking for four to six people.

- Heavy-duty ovenproof skillets with fitted lids are well worth the investment. A seasoned cast-iron skillet is a kitchen must, and with proper care it can last a lifetime. Some brands can be purchased preseasoned, but seasoning it yourself is pretty easy to do. To season a new cast-iron skillet, coat the skillet with cooking oil, bake it in a 350°F oven for 1 hour, then dry it with paper towels. Anytime you cook in it, wash it with soapy water, dry it well, then rub it with more oil. Enamel skillets combine the advantages of cast iron (holds heat very well, providing an even, consistent temperature) with being easy to maintain. They are very durable, nonstick, and the interior resists staining and dulling.

- Nonstick skillets make cleanup a breeze. I have a set in various sizes from 8 inches to 12 inches. They are inexpensive and sturdy enough for everyday cooking. However, many are not ovenproof, so you'll want to use them on the stovetop only.

THE BAKING DISH

Every kitchen needs a trusty casserole dish. Yes, they are good for baking casseroles—as their name implies—but they can also be used to roast chicken, vegetables, and other savory dishes, and can go straight from the oven to the dinner table, doubling as a serving dish. Baking dishes come in all sorts of sizes, shapes, and materials, such as glass, metal, or ceramic, as well as a range of prices. Most types will work for the recipes in this book, so you can make your selection based more on aesthetics and price point. Impressive entrées like Garlic-Dijon Roasted Pork Tenderloin with Potatoes and Green Beans (page 98), Pesce Primavera (page 110), and Honey-Mustard Chicken Bake (page 86) are naturals for the baking dish.

Baking Dish Basics

- I used a 3-quart 9 x 13-inch baking dish made of ceramic for the recipes in this book.

- Look for a baking dish that has sides that are at least 2 inches tall.

- Some come with lids, but if yours doesn't, use foil to cover the top if the recipe calls for it to be covered.

THE DUTCH OVEN

The Dutch oven is such a useful pot and is quite beautiful to boot. Made of cast iron that's coated in enamel, steel, or ceramic, this piece of equipment can be used to simmer on the stovetop and braise in the oven, then is simply placed on the table for family-style serving. Dutch ovens range in price from $50 to more than $300 for more expensive brands like Le Creuset or Staub. The pricier pots are an investment, but they are well worth the money, as you're paying for quality—heavy, durable cast iron that retains heat well, is made of easy-to-clean and scratch-resistant enamel, comes with a heavy lid that locks in moisture, and has sturdy handles. This is the kind of item that you'll keep for a lifetime, and even pass down to your kids.

If you don't have a Dutch oven, a large, heavy pot will work well for these recipes. Just be sure to use one that has a heavy bottom, so that the heat will conduct well and evenly.

Everything from Creamy Cheddar-Broccoli Soup (page 243) and Mussels in Garlicky White Wine Sauce (page 235) to Cheesy Turkey Taco Chili Mac (page 223) and Chicken Fajita Pasta (page 219) is well-suited to Dutch ovens.

Dutch Oven Basics

- A 5-quart or 6-quart Dutch oven or stockpot will work perfectly for the recipes in this book.

- You'll find both round and oval versions of Dutch ovens; either shape will perform well, so take your pick!

- I recommend getting one with a tight-fitting lid, though covering the pot with foil will work, too (those lids have a way of getting lost!).

THE ELECTRIC PRESSURE COOKER

Pressure cookers have come a long way since the older stovetop models our parents used that were the cause of many mishaps. If one ever exploded in your home and left splatters of stew all over the kitchen ceiling, you've probably never forgotten and have a healthy skepticism for this appliance! Today, modern electric pressure cookers are much more foolproof and have safety mechanisms that prevent such disasters from happening. This appliance is my most effective tool for achieving the goal of a super fast dinner, because it is such a time-saver.

Most electric pressure cookers are multipurpose cookers, meaning they can also slow cook, steam, sauté, cook rice, and even make yogurt. In this book, I use the pressure cooking function only, which creates a high pressure (steam pressure) environment that cooks food faster than if it had been prepared on the stove or in the oven. Coq au Vin (page 128), for example, is ready in about 30 minutes start to finish, whereas it takes about 2½ hours on the stovetop. In terms of convenience, it's very similar to the slow cooker—you can throw everything in and walk away—but the difference is speed. The pressure cooker will get dinner on the table *fast*, so you can have Caldo de Papa (Potato and Short Rib Soup) (page 148), Instant Spaghetti and Meat Sauce (page 143), or Turkey Cheeseburger Soup (page 140) on the table in no time.

Electric Pressure Cooker Basics

- All the recipes in this book were tested in a 6-quart Instant Pot. Similar machines from other manufacturers, such as Breville or Fagor, will give you the same results. Before making a purchase, you'll want to do your research to see which machine is best for you.

- The 6-quart model is perfect for dinner for a family of four. If you have a larger family, you might want to look into the 8-quart model.

- Before using your pressure cooker for the first time, be sure to read the manual to learn the basics about the lid, pressure valve, outer body, inner pot, steamer rack, and condensation reservoir.

- Many models have a sauté function, which allows you to sauté in the same pot, much like a burner on the stove. Perfect for browning meat and vegetables, it negates the need to use a separate skillet. If your machine doesn't have this function, sauté the ingredients in a pan over medium heat, then add them to the pressure cooker.

- The steam valve allows the pressure cooker to build pressure and release it. It has two positions: a lock position for sealing and an open position for venting. When pressure cooking, the valve must be in the sealing position.

- The metal pressure valve indicates when the cooker is pressurized. When it reaches pressure, the valve will pop up and lock the lid. When the pressure is released, it will drop, allowing you to open the lid. You can use the quick-release method mentioned in the recipes by turning the steam valve to venting to allow the steam to release quickly.

- Most pressure cookers come with a steamer rack with handles. It sits at the bottom of the inner pot, usually over water or liquid. The handles make it easy to lift food out. If yours doesn't have a handle, you can make a sling with foil.

- There's a popular "pot-in-pot" cooking method that I used in two recipes: Unstuffed Cabbage Bowls (page 157) and Pot-in-Pot Puerto Rican Rice and Beans (page 167). This technique allows you to cook something in the main pot of the pressure cooker, and at the same time, something else (like rice) in a bowl that you set inside of it. It's pretty handy—just be sure to use an ovenproof glass or stainless-steel bowl that will sit far enough below the lid that the cooker can be properly closed.

THE AIR FRYER

Air fryers give you that delicious "fried food" result—crispy, crunchy outside, moist inside—without having to actually fry your food in fat. How? It circulates hot air around your food (like a convection oven). Since you barely need any oil at all, you end up with lighter, healthier dishes, and favorites such as Breaded Popcorn Shrimp with Tartar Sauce (page 202) and Spicy Fried Chicken Sandwiches (page 175) aren't the indulgence they usually are. You also have less mess and easier cleanup; no more oil splatters or having to deal with hot oil! Plus, it heats up very quickly, so cook times are shorter.

In my experimenting, I was surprised to discover that you can do more than "fry" in these machines. I've had great results "baking" bread in them! Be sure to try the Margherita Pizzas (page 209) as well as the other dishes that use the pizza dough recipe—Chicken, Pesto, and Cheese Stromboli (page 180) and Italian Sausage and Pepper Calzones (page 189). It's also great for reheating leftovers without creating the rubbery texture you would get with a microwave.

Air Fryer Basics

- All brands function in the same basic manner—by circulating hot air—but there are a bunch of different bells and whistles, as well as sizes, to choose from. There's a wide range in price, too—on average, they start at $70 and can go up to $400. Weigh your options when choosing which one is right for you.

- Most air fryers come in a smaller, rounded shape with a deep basket compartment. However, some toaster ovens with convection heating capabilities now have air fryer settings and basket inserts. Many people like this option if they want a toaster oven and air fryer all in one device. The recipes will work well in either style air fryer.

- Most air fryers are pretty small; they're able to cook between 1.8 and 2.5 pounds of food. I used the 3-quart size NuWave Brio and Phillips XL models when testing recipes to see if a higher priced brand gave me results similar to a less expensive brand, and with 99 percent of recipes, they both worked great. There are larger models that can even cook a whole chicken or turkey, though I haven't tried those out.

- Air fryers are basically mini ovens. Because of their smaller size, it's important not to overload the basket. Place your food in a single layer and cook in batches. Once everything is cooked, I like to stack all the food back into the basket and heat it for 1 more minute so everything is served hot at the same time.

- If you want to convert your favorite recipes that are written for the oven, a good rule of thumb is to reduce the suggested temperature by 25° to 50°F, and to reduce the cook time by 20 to 40 percent. The same rule applies to frozen items. I usually test one piece of food first to get the timing right.

- Always remember to flip whatever you are cooking halfway through the cooking time. Food browns more on the bottom, so turning it browns both sides perfectly.

- You can open and close the air fryer to check for doneness without affecting the outcome of the dish. So if you're not sure if something is ready, simply peek in.

THE SLOW COOKER

Dinner that practically cooks itself while you're away? Score! With a little advance planning, you can save precious time in the evening. And you can't beat the ease of having to simply combine a few ingredients in the machine, turn it on, and forget it. Then you can come home to a hearty, home-cooked meal hours later. It's well known that slow cookers turn out excellent soups, like Split Pea Soup with Smoked Turkey (page 258), and it does wonders turning tough cuts of meat into meltingly tender meals, as with Pot Roast with Potatoes and Vegetables (page 262). But you may be surprised to learn that you can also make excellent Spinach and Cheese Manicotti (page 271), and Italian Stuffed Cubanelle Peppers (page 255). It's certainly no one-trick pony!

Slow Cooker Basics

- Choose a slow cooker that allows you to adjust the time in 30-minute increments and that automatically switches to "warm" when ready.

- As tempting as it seems, resist the urge to open the lid. It takes a while for the slow cooker to reach temperature, and every time you open the lid, it adds about 15 minutes to your cook time.

- Different models cook at different temperatures. Some are hotter, while others are less so. You will have to make adjustments to the cook time accordingly once you get to know your slow cooker.

- For the sake of the one-pot concept for this book, I had to find a workaround for sautéing aromatics like onion and garlic, which taste much better than when they're tossed into the slow cooker raw. I discovered that microwaving them until soft was a quick, simple solution with results that made me happy.

- One great thing I discovered while testing recipes for this book is that you can skip the step of browning ground meat before cooking it in a slow cooker. You don't lose a thing in flavor. What a time-saver! Try it out in my Tex-Mex Turkey Tacos (page 261).

THE GRILL

As soon as the weather gets warm, we love grilling outdoors for both weeknight dinners as well as weekend entertaining. Grilling food is so easy, though it can take some practice to get the heat right and to know when your dish is fully cooked. But hey, it's a pretty tasty practice! If you have space in your yard and are considering purchasing a grill, the big question is: gas or charcoal? Both are great, but have their pros and cons.

Grill Basics

- Charcoal kettle-style grills, such as those by the popular brand Weber, are ideal for people who don't want to invest a lot of money in a grill. They are affordable and portable, and perfect for grilling everything from steaks and burgers to vegetables. A plus to owning a charcoal grill is the delicious smoky flavor you can't get with gas grills. They also can maintain a higher heat than do gas grills, so foods get a better char. However, there are quite a few downsides with charcoal grills (especially on weeknights), all related to convenience and ease. They are harder to light than gas grills and take longer to get up to temperature. The live fire means there can be flare-ups that can burn the food; and it's tougher to control and gauge the temperature. If you're cooking for a long time, the coals slowly lose heat and you'll need to add more. Lastly, cleanup is messier since you have ash to discard.

- I personally love my gas grill because it offers convenience and heat control. If I want a quick dinner, I can easily light up my grill any night of the week, throw on some chicken or burgers, and have dinner ready fast. It's easy to preheat and you'll be ready to cook in 10 minutes. You also have more control over the heat, which you can raise and lower rapidly. The downside is that gas can be dangerous, as it is explosive if not handled properly. Gas grills also tend to be more expensive than charcoal grills.

THE GRILL PAN

I like grill pans because you can grill all year long, no matter what the weather is like outside. There are many grill pans on the market these days, in all price ranges, but not all are created equal. Look for a pan that has raised ridges: These mimic the cooking surface of an outdoor grill, which gives foods distinctive marks and also lifts the food out of the grease and drippings that accumulate in the grooves. Food that cooks directly in oil in a flat hot skillet is "sautéed" or "seared," but when suspended by the ridges in a grill pan, it is "grilled." Anything cooked on a grill can also be cooked on a grill pan, so the grilling chapter is very versatile. Grilled Lamb Chops with Mint Chimichurri (page 285), Grilled Lemon-Chili Shrimp Summer Salad (page 289), and Chicken-Avocado Burgers with Jalapeño Slaw (page 278) will all be perfectly delicious whether cooked in a grill pan or outside on a grill.

Grill Pan Basics

- Heavy, cast-iron grill pans, such as those made by Staub and Lodge, are affordable, excellent options because they retain heat well and distribute that heat evenly. The downside is that they aren't nonstick and will require care to prevent rust from forming. To feed a large crowd, look for the type that fits over two burners, so you get a lot of surface area.

- Enamel cast-iron grill pans from brands like Le Creuset are more expensive but offer the advantages of heavy cast iron with a durable enamel surface for easy cleanup. They also come in several sizes and colors.

- Nonstick grill pans, such as ones made by Calphalon, have an anodized aluminum interior and a nonstick surface. They have a lower heat capacity than cast iron, meaning that, even though they will heat up quickly, they'll never hold heat as well as cast-iron pans. The positives: They are lightweight and very easy to clean.

TEMPERATURE TIP

To test the doneness of meat, use an instant-read thermometer.

A NOTE ABOUT SALT

You may be surprised to learn that different brands and types of salt can vary widely in how salty they are. I used Diamond Crystal kosher salt for the recipes in this book. If you use another kind, just remember to taste as you go and understand that the sodium numbers in the nutrition information will change.

Skillet

Fiesta Chicken and Carrot "Rice" SERVES 4

Q GF

I love turning veggies into "rice." And not just cauliflower: I do this with any firm vegetable, including carrots, sweet potatoes, broccoli, and others. It's a great way to incorporate more veggies into your meal. Here, my "rice" is studded with corn and black beans, and transformed into a hearty meal with the addition of chicken smothered in salsa, jalapeños, and cheese. It's a dish worthy of an *¡olé!*

14 ounces carrots (5 medium or 3 to 4 large), peeled and cut into 1-inch pieces

2 boneless, skinless chicken breasts (8 ounces each), each cut in half crosswise

1½ teaspoons kosher salt

¼ teaspoon garlic powder

Freshly ground black pepper

Olive oil spray (I like my Misto or Bertolli)

2 teaspoons olive oil

1 cup chopped white onion

1 small fresh jalapeño pepper, seeded and minced, plus ½ jalapeño, thinly sliced

2 garlic cloves, minced

1½ cups corn kernels, fresh or frozen

1 cup canned black beans,* rinsed and drained

2 tablespoons chopped fresh cilantro

Juice of ½ lime

4 tablespoons jarred salsa

4 slices pepper Jack cheese (21 grams each)

FOR SERVING

¼ cup chopped fresh tomatoes

2 tablespoons chopped fresh cilantro

2 tablespoons chopped scallions

4 ounces diced avocado (from 1 small Hass)

*Read the label to be sure this product is gluten-free.

PER SERVING	1 piece chicken + 1 cup veggies
CALORIES	451
FAT	17.5 g
SATURATED FAT	6.5 g
CHOLESTEROL	99 mg
CARBOHYDRATE	40 g
FIBER	11.5 g
PROTEIN	37 g
SUGARS	10 g
SODIUM	993 mg

In a food processor, working in small batches, pulse the carrots a few times until they resemble grains of rice (don't overprocess). Spoon the carrots into a kitchen towel and squeeze out any excess liquid.

Place each piece of chicken between two sheets of plastic wrap. Using a rolling pin, gently pound each piece until it is about ½ inch thick. Season with ¾ teaspoon of the salt, the garlic powder, and black pepper to taste.

Heat a large deep nonstick skillet over high heat. Spray it with oil and cook the chicken until browned and just cooked through, about 2 minutes per side. Transfer the chicken to a plate.

Reduce the heat under the skillet to medium and add the 2 teaspoons oil, the onion, minced jalapeño, and garlic. Cook, stirring, until fragrant, about 2 minutes. Add the riced carrots, increase the heat to high, and add the remaining ¾ teaspoon salt and black pepper to taste. Cook, stirring, until the carrots are crisp-tender, about 6 minutes. Add the corn and beans and cook, stirring, until heated through, 1 to 2 minutes. Stir in the cilantro and the lime juice.

Place the chicken over the "rice." Top each piece with 1 tablespoon salsa, a few jalapeño slices, and a slice of cheese. Reduce the heat to low, cover, and cook until the chicken is cooked through, about 5 minutes. Top each serving with the tomatoes, cilantro, scallions, and avocado.

Chicken Cordon Bleu with Asparagus SERVES 4

I love making chicken cordon bleu, a delicious breaded, rolled, and baked dinner of chicken stuffed with ham and cheese. One day, I wanted to cook something using the same ingredients, but that was quicker to make. And that's how I came up with this dish: lazy chicken cordon bleu that's all made in one skillet and is a fan favorite on my blog. In this version, I added the asparagus right to the skillet to make it a complete meal.

4 thin-sliced chicken breast cutlets (4 ounces each)

3/4 teaspoon kosher salt

Freshly ground black pepper

1/4 cup all-purpose flour, wheat or gluten-free

3/4 cup reduced-sodium chicken broth*

1 tablespoon fresh lemon juice

1/2 tablespoon Dijon mustard

1/2 teaspoon unsalted butter

1 1/2 teaspoons olive oil

3/4 pound asparagus, tough ends trimmed

4 thin slices (3 ounces total) low-sodium deli ham* (I like Boar's Head)

4 slices (3 ounces total) reduced-fat Swiss cheese (I like Alpine Lace)

Chopped fresh parsley, for garnish

*Read the label to be sure this product is gluten-free.

PER SERVING	1 chicken cutlet + 3 ounces asparagus
CALORIES	243
FAT	10.5 g
SATURATED FAT	4 g
CHOLESTEROL	99 mg
CARBOHYDRATE	11 g
FIBER	2 g
PROTEIN	37 g
SUGARS	4 g
SODIUM	751 mg

Season the chicken with the salt and pepper to taste. Place the flour in a shallow dish. Lightly dredge both sides of the chicken in the flour, shaking off any excess. Reserve the flour.

In a small bowl, combine the chicken broth, lemon juice, mustard, and 1 teaspoon of the reserved flour. Whisk until smooth.

In a large nonstick skillet, melt the butter over medium-high heat. Add 1 teaspoon of the olive oil and 2 of the chicken cutlets. Cook until slightly golden, 2 minutes per side, and transfer to a plate. Add the remaining 1/2 teaspoon olive oil and remaining 2 chicken cutlets and cook until slightly golden, 2 minutes per side. Transfer to the plate with the other pieces of chicken.

Reduce the heat to medium-low, add the chicken broth mixture, and cook, whisking and using a wooden spoon to scrape up any bits stuck to the bottom of the pan, until reduced slightly, about 2 minutes. Add the asparagus, cover, and simmer until just about tender, about 5 minutes. Return the chicken to the skillet, setting it over the asparagus, and top each piece with a slice of ham and a slice of cheese. Cover the skillet and cook until the cheese melts, 3 to 4 minutes.

To serve, use a spatula to transfer the chicken and asparagus to 4 plates. Spoon the remaining sauce from the skillet over the chicken and garnish with the parsley.

Lemon Chicken and Brown Rice Pilaf SERVES 4

I love rice pilaf and often make my own homemade version of Rice-A-Roni so I can control what goes into it. Simple tweaks, like using whole-grain pasta and brown rice, make the dish a bit healthier than the boxed version, and pairing it with lemon chicken brightens everything up. Although I typically don't cook with parboiled rice, I don't mind it at all when it comes to brown rice, especially since brown rice can take a while to cook in the skillet. I've tried all the brands sold in my supermarket and found Minute Rice to have the best taste and texture.

2 boneless, skinless chicken breasts (8 ounces each)

2 tablespoons fresh lemon juice

1 teaspoon minced garlic

1 teaspoon dried oregano

¾ teaspoon kosher salt

Olive oil spray (I like my Misto or Bertolli)

1 tablespoon unsalted butter

1 ounce (¼ cup) broken vermicelli, whole wheat or gluten-free

2 cups parboiled brown rice (I used Minute Rice)

1 tablespoon chicken bouillon* (I like Better Than Bouillon)

⅓ cup frozen petite peas

1 lemon, ½ thinly sliced, ½ cut into wedges

Chopped fresh parsley, for garnish

*Read the label to be sure this product is gluten-free.

PER SERVING	1 piece chicken + 1 cup rice
CALORIES	377
FAT	7.5 g
SATURATED FAT	2.5 g
CHOLESTEROL	80 mg
CARBOHYDRATE	50 g
FIBER	3 g
PROTEIN	27 g
SUGARS	1 g
SODIUM	881 mg

SKINNY SCOOP

Each brand of rice will yield a different amount, so if you don't use Minute Rice, make adjustments to the measurements of rice and liquid to end up with the same results.

Cut the chicken lengthwise into 4 thin cutlets. Put the chicken in a large zip-top plastic bag and add the lemon juice, garlic, oregano, and salt. Marinate in the refrigerator for at least 30 minutes and up to 1 hour.

Heat a large nonstick skillet (one that has a fitted lid) over high heat. Spray the skillet with oil. Remove the chicken from the marinade (discard the marinade). Add the chicken to the skillet and cook until it is browned on both sides and almost cooked through, 3 to 4 minutes per side. Transfer the chicken to a plate and loosely tent with a piece of foil to keep warm.

Wipe the skillet with a damp paper towel, reduce the heat to medium, and add the butter to the skillet. Once melted, add the vermicelli and cook, stirring constantly, until golden brown, 1 to 1½ minutes (be careful not to burn it). Add the rice and cook, stirring to coat the rice with the butter, until toasted, about 2 minutes. Add 2 cups water, stir in the chicken bouillon and peas, and bring the mixture to a boil. Reduce the heat to low, cover, and cook for 7 minutes, until the rice is almost done. Uncover the skillet and arrange the chicken and lemon slices over the rice. Cover and continue cooking until the chicken is heated through and fully cooked in the center and the liquid is absorbed, 2 to 3 minutes. Remove the pan from the heat and let sit covered for 3 minutes.

Garnish with the parsley and serve with the lemon wedges on the side.

SKINNY SCOOP

If your kids don't like peas, you can use carrots or chopped broccoli instead.

Spicy Stir-Fried Chicken and Shredded Brussels Bowls SERVES 2

Brussels sprouts in a *stir-fry*? Why not! Although you'll probably never see this dish on a Chinese takeout menu, I love making stir-fries with uncommon ingredients. Shred the sprouts very thinly with a sharp knife or buy them pre-shredded, and make sure your pan is really hot so that they brown a little on the edges—yum! This low-carb dish is so loaded with veggies that you won't even miss the rice.

1 teaspoon grapeseed or canola oil

1/2 pound 93% ground chicken

3 tablespoons reduced-sodium soy sauce*

1/4 teaspoon crushed red pepper flakes

1/2 small onion, chopped

2 garlic cloves, minced

1/2 teaspoon grated fresh ginger

3 cups (7 ounces) shredded Brussels sprouts

1/2 cup shredded carrots

1/4 cup sliced red bell pepper

2 ounces sliced shiitake mushrooms

1/2 tablespoon Shaoxing (Chinese rice wine), mirin, or dry sherry

1 teaspoon toasted sesame oil

1 medium scallion, sliced, for garnish

*Read the label to be sure this product is gluten-free.

PER SERVING	1³/₄ cups
CALORIES	318
FAT	14.5 g
SATURATED FAT	3.5 g
CHOLESTEROL	98 mg
CARBOHYDRATE	23 g
FIBER	7.5 g
PROTEIN	27 g
SUGARS	7 g
SODIUM	926 mg

In a large nonstick skillet or wok, heat 1/2 teaspoon of the grapeseed oil over high heat. When the pan is hot and almost smoking, add the chicken, 1/2 tablespoon of the soy sauce, and the pepper flakes and brown the chicken, using a wooden spoon to break it into small pieces as it cooks, 3 to 4 minutes. Add the onion, garlic, and ginger and cook, stirring, until softened, 2 to 3 minutes. Transfer to a medium bowl.

To the pan, add the remaining 1/2 teaspoon grapeseed oil, the Brussels sprouts, and carrots. Cook, stirring, until browned, about 5 minutes. Add the bell pepper and mushrooms. Pour in the remaining 2 1/2 tablespoons soy sauce, rice wine, and sesame oil. Cook, stirring occasionally, until the vegetables are crisp-tender, about 2 minutes. Return the chicken to the skillet, stir, and reheat for about 30 seconds. Remove the pan from the heat, garnish with the scallion, and divide between 2 bowls.

SKINNY SCOOP

The trick to a stress-free stir-fry? Have all your ingredients prepped and ready before you start.

Bacon-Wrapped BBQ Ranch Chicken Salad SERVES 4

Want the juiciest chicken breasts? Wrap them in bacon! This super simple technique is delicious and so versatile. I especially love to serve this chicken over greens with BBQ sauce and a homemade ranch dressing, as I've done here. One of my other favorite ways to enjoy it, especially when I want something warm, is to plate it with roasted vegetables, such as cauliflower, broccoli, and/or Brussels sprouts.

4 boneless, skinless chicken breasts (8 ounces each)

Freshly ground black pepper

8 slices center-cut bacon

8 cups chopped romaine lettuce

4 medium campari tomatoes, cut into wedges

4 ounces sliced avocado (from 1 small Hass)

4 tablespoons store-bought barbecue sauce

Chive Ranch Dressing (opposite) or ¾ cup store-bought ranch-style dressing

PER SERVING	1 salad
CALORIES	496
FAT	19.5 g
SATURATED FAT	4.5 g
CHOLESTEROL	156 mg
CARBOHYDRATE	21 g
FIBER	5.5 g
PROTEIN	58 g
SUGARS	12 g
SODIUM	774 mg

SKINNY SCOOP

When I buy bacon, I look for the center-cut kind—it's leaner than standard strips since it's cut close to the bone. If you don't eat pork, turkey bacon is perfectly fine.

Preheat the oven to 400°F.

Season the chicken breasts with pepper. Tightly wrap 2 strips of bacon around each chicken breast.

Heat a large ovenproof or cast-iron skillet over medium-high heat. Sear the chicken until the bacon is crisp, about 2 minutes per side. Drain any fat that accumulates in the pan.

Transfer the pan to the oven and roast until the chicken is cooked through and a thermometer registers 160°F, about 12 minutes. Transfer the chicken to a cutting board, tent it with foil, and let it rest for 5 minutes before slicing.

Divide the lettuce, tomatoes, avocado, and sliced chicken among 4 plates. Drizzle each with 1 tablespoon of the barbecue sauce and 3 tablespoons of the ranch dressing, and serve.

CHIVE RANCH DRESSING

Makes ¾ cup

½ cup low-fat (1%) buttermilk

¼ cup light mayonnaise

¼ cup finely chopped fresh chives

¼ teaspoon garlic powder

¼ teaspoon onion powder

¼ teaspoon dried parsley

¼ teaspoon dried basil

Freshly ground black pepper

In a small bowl, whisk together the buttermilk, mayonnaise, chives, garlic powder, onion powder, dried parsley, and dried basil until combined. Season with pepper.

PER SERVING	3 tablespoons	CARBOHYDRATE	3 g
CALORIES	63	FIBER	0 g
FAT	5.5 g	PROTEIN	1 g
SATURATED FAT	1 g	SUGARS	2 g
CHOLESTEROL	6 mg	SODIUM	134 mg

Chicken Saltimbocca with Spinach SERVES 4

Finding a dish my whole family will eat is one of life's small challenges, and I know I'm not alone here. Instead of making everyone a separate meal (who has the time or the energy for that?), I find creative ways to make it work. This dish (which happens to be one of my favorite guilty pleasures at Italian restaurants) is one of those miracle meals that makes everyone happy, with a few adjustments, of course. For example, to get Madison to eat this, I simply serve her the chicken cutlet (with some lemon) separate from the cheese and prosciutto, which I put on the side (kids!). Madison prefers her veggies raw, so rather than giving her wilted spinach, I add some raw leaves to her salad. Small steps, but talk about a happy meal!

2 boneless, skinless chicken breasts (8 ounces each), halved horizontally to make a total of 4 cutlets

½ teaspoon kosher salt

⅓ cup seasoned bread crumbs, regular or gluten-free

2 large egg whites

1½ tablespoons olive oil

½ teaspoon unsalted butter

Olive oil spray (I like my Misto or Bertolli)

¾ cup reduced-sodium chicken broth*

1 teaspoon fresh lemon juice

1 teaspoon all-purpose flour, wheat or gluten-free

10 cups (about 6 ounces) baby spinach

2 thin slices prosciutto (1 ounce total), cut in half

3 ounces part-skim mozzarella, cut into 4 thin slices

1 tablespoon chopped fresh sage, for garnish

*Read the label to be sure this product is gluten-free.

PER SERVING	1 chicken cutlet + spinach
CALORIES	297
FAT	13 g
SATURATED FAT	4 g
CHOLESTEROL	92 mg
CARBOHYDRATE	8 g
FIBER	1.5 g
PROTEIN	36 g
SUGARS	1 g
SODIUM	901 mg

Sprinkle the chicken cutlets with the salt. Place the bread crumbs in a shallow bowl. In another shallow bowl, beat the egg whites. Dip the cutlets in the egg whites and then in the bread crumbs, shaking off any excess.

Heat a large nonstick skillet over medium-high heat. Add the olive oil and butter. When hot, swirl around to coat the bottom of the pan. Add the cutlets and cook until browned on the bottom, about 5 minutes. Spritz the top of the chicken with oil, turn the cutlets, and cook until golden brown on the second side and cooked through, about 5 minutes. Transfer to a plate. Wipe out the skillet with a damp paper towel.

In a small bowl, whisk together the chicken broth, lemon juice, and flour until smooth.

Add the chicken broth mixture to the skillet and bring to a simmer over medium-low heat, whisking constantly. Cook, whisking constantly, until reduced slightly, 2 to 3 minutes. Add the spinach and stir to coat with the liquid. Return the chicken to the skillet and top each piece with ½ slice prosciutto and 1 slice mozzarella. Cover the skillet and cook until the cheese melts and the spinach wilts, 3 to 4 minutes.

Use a spatula to transfer the chicken and spinach to a serving platter. Garnish with the sage and serve.

Weeknight Chicken Souvlaki SERVES 4

Q

Tommy's a happy man when he knows I'm whipping this up for dinner. Rather than grilling pieces of chicken on skewers, I love using this quick method, which is similar to a stir-fry. I prefer boneless, skinless chicken thighs over breast meat, because they have more fat and flavor. With the pita bread, tzatziki, and tons of fresh veggies, this is a bright, fresh, crowd-pleasing meal!

TZATZIKI

½ English cucumber, peeled, seeded, and grated

1 cup 2% Greek yogurt

1 garlic clove, crushed through a garlic press

1 tablespoon chopped fresh chives

1 tablespoon chopped fresh mint

¼ teaspoon kosher salt

Freshly ground black pepper

CHICKEN

1¼ pounds boneless, skinless chicken thighs, trimmed and cut into ½-inch-thick strips

1 large onion, cut into ½-inch-thick slices

1 tablespoon extra-virgin olive oil

3 tablespoons fresh lemon juice

2 tablespoons chopped fresh oregano

2 garlic cloves, crushed through a garlic press

1 teaspoon kosher salt

Freshly ground black pepper

Olive oil spray (I like my Misto or Bertolli)

FOR SERVING

4 large whole wheat pocketless pitas or flatbread (about 3 ounces each), warmed

1 cup chopped romaine lettuce

½ English cucumber, chopped

1 medium tomato, chopped

¼ cup sliced red onion

4 lemon wedges

PER SERVING	¾ cup chicken/onion mixture + 1 pita + salad + ⅓ cup tzatziki
CALORIES	494
FAT	15.5 g
SATURATED FAT	3.5 g
CHOLESTEROL	140 mg
CARBOHYDRATE	54 g
FIBER	6.5 g
PROTEIN	45 g
SUGARS	10 g
SODIUM	845 mg

For the tzatziki: Squeeze any excess liquid from the grated cucumber and place the cucumber in a small bowl. Add the yogurt, garlic, chives, mint, salt, and pepper to taste. Stir well.

For the chicken: In a medium bowl, toss together the chicken, onion, olive oil, lemon juice, oregano, garlic, salt, and pepper to taste. Let stand for at least 15 minutes.

Heat a large, deep skillet over high heat until very hot. Spray with oil and add the chicken and onion along with any marinade. Cook, turning 5 or 6 times, until the liquid evaporates and the chicken and onion are tender and browned on the edges, 12 to 14 minutes.

To serve, place the warm pitas on 4 plates and pile on a generous ¾ cup of the chicken/onion mixture. Top with the lettuce, cucumber, tomato, red onion, and ⅓ cup of the tzatziki. Serve with the lemon wedges.

SKINNY SCOOP

The chicken and onion need to marinate for at least 15 minutes, but you can also marinate them overnight for even more flavor.

Mom's Skillet Chicken Pot Pie SERVES 8

This is a simplified version of my mom's chicken pot pie, a comfort dish I grew up with. Hers is a bit different from most pot pies, as it isn't filled with a white, goopy sauce. Instead she uses the meat of a whole chicken—which has more flavor and a better texture than breast meat only—as well as lots of parsley, onion, celery, and other vegetables. Making Mom's original version is a two-day process involving dirtying quite a few pots and pans. I streamlined her recipe by using a cooked rotisserie chicken from the supermarket, which works brilliantly. Also, by making it all in one skillet, the crust is only on top, shaving off lots of calories.

1 whole rotisserie chicken (about 2¼ pounds)

1 tablespoon olive oil

1 medium onion, chopped

½ cup chopped fresh parsley

3 celery stalks, chopped

1 (16-ounce) package frozen mixed vegetables

3¾ cups chicken broth

½ teaspoon kosher salt

⅛ teaspoon freshly ground black pepper

¼ cup cornstarch

1 refrigerated pie crust (from a 14-ounce package)

1 large egg, beaten

PER SERVING	one-eighth pie
CALORIES	333
FAT	14.5 g
SATURATED FAT	4.5 g
CHOLESTEROL	87 mg
CARBOHYDRATE	26 g
FIBER	3.5 g
PROTEIN	25 g
SUGARS	1 g
SODIUM	578 mg

Preheat the oven to 425°F.

Remove the meat from the chicken and shred it with two forks (discard the skin and bones). You should have about 5 cups chicken (about 20 ounces).

In a 10½-inch ovenproof cast-iron or enamel skillet, heat the oil over medium heat. Add the onion and parsley and cook, stirring, until the onion is almost softened, 2 to 3 minutes. Add the celery and cook, stirring, until the vegetables are soft, 3 to 5 minutes. Add the shredded chicken, frozen mixed vegetables, 2 cups of the chicken broth, salt, and pepper. Stir well and bring to a boil. Reduce the heat to medium-low and cook, stirring, for 10 minutes to meld the flavors.

Meanwhile, in a small bowl, combine the remaining 1¾ cups chicken broth and the cornstarch and stir until the cornstarch is dissolved. Stir into the chicken mixture and cook, stirring, until thickened, 4 to 6 minutes. Remove the pan from the heat.

Using a rolling pin, roll out the pie dough until it is about 12 inches in diameter. Place it over the chicken filling. Crimp the edges and, using a knife, make small slits in the top. Brush the top with the beaten egg.

Bake until the crust is golden and the filling is bubbling, about 30 minutes. Let cool slightly. Cut into 8 wedges and serve.

Cheesy Turkey, Leek, and Potato Gratin SERVES 6

This dish is comfort food with a capital C. Sure, it's a little more decadent than most of my dishes, but it's a must-make on those nights you're craving something warm, delicious, and cozy. Tommy absolutely fell in love with this dish—it's satisfying, and maybe even a little dangerous since it's too tempting to take a second helping!

1 cup 1% milk

3 sprigs of fresh thyme plus
½ teaspoon fresh thyme leaves

2 sprigs of fresh rosemary

2 teaspoons kosher salt

1 tablespoon unsalted butter

1½ cups halved and sliced leeks, white parts only (3 to 4 large), rinsed well

2 pounds 93% lean ground turkey

3 garlic cloves, minced

¼ teaspoon freshly ground black pepper

1 (15-ounce) can low-sodium chicken broth*

2 cups frozen peas and carrots

3 tablespoons chopped fresh parsley

¼ cup cornstarch

1 pound Yukon Gold potatoes (about 4 medium), peeled and cut into ⅛-inch-thick slices

2 tablespoons freshly grated Parmesan cheese

1 packed cup (4 ounces) shredded Gruyère cheese*

*Read the label to be sure this product is gluten-free.

PER SERVING	1½ cups
CALORIES	481
FAT	22 g
SATURATED FAT	8.5 g
CHOLESTEROL	141 mg
CARBOHYDRATE	31 g
FIBER	4 g
PROTEIN	40 g
SUGARS	6 g
SODIUM	837 mg

Adjust an oven rack to the second highest position and preheat the oven to 375°F.

In a large, deep ovenproof cast-iron or enamel 12-inch skillet with a fitted lid, combine the milk, thyme sprigs, rosemary sprigs, and ¼ teaspoon salt and bring to a simmer over low heat. Simmer, being careful not to let it boil, for 5 minutes to let the herbs infuse with the milk. Pour into a small bowl and set aside.

Wipe out the skillet, set it over medium heat, and add the butter. Once melted, add the leeks and cook, stirring, until softened, 4 to 5 minutes. Increase the heat to high, then add the ground turkey, garlic, black pepper, and remaining 1¾ teaspoons salt and brown the meat, using a wooden spoon to break it into small pieces as it cooks, about 10 minutes. Add 1 cup of the chicken broth, the peas and carrots, 2 tablespoons of the parsley, and the ½ teaspoon thyme leaves and cook, stirring, until heated through, 3 to 4 minutes.

In a small bowl, whisk together the remaining chicken broth and the cornstarch. Pour over the turkey mixture and cook, stirring, until thickened, 3 to 4 minutes. Cover with the sliced potatoes by overlapping them in a spiral, starting from the outside and working your way to the center. Discard the rosemary and thyme sprigs from the milk mixture and pour it over the potatoes. Sprinkle the top with the Parmesan, then the Gruyère. Cover the skillet tightly with the lid (or use foil). Bake until the potatoes are tender, about 1 hour. Uncover, switch the oven to broil, and broil until the cheese is slightly browned and golden, about 3 minutes. Garnish with the remaining parsley.

Shepherd's Pie with Cauliflower Crust SERVES 4

Lean and low-carb, this healthier take on shepherd's pie is made with ground turkey and lots of veggies, and is topped with cauliflower mash instead of the traditional mashed potatoes. It's a great dish to assemble ahead of time and then pop in the oven when you're ready to eat.

6 cups cauliflower florets
(1½ pounds, from 1 large head)

⅓ cup low-fat (1%) buttermilk

2 tablespoons unsalted butter

1¾ teaspoons kosher salt

Freshly ground black pepper

1 medium onion, chopped

2 carrots, finely chopped

1 celery stalk, chopped

2 garlic cloves, minced

1½ pounds 93% lean ground turkey

¾ cup chopped mushrooms

2 tablespoons all-purpose flour, wheat or gluten-free

1 cup reduced-sodium chicken broth*

2 teaspoons tomato paste

1 teaspoon Worcestershire sauce*

½ cup fresh or frozen corn kernels

½ cup fresh or frozen green peas

1 teaspoon chopped fresh rosemary

1 teaspoon chopped fresh thyme

Sweet paprika, for topping

Chopped fresh parsley, for garnish

*Read the label to be sure this product is gluten-free.

PER SERVING	1⅓ cups
CALORIES	440
FAT	21 g
SATURATED FAT	7.5 g
CHOLESTEROL	142 mg
CARBOHYDRATE	28 g
FIBER	7.5 g
PROTEIN	40 g
SUGARS	10 g
SODIUM	890 mg

SKINNY SCOOP

To change it up, you can do a mix of half potatoes and half cauliflower, and you can even add cheddar cheese to the topping.

Adjust an oven rack to the second highest position and preheat the oven to 425°F.

Heat a 10½-inch ovenproof skillet over medium heat. Add the cauliflower and 1 cup water, cover, and cook until tender, 10 to 12 minutes. Drain and transfer to a large bowl. Add the buttermilk, 1 tablespoon of the butter, ¾ teaspoon of the salt, and black pepper to taste. Using an immersion blender (or regular blender or food processor), puree the cauliflower until it has the consistency of lumpy mashed potatoes, being careful not to overprocess.

In the same skillet, melt the remaining 1 tablespoon butter over medium-high heat. Add the onion, carrots, and celery and cook, stirring, just until softened, 5 to 6 minutes. Add the garlic and cook, stirring, until fragrant, about 30 seconds. Add the turkey, remaining 1 teaspoon salt, and black pepper to taste. Brown the meat, using a wooden spoon to break it into small pieces as it cooks, about 5 minutes. Add the mushrooms and cook, stirring, until softened, about 3 minutes. Sprinkle the mixture with the flour and cook, stirring, until golden, about 1 minute. Stir in the chicken broth, tomato paste, Worcestershire sauce, corn, peas, rosemary, and thyme. Bring to a boil, reduce the heat to medium, and simmer until the flavors meld, 10 to 12 minutes. Remove from the heat.

Spoon the cauliflower mash over the meat and spread it into an even layer. Dust with paprika. Bake until hot and bubbling, about 20 minutes. Switch the oven to broil and broil about 6 inches from the heating element until the top is lightly browned, 6 to 8 minutes (be careful not to let it burn). Garnish with the parsley, and serve.

SKILLET

Pork Chops Pizzaiola
with Arugula Salad SERVES 4

Pizzaiola sauce gets its name because it features the typical pizza ingredients of olive oil, garlic, oregano, and tomatoes. Usually served with steak or chicken, it's also a great way to jazz up pork chops for a quick weeknight meal. The sauce is so good you'll want to serve it with some crusty bread on the side for dunking. If you don't mind dirtying two pots, you can pour it over pasta, too.

PORK CHOPS

Olive oil spray (I like my Misto or Bertolli)

4 thin bone-in center-cut pork loin chops (8 ounces each)

½ teaspoon kosher salt

Freshly ground black pepper

1 teaspoon olive oil

4 garlic cloves, chopped

1¾ cups canned crushed tomatoes (I like Tuttorosso)

1 sprig of fresh oregano, stemmed and leaves chopped

¼ teaspoon crushed red pepper flakes (optional)

1 tablespoon chopped fresh parsley, plus more for garnish

¼ cup freshly grated Parmigiano-Reggiano cheese

4 fresh basil leaves, chopped

SALAD

6 cups (4 ounces) baby arugula

2 tablespoons extra-virgin olive oil

1 tablespoon red wine vinegar

Freshly ground black pepper

4 ounces Italian bread, whole wheat or gluten-free, cut into 4 pieces

PER SERVING	1 chop + ⅓ cup sauce + 1½ cups salad + 1 ounce bread
CALORIES	511
FAT	20 g
SATURATED FAT	5 g
CHOLESTEROL	162 mg
CARBOHYDRATE	24 g
FIBER	4 g
PROTEIN	58 g
SUGARS	8 g
SODIUM	795 mg

For the pork chops: Heat a large skillet over high heat and spray with oil. Season the chops with the salt and pepper to taste. Add 2 of the pork chops to the hot skillet and cook until browned on both sides, 1½ to 2 minutes per side. Transfer to a plate and repeat with the remaining chops.

Reduce the heat to medium-low. Add the oil and garlic and cook, stirring, until golden, about 1 minute. Stir in the tomatoes, oregano, pepper flakes (if using), parsley, and black pepper to taste. Reduce the heat to low, stir in the Parmigiano-Reggiano and basil, and let cook for 5 minutes.

Return the chops to the skillet along with any juices. Cover and cook for 5 minutes. Flip the chops and cook until a thermometer registers 145°F and the chops are cooked through but still juicy, about 2 more minutes.

Meanwhile, for the salad: In a large bowl, toss the arugula with the olive oil, vinegar, and black pepper to taste.

Transfer the chops to 4 plates, spoon the tomato sauce over the chops, and garnish with the parsley. Divide the salad among the plates and serve with the bread.

SKINNY SCOOP

I prefer the fresh flavor of the sauce that you get with the quick cooking time, but you can also make this dish in a pressure cooker. The flavor will change, but the pork will come out tender if you cook it on high pressure for 6 to 8 minutes after sautéing. Be sure to cover the chops with sauce to keep them submerged before cooking under pressure.

Cheesy Pork Chops with Mushrooms and Wilted Spinach SERVES 4

These easy pork chops are great topped with any kind of cheese—I've tried them with Gouda, mozzarella, and Swiss, and have loved them all. They come out juicy every time; the trick is to make sure your chops are 1 inch thick, not the thinner cuts. The simple pan sauce is so easy and definitely takes the whole dish to another level.

4 boneless center-cut pork loin chops (5 ounces each), 1 inch thick

Kosher salt and freshly ground black pepper

1 teaspoon olive oil

6 tablespoons chopped shallots

16 cups (10 ounces) baby spinach

1 tablespoon unsalted butter

¾ cup low-sodium chicken broth*

2 teaspoons Dijon mustard

10 ounces cremini mushrooms, sliced

3 ounces shredded Gouda, Swiss, or mozzarella cheese*

Chopped fresh parsley, for garnish

*Read the label to be sure this product is gluten-free.

PER SERVING	1 chop + ⅓ cup mushrooms + ½ cup spinach
CALORIES	379
FAT	19.5 g
SATURATED FAT	9 g
CHOLESTEROL	110 mg
CARBOHYDRATE	8 g
FIBER	3 g
PROTEIN	41 g
SUGARS	3 g
SODIUM	628 mg

Preheat the oven to 200°F.

Season the pork with ½ teaspoon salt and pepper to taste.

In a large skillet, heat the oil over medium heat. Add 2 tablespoons of the shallots and cook, stirring, until softened, about 2 minutes. Gradually add the spinach, letting it wilt before adding another handful. Season with ⅛ teaspoon salt and pepper to taste. Cook, stirring, until all of the spinach is wilted, about 2 minutes. Transfer the spinach to an ovenproof platter and place in the oven to keep warm.

To the skillet, add ½ tablespoon of the butter. When hot, add the pork chops and cook until browned on one side, about 7 minutes. Flip the chops and cook until browned and a thermometer inserted in the thickest part of the pork registers 145°F, and the chops are cooked through but still juicy, about 8 minutes. Transfer the chops to the platter with the spinach and place in the oven to keep warm.

In the skillet, melt the remaining ½ tablespoon butter. Add the remaining 4 tablespoons shallots and cook, stirring, until softened, about 2 minutes. Add the broth, using a wooden spoon to scrape up any browned bits stuck to the bottom of the pan. Stir in the mustard, then add the mushrooms, ¼ teaspoon salt, and pepper to taste. Cook, stirring occasionally, until the mushrooms are tender, about 3 minutes. Return the chops to the skillet, spooning the mushrooms over the chops. Top the chops with the cheese and cover the pan. Remove the pan from the heat and leave covered until the cheese melts, 2 to 3 minutes.

Divide the spinach among 4 plates. Top with the chops, garnish with the parsley, and serve.

Shrimp Quesadillas with Stuffed Avocados SERVES 4

Making quesadillas is so fast, they're perfect for weeknight cooking. The stuffed avocados are light and fresh, adding a nice balance to the cheese and mild spice. Since I use cooked shrimp, the whole thing comes together in less than 15 minutes. You could also make these with lump crabmeat instead of shrimp, if you prefer.

SHRIMP SALSA

2 tablespoons finely chopped red onion

Juice of 1 lime

Kosher salt

8 ounces cooked peeled shrimp, finely chopped

1 medium tomato, seeded and chopped

1 fresh jalapeño pepper, seeded and finely chopped

1 tablespoon minced fresh cilantro, plus more for garnish

8 ounces avocado (from 2 small Hass)

QUESADILLAS

Cooking spray (I like my Misto or Bertolli)

8 (6-inch) gluten-free flour tortillas (I like Siete Cassava and Coconut Tortillas)

1⅓ cups (5¼ ounces) shredded reduced-fat Mexican cheese blend*

*Read the label to be sure this product is gluten-free.

PER SERVING	1 quesadilla + 1 stuffed avocado half
CALORIES	416
FAT	21 g
SATURATED FAT	9 g
CHOLESTEROL	131 mg
CARBOHYDRATE	34 g
FIBER	5.5 g
PROTEIN	28 g
SUGARS	4 g
SODIUM	999 mg

SKINNY SCOOP

I'm obsessed with Siete brand Cassava and Coconut Tortillas. Available at Whole Foods and online, they're amazing and free of grains, gluten, and dairy. I actually prefer them over wheat-based tortillas because of their taste and texture. That said, whole wheat tortillas would also work.

For the shrimp salsa: In a medium bowl, stir together the onion, lime juice, and ¼ teaspoon salt. Let it sit for 5 minutes. Add the shrimp, tomato, jalapeño, and cilantro. Mix well. Measure out 1 cup of the shrimp salsa for the quesadillas and drain it well to prevent the quesadillas from getting soggy.

Halve the avocados lengthwise. Remove the pits and use a large spoon to scoop out the flesh from the skins in one piece. Place one half on each of 4 plates and top each with a pinch of salt and ⅓ cup of the remaining shrimp salsa.

For the quesadillas: Heat a skillet over high heat. Spray it with oil. Place 1 tortilla in the hot skillet and mound ⅓ cup cheese in the center, leaving about 1 inch around the edges. Add ¼ cup of the reserved drained shrimp salsa and top with another tortilla. Cook until the tortilla is golden brown on the edges and the cheese is fully melted, 1½ to 2 minutes per side. Transfer to a plate to keep warm. Repeat with the remaining ingredients.

Serve hot, garnished with the cilantro and divided among the plates that have the stuffed avocados on the side.

Summer Veggie Zucchini Noodles with Burrata SERVES 2

This dish is basically one big bowl of summer! It's loaded with seasonal veggies and literally comes together in less than 10 minutes. I especially love making this late in the season when my garden tomatoes are at their sweetest. Zucchini noodles keep it light while allowing you to indulge in a generous serving of rich, creamy burrata, the star of the dish.

1 tablespoon extra-virgin olive oil

1 garlic clove, sliced

1 cup halved cherry tomatoes

1 cup sliced asparagus

¾ teaspoon kosher salt

Freshly ground black pepper

1 cup packed baby spinach

1 large or 2 small zucchini (about 14 ounces total), spiralized and cut into 6-inch lengths

¼ cup (1 ounce) freshly grated Parmesan cheese

1 (4-ounce) ball burrata, sliced into 4 pieces

2 tablespoons chopped fresh basil

PER SERVING	1¾ cups
CALORIES	325
FAT	24 g
SATURATED FAT	11.5 g
CHOLESTEROL	50 mg
CARBOHYDRATE	13 g
FIBER	5 g
PROTEIN	20 g
SUGARS	8 g
SODIUM	857 mg

Heat a large skillet over high heat. Add ½ tablespoon of the olive oil and the garlic and cook, stirring, until golden, about 30 seconds. Add the tomatoes, asparagus, ¼ teaspoon of the salt, and pepper to taste. Cook, stirring, until the asparagus is crisp-tender, about 3 minutes. Stir in the spinach and cook until wilted, about 1 minute. Transfer to a medium bowl.

To the pan, add the remaining ½ tablespoon oil, the zucchini noodles, remaining ½ teaspoon salt, and pepper to taste. Cook, stirring, until slightly undercooked, about 1 minute.

Divide the zucchini noodles between 2 plates. Top each with half of the reserved vegetables, the Parmesan, burrata slices, and fresh basil. Serve immediately.

SKINNY SCOOP

The trick to avoiding watery zucchini is to *under*cook it. It will continue cooking in the hot skillet, so transfer it to a plate as soon as it's ready to prevent it from overcooking. Alternatively, you can serve this over raw zucchini noodles.

Garlicky Shrimp with Smashed Chickpea "Mofongo" SERVES 4

This classic Puerto Rican comfort food is typically made with fried mashed green plantains, garlic, and pork rinds—and it is completely delicious. My healthier version replaces the fried plantains with mashed chickpeas, and topped with the delicious, garlicky shrimp in tomato sauce, it tastes almost like the real thing.

SMASHED CHICKPEAS

2 teaspoons extra-virgin olive oil

1 medium onion, chopped

½ teaspoon kosher salt

Freshly ground black pepper

4 garlic cloves, minced

1½ teaspoons ground cumin

2 (15-ounce) cans reduced-sodium chickpeas,* rinsed and drained

¾ teaspoon sazón seasoning, homemade (see page 127) or store-bought (I like Badia Sazón Tropical)

SHRIMP

1 tablespoon extra-virgin olive oil

½ medium onion, finely chopped

½ green bell pepper, finely chopped

¼ cup minced garlic

¼ cup dry white wine

2 (8-ounce) cans tomato sauce

½ teaspoon ground cumin

½ teaspoon sazón seasoning, homemade (see page 127) or store-bought (I like Badia Sazón Tropical)

¼ teaspoon dried oregano

1 pound peeled and deveined jumbo shrimp (about 24)

2 tablespoons sliced green olives

Chopped fresh cilantro, for garnish

*Read the label to be sure this product is gluten-free.

PER SERVING	¾ cup chickpeas + 1 cup shrimp and sauce
CALORIES	412
FAT	10.5 g
SATURATED FAT	1 g
CHOLESTEROL	135 mg
CARBOHYDRATE	45 g
FIBER	13 g
PROTEIN	35 g
SUGARS	12 g
SODIUM	1,357 mg

For the smashed chickpeas: Preheat the oven to 200°F.

In a large, deep skillet, heat the olive oil over medium heat. Add the onion, salt, and black pepper to taste and cook, stirring, until softened, 4 to 5 minutes. Increase the heat to medium-high. Add the garlic and cumin and cook, stirring, for 1 minute. Add the chickpeas and cook, stirring, until heated through, about 5 minutes. Using a potato masher or fork, crush the chickpeas in the pan. Stir in 1 cup water and the sazón seasoning. Bring the mixture to a simmer, reduce the heat to medium, and cook until the water is evaporated, 1 to 2 minutes. Transfer to an ovenproof dish and set in the oven to keep warm.

For the shrimp: Use a paper towel to wipe the skillet clean. Set the skillet over medium heat and add the olive oil. Add the onion, bell pepper, and garlic. Cook, stirring, until the onion is translucent, 3 to 4 minutes. Add the wine and cook, stirring gently, until slightly reduced, about 1 minute. Add 1 cup water, the tomato sauce, cumin, sazón, and oregano. Bring the sauce to a simmer, cover, reduce the heat to low, and let cook until the flavors meld, about 10 minutes. Add the shrimp and olives and cook, uncovered, until the shrimp is fully cooked through, stirring occasionally, 4 to 5 minutes total. Divide the chickpeas among 4 bowls. Top each with a generous cup of shrimp and sauce. Garnish with cilantro.

Seafood and Chicken Paella SERVES 4

Paella, the national dish of Spain, has held a place of honor in Spanish homes for centuries. It's typically cooked in a special skillet called a *paellera*, but you don't need a fancy pan to make it— a large skillet with a fitted lid works just fine. There are many variations of this dish; you can easily substitute mussels for the clams, for instance (just be sure to thoroughly scrub them before using). Or eliminate the chicken altogether and use more seafood. To round out the meal, serve this with a light salad and a glass of Spanish red wine. Cheers!

8 littleneck clams

7 ounces peeled and deveined jumbo shrimp (about 12)

1 tablespoon fresh lemon juice

¼ teaspoon Old Bay seasoning

½ pound boneless, skinless chicken breast, cut into 1-inch pieces

¾ teaspoon sweet paprika

¼ teaspoon dried oregano

1½ teaspoons kosher salt

Freshly ground black pepper

Olive oil spray (I like my Misto or Bertolli)

2½ teaspoons olive oil

1 small (1¾-ounce) dried chorizo link, thinly sliced

¼ cup chopped onion

2 garlic cloves, minced

1¼ cups uncooked short- or medium-grain white rice

½ cup finely chopped tomatoes

2½ cups unsalted chicken broth*

¼ teaspoon saffron threads

1 bay leaf

½ red bell pepper, thinly sliced

¼ cup frozen green peas

1 tablespoon chopped fresh parsley, for garnish

*Read the label to be sure this product is gluten-free.

PER SERVING	1¾ cups
CALORIES	491
FAT	10 g
SATURATED FAT	2.5 g
CHOLESTEROL	155 mg
CARBOHYDRATE	55 g
FIBER	2.5 g
PROTEIN	40 g
SUGARS	3 g
SODIUM	994 mg

Clean the clams and soak in cold water for 20 minutes to let them release sand. Lift them out of the water (don't pour them out, or the sand will get in the clams again) and set aside.

Place the shrimp in a large bowl and season with ½ tablespoon of the lemon juice and the Old Bay.

Season the chicken with the remaining ½ tablespoon lemon juice, ¼ teaspoon of the paprika, the oregano, ½ teaspoon of the salt, and black pepper to taste.

Heat a large, deep nonstick skillet over high heat. When hot, spray the skillet with oil and add the chicken. Cook, stirring, until browned, about 4 minutes. Reduce the heat to medium and push the chicken to the outer edges of the skillet. Pour 1 teaspoon of the oil into the center of the pan and add the chorizo, onion, and garlic. Cook, stirring and trying not to disturb the chicken, until the onion is softened, about 3 minutes. Stir together the vegetables and chicken, then push the mixture to the outer edges of the skillet. Pour the remaining 1½ teaspoons oil into the center of the pan and add the rice, stirring to coat it with the oil.

(recipe continues)

Cook, stirring the rice occasionally, and trying not to disturb the chicken and vegetables, until slightly toasted, about 3 minutes. Add the tomatoes, chicken broth, saffron threads (crumbled between your fingers), bay leaf, and remaining ½ teaspoon paprika and 1 teaspoon salt. Stir well and bring to a boil, stirring once. Arrange the bell pepper slices over the rice, reduce the heat to low, cover with a fitted lid, and cook for 15 minutes.

Uncover and top with the clams, shrimp, and peas. Cover again and cook until the clams open and the shrimp are cooked through, about 12 minutes. Discard any clams that haven't opened.

Uncover the skillet, increase the heat to medium-high, and cook to toast the bottom of the rice (you should hear it sizzling), 2 to 3 minutes. Discard the bay leaf, garnish with the parsley, and serve.

Seafood Fried Brown Rice SERVES 4

Fried rice is one of my favorite Chinese take-out dishes, and it's one of the biggest reasons I could never live on a strictly low-carb diet! Sure, cauliflower rice can be used in place of the grain, but since this dish is loaded with shrimp, scallops, peas, and carrots—all low-calorie foods—I don't think twice about using brown rice, as it's the perfect choice for a satisfying meal.

2 large eggs

Pinch of kosher salt

Freshly ground black pepper

Cooking spray (I like my Misto or Bertolli)

½ tablespoon toasted sesame oil

½ tablespoon grapeseed or canola oil

½ medium onion, chopped

4 scallions, white parts finely chopped, green parts cut into ¼-inch lengths

½ pound peeled and deveined large shrimp, chopped

½ pound bay scallops

3 garlic cloves, minced

1 teaspoon grated fresh ginger

3 cups leftover cooked short-grain brown rice, cold

1 cup frozen peas and carrots, thawed

3½ tablespoons reduced-sodium soy sauce*

*Read the label to be sure this product is gluten-free.

PER SERVING	1²/3 cups
CALORIES	366
FAT	8.5 g
SATURATED FAT	1.5 g
CHOLESTEROL	174 mg
CARBOHYDRATE	45 g
FIBER	4.5 g
PROTEIN	26 g
SUGARS	3 g
SODIUM	1,016 mg

In a small bowl, whisk together the eggs; add salt and pepper to taste.

Heat a large nonstick wok or deep skillet over high heat. Spray it with oil, add the eggs, and quickly cook, stirring to scramble, until just set, 1 to 2 minutes. Transfer to a plate.

Let the wok get very hot. Add both oils, the onion, and the scallion whites and cook, stirring, for 30 seconds. Add the shrimp and stir-fry for 1 minute. Add the scallops, garlic, and ginger and stir-fry until the seafood is just turning opaque and the garlic and ginger are fragrant, 1 more minute. Stir in the rice and peas and carrots and toss well. Spread the mixture over the surface of the wok and cook, undisturbed, for 3 minutes. Toss, spread back out, and cook undisturbed for 2 more minutes. Add the soy sauce and stir-fry for 1 minute. Add the egg and the scallion greens and stir-fry for 30 seconds. Remove the pan from the heat and serve right away.

Jalapeño Popper Frittata with Pico de Gallo SERVES 4

Frittatas are my default when I need a quick, easy, filling, and cheap meal. It's also the ultimate clean-out-your-fridge dish. Step up your frittata game with a little kick, inspired by the popular appetizer jalapeño poppers! This version uses basic ingredients that I usually have on hand—eggs, cheese, bacon, and avocados—plus the star of the recipe, jalapeños.

FRITTATA

4 large eggs

6 large egg whites

1/2 cup whipped cream cheese, at room temperature

1 teaspoon kosher salt

Freshly ground black pepper

4 slices center-cut bacon, chopped

2 large fresh jalapeño peppers, seeded, 1 minced and 1 thinly sliced

1/3 cup finely chopped shallots

2 garlic cloves, minced

1/2 cup (2 ounces) shredded cheddar cheese*

PICO DE GALLO

1 cup chopped tomatoes

1/3 cup chopped onion

1/4 cup chopped fresh cilantro

Juice of 1/2 lime

Pinch of kosher salt

Freshly ground black pepper

4 ounces thinly sliced avocado (from 1 small Hass)

*Read the label to be sure this product is gluten-free.

PER SERVING	1 wedge + 1/3 cup pico de gallo + 1 ounce avocado
CALORIES	308
FAT	21 g
SATURATED FAT	9 g
CHOLESTEROL	223 mg
CARBOHYDRATE	12 g
FIBER	3.5 g
PROTEIN	20 g
SUGARS	5 g
SODIUM	756 mg

For the frittata: Adjust an oven rack to the second highest position and preheat the oven to 350°F.

In a medium bowl, whisk together the whole eggs, egg whites, cream cheese, salt, and pepper to taste until most of the cream cheese is mixed in and only small chunks remain. Set aside.

Put the bacon in a cold skillet, set the skillet over medium heat, and cook, stirring occasionally, until the bacon is cooked without getting too crisp, about 6 minutes.

To the skillet, add the minced jalapeño, shallots, and garlic. Cook, stirring, until the vegetables are softened, about 2 minutes. Spread everything out in an even layer in the bottom of the skillet. Pour the egg and cream cheese mixture into the skillet and top with the cheddar and sliced jalapeño.

Bake until the eggs are set, about 12 minutes.

Meanwhile, for the pico de gallo: In a small bowl, combine the tomatoes, onion, cilantro, lime juice, salt, and pepper to taste.

Switch the oven to high broil and broil the frittata 4 to 6 inches from the heating element until the top is browned and crisp, 3 to 4 minutes.

To serve, using a spatula, carefully slide the frittata out of the skillet onto a cutting board and cut into 4 wedges. Serve each wedge topped with the avocado and pico de gallo.

SKINNY SCOOP

Jalapeños may vary in heat. If you like extra spice, leave in the seeds and membranes.

Spicy Carrot "Fideos" Secos   SERVES 2

Fideos secos, also known as *sopa seca* or Mexican "dry soup," is typically made with thin spaghetti cooked in a guajillo pepper and tomato sauce, topped with avocado, queso fresco, and sometimes *chicharrón* (fried pork rinds). This grain-free version replaces the pasta with carrots—and I have to say, they just might be the tastiest carrots I've ever eaten (and this is coming from a girl who doesn't really like carrots). Spiralized carrots are great as a pasta swap in dishes like this where you want a noodle with a good bite. Zucchini tends to get watery if cooked too long, but the carrots stay firm, creating a very pasta-like experience.

1 large (13-ounce) carrot (at least 2 inches thick)

2 dried guajillo chiles,* stemmed, split open, and seeded

4 teaspoons olive oil

⅓ cup chopped onion

3 garlic cloves

2 medium tomatoes, quartered

1 teaspoon adobo sauce (from a can of chipotle peppers in adobo sauce)

½ teaspoon ground cumin

¾ teaspoon kosher salt

4 ounces thinly sliced avocado (from 1 small Hass)

2 ounces (scant ½ cup) crumbled queso fresco

1 tablespoon chopped fresh cilantro

*Read the label to be sure this product is gluten-free.

PER SERVING	1¼ cups noodles + 2 ounces avocado
CALORIES	391
FAT	25 g
SATURATED FAT	6.5 g
CHOLESTEROL	20 mg
CARBOHYDRATE	38 g
FIBER	12 g
PROTEIN	11 g
SUGARS	17 g
SODIUM	789 mg

SKINNY SCOOP

A heavy-duty spiralizer, such as an Inspiralizer or the KitchenAid attachment, is recommended for this dish. To make carrot noodles, look for thick carrots, at least 2 inches in diameter. As an alternative, you could use preshredded carrots from the store.

Using the widest noodle blade of your spiralizer, spiralize the carrot, then cut the "noodles" into 6-inch lengths. Set aside on a plate.

Soak the guajillo chiles in a bowl of ½ cup hot water until softened, about 30 minutes. Transfer the chiles and soaking liquid to a blender.

Heat a large skillet over medium-high heat. Add 1 teaspoon of the oil, the onion, and garlic and cook, stirring, until the onion is golden brown, 3 to 4 minutes. Transfer the mixture to the blender. Add the tomatoes, adobo sauce, cumin, and ¼ teaspoon of the salt to the blender and blend well.

In the same skillet, heat the remaining 3 teaspoons oil over medium-high heat. Add the carrot noodles and the remaining ½ teaspoon salt. Cook, stirring, until softened, about 5 minutes. Pour the sauce from the blender over the carrots, increase the heat to high, and cook, stirring occasionally, until the sauce thickens, about 5 minutes.

To serve, divide the carrot noodles between 2 bowls. Top each with half the avocado, queso fresco, and cilantro.

Beef Bibimbap Bowls with Riced Carrots SERVES 2

Inspired by one of my favorite Korean rice dishes, this great big bowl of carrot "rice" will fill you up but won't weigh you down. The best part? How versatile this dish is: You can swap out the carrots for cauliflower "rice" (available precut in most supermarkets today), replace the beef with ground turkey or even pork, and you can top the bowls with kimchi or pickled veggies, if you wish. The egg on top is the pièce de résistance, so don't leave it out!

14 ounces carrots (5 medium or 3 to 4 large), peeled and roughly chopped

3 teaspoons toasted sesame oil

1 medium yellow onion, chopped

1 garlic clove, minced

6 ounces 90% lean ground beef, preferably grass-fed

1 tablespoon gochujang,* plus more for serving

3 tablespoons reduced-sodium soy sauce*

4 ounces sliced shiitake mushrooms

3 cups (about 2 ounces) baby spinach

Pinch of kosher salt

½ cup seeded cucumbers, cut into matchsticks

2 tablespoons sliced scallions

1 teaspoon sesame seeds

Cooking spray (I like my Misto or Bertolli)

2 large eggs

Bean sprouts (optional)

*Read the label to be sure this product is gluten-free.

PER SERVING	1 bowl
CALORIES	495
FAT	21.5 g
SATURATED FAT	6 g
CHOLESTEROL	241 mg
CARBOHYDRATE	46 g
FIBER	10.5 g
PROTEIN	31 g
SUGARS	24 g
SODIUM	1,261 mg

SKINNY SCOOP

Gochujang is a must in Korean cuisine. A savory, sweet, spicy red chile paste, it's so thick it often needs to be thinned out. Annie Chun's makes a great prepared variety, which you can find in the Asian aisle in most supermarkets.

Preheat the oven to 200°F.

In a food processor, working in small batches, pulse the carrots a few times until they resemble grains of rice (don't overprocess or it will get mushy). Spoon the carrots into a kitchen towel, cheesecloth, or paper towels and squeeze out any excess liquid.

In a large skillet, heat 1 teaspoon of the sesame oil over medium heat. Add the onion and cook, stirring, until translucent, about 3 minutes. Add the garlic and cook, stirring, until fragrant, 1 minute. Add the beef, increase the heat to high, and brown the meat, using a wooden spoon to break it into small pieces as it cooks, about 5 minutes. Add the 1 tablespoon gochujang and 1 tablespoon of the soy sauce. Cook, stirring, for 30 seconds, until combined. Transfer to an ovenproof bowl and set the bowl in the oven to keep the mixture warm.

Wipe the skillet clean with a damp paper towel and set it over high heat. When hot, add 1 teaspoon of the sesame oil, then the riced carrots and remaining 2 tablespoons soy sauce. Cook, stirring, until softened, 7 to 8 minutes. Divide evenly between 2 bowls (about ¾ cup for each).

Reduce the heat to medium-high and add the remaining 1 teaspoon sesame oil. Add the mushrooms and cook, stirring, until almost soft, about 3 minutes. Add the spinach and a few drops of water, cover the

pan, and cook until the spinach has wilted, about 1 minute. Season with the salt and divide between the 2 bowls of carrot rice. Top each bowl with ½ cup beef and ¼ cup cucumber. Garnish with the scallions and sesame seeds.

Wipe the skillet clean with a damp paper towel and spray with oil. Set the skillet over medium-low heat and crack the eggs into the skillet. Cover and cook until the yolks are set but still runny, about 2 minutes, or longer if desired. Slide an egg on top of each bowl. Top with bean sprouts (if using)

Skillet Spinach and Feta Pie SERVES 6

Inspired by spanakopita, one of my favorite Greek dishes, I created this dish as an easy alternative to the traditional savory pie, which uses a lot more phyllo and butter. Loaded with spinach and feta cheese, each bite takes me back to Old Town of Rhodes, one of my favorite places I've visited in Greece. I love to make a big garden salad—with lots of cucumber, bell peppers, tomatoes, and olives—to go with it.

2 teaspoons olive oil

1½ cups finely chopped scallions

1¼ cups chopped plum tomatoes (about 4)

3 garlic cloves, minced

3 (10-ounce) packages frozen chopped spinach, thawed and squeezed dry

3 tablespoons chopped fresh dill

⅓ cup chopped fresh parsley

¾ teaspoon kosher salt

Olive oil spray (I like my Misto or Bertolli)

7 large eggs, beaten

1⅔ cups (8 ounces) crumbled feta cheese

⅓ cup (1½ ounces) freshly grated Parmesan cheese

Freshly ground black pepper

6 sheets phyllo dough

1 tablespoon unsalted butter, melted

PER SERVING	1 wedge
CALORIES	360
FAT	21 g
SATURATED FAT	10.5 g
CHOLESTEROL	262 mg
CARBOHYDRATE	22 g
FIBER	5.5 g
PROTEIN	23 g
SUGARS	4 g
SODIUM	958 mg

Preheat the oven to 375°F.

Heat a 10-inch ovenproof skillet over medium-low heat. Add the olive oil, scallions, and tomatoes and cook, stirring, until the tomatoes soften, about 8 minutes. Add the garlic and cook, stirring, until fragrant, 30 more seconds. Add the spinach, dill, parsley, and salt. Cook, stirring, until heated through, about 2 minutes. Transfer to a large bowl and let cool for 5 minutes.

Wipe out the skillet with a paper towel and spray it with oil.

To the bowl of the spinach mixture, add the eggs, feta, Parmesan, and pepper to taste. Stir well. Transfer the mixture to the skillet and spread it evenly in the bottom. Top with 1 sheet of phyllo and carefully trim the excess. Using a pastry brush, gently brush the phyllo with butter. Top with another sheet of phyllo, trim the edges, and brush with butter. Repeat the process with the remaining 4 sheets phyllo.

Bake until the phyllo is golden brown, 40 to 45 minutes. Let cool for 5 minutes. Slice into 6 wedges and serve.

Veggie-Loaded Zucchini Noodle Primavera SERVES 2

Need a 15-minute, veggie-loaded dish? This is it! A low-carb makeover of a vegetarian Italian classic, this meal is super quick to whip up and will disappear from your dinner table even faster because it's *that* good. Although primavera is not typically topped with melted mozzarella, I love the addition, and you can get away with it because this dish is so light.

1 medium zucchini (about 9 ounces)

2 teaspoons extra-virgin olive oil

¼ cup chopped red onion

¼ cup chopped celery

¼ cup chopped carrot

1 tablespoon minced shallot

1 garlic clove, minced

1 cup bite-size pieces broccoli florets

¼ teaspoon kosher salt

Freshly ground black pepper

2 cups store-bought marinara sauce

1 tablespoon freshly grated Pecorino Romano cheese (I like Locatelli)

3 ounces fresh mozzarella cheese, thinly sliced

Chopped fresh basil, for garnish

PER SERVING	2 cups
CALORIES	329
FAT	15.5 g
SATURATED FAT	6.5 g
CHOLESTEROL	25 mg
CARBOHYDRATE	29 g
FIBER	7.5 g
PROTEIN	19 g
SUGARS	10 g
SODIUM	1,098 mg

Using the widest noodle blade of your spiralizer, spiralize the zucchini, then cut the "noodles" into 6-inch lengths.

In a medium skillet, heat the oil over medium-low heat. Add the red onion, celery, carrot, shallot, and garlic and cook, stirring, until tender, about 5 minutes. Add the broccoli, salt, and pepper to taste. Add the marinara sauce, increase the heat to medium, and simmer until the vegetables are crisp-tender, about 3 minutes. Add the zucchini noodles and pecorino. Cook, stirring, until the zucchini is crisp-tender, about 1½ minutes. Top with the mozzarella, cover, and cook until the mozzarella is melted, 1 to 2 more minutes.

Divide evenly between 2 plates and garnish with the basil.

SKINNY SCOOP

To make this fit in to the theme of "one pot," I've suggested using jarred marinara sauce, but you can absolutely use your own homemade sauce. I'm pretty picky about store-bought sauce, but I highly recommend DeLallo's Pomodoro Fresco, which you can buy on their website. It's the best one out there!

Mediterranean Shrimp and Pearl Couscous SERVES 4

This recipe is super easy and crazy good! Perfect for the summer, it's made with Israeli couscous (the larger, more pearl-like variety), shrimp, and fresh cherry tomatoes as the star of the dish. The warm couscous softens the feta cheese, making it just irresistible. Get ready to dig in.

2 cups halved cherry tomatoes (10 ounces)

1/3 cup sliced pitted Kalamata olives

1/4 cup crumbled feta cheese

1 tablespoon capers, drained

Freshly ground black pepper

1/4 teaspoon kosher salt

1 pound peeled and deveined extra-large shrimp

1 teaspoon olive oil

3 garlic cloves, minced

2 cups low-sodium chicken broth*

1 1/2 cups pearl couscous, wheat or gluten-free

Juice of 1/2 lemon

2 tablespoons chopped fresh parsley, for garnish

1/4 teaspoon grated lemon zest, for garnish

*Read the label to be sure this product is gluten-free.

PER SERVING	1¾ cups
CALORIES	394
FAT	6 g
SATURATED FAT	1.5 g
CHOLESTEROL	144 mg
CARBOHYDRATE	53 g
FIBER	1.5 g
PROTEIN	30 g
SUGARS	2 g
SODIUM	680 mg

In a large bowl, combine the tomatoes, olives, feta, and capers. Season with the pepper.

Sprinkle the salt over the shrimp. Heat a large deep skillet over medium-high heat. When hot, add the oil, then the shrimp, and cook until opaque, 2½ minutes per side, stirring in the garlic for the last minute. Transfer to the bowl of the tomato mixture.

Add the broth to the skillet, increase the heat to high, and bring to a boil. Add the couscous, stir, cover, and reduce the heat to medium. Cook until all the liquid is absorbed, 10 to 12 minutes. Fluff with a fork and add to the bowl of the shrimp and tomato mixture. Add the lemon juice and toss well.

Divide among 4 bowls, garnish with the parsley and lemon zest, and serve.

Lazy Veggie Lasagna SERVES 4

When I was a kid, I always loved helping my mom make lasagna—it was an all-day affair because she usually whipped up more than one for holidays. But why save this dish for special occasions when you can make a quick weeknight version in a single skillet? No draining the noodles or layering the pasta; everything cooks all in one pot at the same time! This meatless version is loaded with vegetables, and no one in my family misses the meat (although you can certainly add some if you want). Leftovers (if you have any!) reheat well the next day.

1 cup (8 ounces) part-skim ricotta cheese, at room temperature

¼ cup freshly grated Parmesan cheese

2 tablespoons chopped fresh parsley, plus more for garnish

½ tablespoon olive oil

½ medium onion, chopped

6 ounces mushrooms, stemmed and thinly sliced

1½ cups broccoli florets (1-inch pieces)

½ cup chopped red bell pepper

3 garlic cloves, chopped

2 cups chopped baby spinach

2 cups jarred marinara sauce

1¼ cups low-sodium vegetable broth*

¼ cup chopped fresh basil

6½ ounces no-boil lasagna noodles (about 11), wheat or gluten-free, broken into 1½-inch pieces

¾ cup (3 ounces) shredded part-skim mozzarella cheese*

*Read the label to be sure this product is gluten-free.

PER SERVING	1¾ cups
CALORIES	492
FAT	14.5 g
SATURATED FAT	7 g
CHOLESTEROL	36 mg
CARBOHYDRATE	62 g
FIBER	7.5 g
PROTEIN	28 g
SUGARS	8 g
SODIUM	979 mg

SKINNY SCOOP

Leftovers can be stored in an airtight container in the refrigerator for up to 4 days.

In a small bowl, combine the ricotta, Parmesan, and parsley.

In a 12-inch ovenproof nonstick skillet with a fitted lid, heat the oil over medium-high heat until shimmering. Add the onion, mushrooms, broccoli, bell pepper, and garlic, and cook, stirring, until the vegetables are tender, about 5 minutes. Add the spinach and cook, stirring, until wilted, about 1 minute. Transfer to a medium bowl.

To the skillet, add the marinara sauce, broth, and basil. Stir to combine and bring to a simmer. Add the noodles, stir to coat, and spread into an even layer, making sure the noodles are submerged in liquid. Return the vegetables to the skillet and reduce the heat to medium. Simmer, covered and stirring occasionally, until the pasta is just tender and the sauce has thickened, about 20 minutes.

Remove the pan from the heat and dollop the ricotta cheese mixture over the lasagna noodles. Sprinkle the mozzarella over the top.

Adjust an oven rack to 6 inches from the heating element and preheat the broiler to high.

Broil until the cheese is melted and slightly browned, 3 to 4 minutes. Divide among 4 plates and garnish with the parsley.

Open-Faced French Onion Burgers   SERVES 4

Instead of sandwiching your burger between two halves of a bun, try this open-faced version served on top of ciabatta. Although the onions take some time to caramelize, it's well worth the wait, since they make these burgers instantly taste gourmet—plus, you can easily make them a day or two ahead and keep them in the fridge. You can skip the bread, if you wish, to make it low-carb and gluten-free.

BURGERS

1 pound 90% lean ground beef

¾ teaspoon kosher salt

Freshly ground black pepper

1 teaspoon Worcestershire sauce

ONIONS

½ tablespoon unsalted butter

2 teaspoons olive oil

10 ounces yellow onions (2 medium), halved and cut into ⅛-inch-thick slices

¼ teaspoon kosher salt

Freshly ground black pepper

1 tablespoon dry sherry wine

¼ cup beef stock

Leaves from 1 sprig of fresh thyme

FOR SERVING

2 ounces Gruyère or Swiss cheese, grated

2 small ciabatta or sourdough rolls, halved

1 teaspoon chopped fresh parsley

PER SERVING	1 burger
CALORIES	373
FAT	20 g
SATURATED FAT	8.5 g
CHOLESTEROL	93 mg
CARBOHYDRATE	17 g
FIBER	1.5 g
PROTEIN	30 g
SUGARS	4 g
SODIUM	561 mg

For the burgers: Gently form the beef into 4 equal patties. Season both sides with the salt and pepper to taste. Sprinkle each patty with ¼ teaspoon Worcestershire sauce. Set aside at room temperature while you cook the onions.

For the onions: In a large nonstick skillet, heat the butter and olive oil over medium heat. Add the onions, salt, and pepper to taste and stir well. Cover and cook for 5 minutes. Uncover, reduce the heat to medium-low, and cook, stirring occasionally, until the onions are caramelized and golden brown, 25 to 30 minutes. Add the sherry and cook, stirring, until reduced, about 1 minute. Add the beef stock and thyme and simmer until the liquid evaporates, 2 to 3 minutes. Transfer to a bowl and cover to keep warm.

Wipe the skillet with a damp paper towel and increase the heat to medium-high. When very hot, add the burgers and cook, flipping once, until browned on both sides and almost cooked to your desired doneness, 5 to 6 minutes for medium-rare.

Reduce the heat to low and evenly divide the onions and cheese over the patties. Cover and cook until the cheese is melted, 2 to 3 minutes. Transfer each patty to one half of a roll, sprinkle with the parsley, and serve.

Sheet Pan &
Baking Dish

Crispy Chicken Schnitzel Dinner SERVES 4

I took one of my childhood favorites, chicken schnitzel—which is usually pounded thin, breaded, and deep-fried in oil—and made it lighter *and* easier by whipping it up in the oven. Double score! To ensure the chicken comes out juicy, I don't pound it, and this prevents it from drying out. Then, I swap out regular bread crumbs for panko to get a crunchier crust, and I put it under the broiler for the last minute of cooking so it really crisps up. Adding potatoes and green beans to the sheet pan turns this into a full meal. The dish would not be complete without the capers and lemon. Perfection!

VEGETABLES

Olive oil spray (I like my Misto or Bertolli)

¾ pound baby red potatoes, quartered

1 pound green beans, trimmed and cut into thirds

2 tablespoons olive oil

2 teaspoons minced garlic

½ teaspoon kosher salt

Freshly ground black pepper

CHICKEN

2 boneless, skinless chicken breasts (8 ounces each), halved horizontally to make a total of 4 cutlets

¼ teaspoon kosher salt

Freshly ground black pepper

2 tablespoons all-purpose flour, wheat or gluten-free

1 large egg, beaten

¾ cup seasoned panko bread crumbs, regular or gluten-free

Olive oil spray (I like my Misto or Bertolli)

½ lemon, plus 4 lemon wedges, for serving

1 tablespoon capers, drained

½ tablespoon chopped fresh parsley

PER SERVING	1 chicken cutlet + 1 cup vegetables
CALORIES	363
FAT	11.5 g
SATURATED FAT	2 g
CHOLESTEROL	119 mg
CARBOHYDRATE	35 g
FIBER	6 g
PROTEIN	31 g
SUGARS	4 g
SODIUM	607 mg

For the vegetables: Preheat the oven to 425°F. Lightly spray an 18 x 13-inch large rimmed sheet pan with oil.

On the prepared pan, toss together the potatoes, green beans, olive oil, garlic, salt, and pepper to taste. Spread the vegetables out in a single layer. Bake until partially cooked, about 20 minutes.

Meanwhile, for the chicken: Season the chicken with the salt and pepper to taste. Put the flour in a shallow plate and put the egg in a medium bowl. Put the panko in another shallow plate. Dredge each chicken cutlet lightly in the flour, then dip in the egg, shaking off the excess. Dredge in the panko, lightly pressing to evenly coat. Set aside on a plate.

Remove the pan of vegetables from the oven, stir them together, then push to one side. Place the chicken on the other side of the pan and spray the tops with oil. Return to the oven and bake until the chicken is golden and the potatoes are cooked through, about 15 minutes. Switch the oven to broil and broil until the top of the chicken is browned slightly, 1 to 2 minutes. Remove the pan from the oven and squeeze the lemon half over the vegetables.

Top the chicken with the capers and parsley, and serve with the lemon wedges on the side.

Spicy Peanut Chicken and Vegetables SERVES 4

This dish was inspired by chicken satay, which is usually served as an appetizer on skewers and drizzled with peanut sauce. (It happens to be one of Tommy's favorite appetizers.) I took those flavors and turned them into a meal you can enjoy any night of the week!

PEANUT SAUCE

2 tablespoons smooth peanut butter

2 tablespoons canned full-fat coconut milk

½ tablespoon reduced-sodium soy sauce*

Juice of ½ lime

1 teaspoon Sriracha sauce

¼ teaspoon grated fresh ginger

CHICKEN

Olive oil spray (I like my Misto or Bertolli)

1½ pounds boneless, skinless chicken breast, sliced into 1-inch-thick strips

2 tablespoons reduced-sodium soy sauce*

Juice of ½ lime

4 garlic cloves, minced

1 teaspoon grated fresh ginger

1 teaspoon kosher salt

2 cups peeled, diced (½-inch) sweet potatoes (about 2 large)

2 cups broccoli florets

1 small red onion, thickly sliced

1 medium red bell pepper, sliced

2 cups sugar snap peas

1 tablespoon toasted sesame oil

2 tablespoons chopped roasted salted peanuts

Chopped fresh cilantro, for garnish

4 lime wedges, for serving

*Read the label to be sure this product is gluten-free.

PER SERVING	1 cup vegetables + 4½ ounces chicken
CALORIES	434
FAT	16 g
SATURATED FAT	4 g
CHOLESTEROL	109 mg
CARBOHYDRATE	29 g
FIBER	6 g
PROTEIN	44 g
SUGARS	7 g
SODIUM	943 mg

For the peanut sauce: In a small bowl, whisk together the peanut butter, coconut milk, soy sauce, lime juice, Sriracha, and ginger until smooth.

For the chicken: Adjust a rack in the center and another rack 4 to 6 inches from the broiler and preheat the oven to 425°F. Spray an 18 x 13-inch large rimmed sheet pan with oil.

In a medium bowl, combine the chicken, soy sauce, lime juice, garlic, ginger, and ½ teaspoon of the salt. Pour half of the peanut sauce over the chicken.

Place the sweet potatoes, broccoli, red onion, bell pepper, and snap peas on the prepared pan and toss with the sesame oil and remaining ½ teaspoon salt.

Roast on the center rack, tossing halfway, until the sweet potatoes are almost tender, about 30 minutes. Nestle the chicken among the vegetables, pour the marinade over the chicken, and roast until the chicken is cooked through, 10 to 12 minutes. Switch the oven to broil, move the pan to the higher rack, and broil until the chicken is browned, 2 to 3 minutes.

Divide among 4 plates, pour the remaining peanut sauce over everything, and garnish with the peanuts and cilantro. Serve with the lime wedges on the side.

Dijon-Maple Chicken with Brussels and Butternut SERVES 4

The glaze in this dish combines spicy Dijon mustard and sweet maple syrup for a nicely balanced flavor that's as delicious on the chicken as it is on the veggies. Brussels sprouts and butternut squash each take to the savory-sweet sauce wonderfully, and the hint of thyme makes it just perfect. I like using soy sauce instead of salt in the glaze because it gives it a fantastic depth of flavor.

Olive oil spray (I like my Misto or Bertolli)

4 tablespoons Dijon mustard

3 tablespoons pure maple syrup

2 tablespoons reduced-sodium soy sauce*

4 large bone-in chicken thighs (6½ ounces each), skin removed and fat trimmed

4 skinless chicken drumsticks (3½ ounces each)

¾ teaspoon kosher salt

Freshly ground black pepper

12 ounces Brussels sprouts, trimmed and halved

12 ounces butternut squash, peeled, seeded, and cut into ¾-inch cubes

6 sprigs of fresh thyme

1½ tablespoons olive oil

*Read the label to be sure this product is gluten-free.

PER SERVING	1 drumstick + 1 thigh + 1 cup vegetables
CALORIES	527
FAT	18.5 g
SATURATED FAT	3.5 g
CHOLESTEROL	264 mg
CARBOHYDRATE	28 g
FIBER	5 g
PROTEIN	59 g
SUGARS	13 g
SODIUM	1,153 mg

Preheat the oven to 425°F. Line an 18 x 13-inch large rimmed sheet pan with foil or parchment and spray with oil.

In a small bowl, combine 3 tablespoons of the mustard, 2 tablespoons of the maple syrup, and the soy sauce.

Season both sides of the chicken with ½ teaspoon of the salt and pepper to taste, then arrange it on the prepared pan.

In a large bowl, combine the Brussels sprouts, butternut squash, thyme, olive oil, and the remaining ¼ teaspoon salt. Season with the pepper and toss well. Arrange the vegetables on the prepared sheet pan in a single layer around the chicken. Pour the Dijon-maple sauce over the chicken, turning to coat completely, and pour any remaining sauce over the vegetables.

Bake until the chicken is cooked through and the vegetables are tender, about 40 minutes.

Meanwhile, in a small bowl, whisk together the remaining 1 tablespoon each mustard and maple syrup.

Brush the mustard/maple mixture over the chicken. Bake for 5 more minutes, until browned, and serve right away.

Chicken Fajitas SERVES 4

When we go out for Mexican food, four out of five times my husband, Tommy, orders chicken fajitas. He's predictable like that. And chicken fajitas were the first dish Tommy cooked for me when we were dating (fun fact!). Fajitas are traditionally grilled, so I wasn't sure what he would think if I changed them up by making them on a sheet pan. The verdict: two thumbs up. Phew!

CHICKEN AND VEGETABLES

¼ cup pineapple juice

Grated zest and juice of 1 lime

1 tablespoon olive oil

¼ cup chopped onion

2 garlic cloves, minced

1 teaspoon chili powder*

1 teaspoon ground cumin

1 teaspoon dried oregano

½ teaspoon smoked paprika

1 teaspoon kosher salt

1 pound boneless, skinless chicken breasts, cut lengthwise into 1½-inch-thick strips

Cooking spray (I like my Misto or Bertolli)

1 green bell pepper, cut into ¼-inch-wide slices

1 red bell pepper, cut into ¼-inch-wide slices

1 large onion, cut into ¼-inch-wide slices

Freshly ground black pepper

GUACAMOLE

4 ounces avocado (from 1 small Hass)

Juice of ½ lime

¼ teaspoon kosher salt

2 teaspoons chopped fresh cilantro

FOR ASSEMBLY

8 corn tortillas

½ cup (2 ounces) shredded reduced-fat Mexican cheese blend*

*Read the label to be sure this product is gluten-free.

PER SERVING	**2 fajitas**
CALORIES	**405**
FAT	**15 g**
SATURATED FAT	**3.5 g**
CHOLESTEROL	**81 mg**
CARBOHYDRATE	**38 g**
FIBER	**8 g**
PROTEIN	**33 g**
SUGARS	**7 g**
SODIUM	**632 mg**

For the chicken and vegetables: In a liquid measuring cup, whisk together the pineapple juice, lime zest, lime juice, olive oil, onion, garlic, chili powder, cumin, oregano, smoked paprika, and ½ teaspoon of the salt.

Place the chicken in a large zip-top plastic bag and add the marinade. Massage the marinade into the chicken, making sure to evenly coat all the pieces. Refrigerate for at least 1 hour or as long as overnight.

Adjust an oven rack in the center and another 4 to 6 inches from the broiler and preheat the oven to 400°F. Spray a large rimmed sheet pan with oil and set aside (you can also line it with foil, then spray).

Remove the chicken from the marinade, shaking off any excess, and place it on the prepared pan. Pour the marinade into a large bowl, add the bell peppers and onion, and toss well. Spread the vegetables evenly on the pan around the chicken and sprinkle with the remaining ½ teaspoon salt and pepper to taste. Toss to coat and spread out evenly in the pan.

(recipe continues)

Bake on the center rack until the chicken is almost cooked through, about 15 minutes.

Meanwhile, for the guacamole: Mash the avocado in a small bowl with a fork. Add the lime juice, salt, and cilantro, and stir to combine. Set aside.

Switch the oven to high broil. Give the vegetables and chicken a good toss, move to the top rack, and broil until the vegetables are slightly charred and the chicken is cooked through, 4 to 5 minutes. Remove the pan from the oven and transfer the chicken to a cutting board. Place the tortillas directly on the top oven rack and broil until warm and slightly charred, about 1 minute. Slice the chicken into smaller pieces and mix with the vegetables.

To assemble, evenly distribute the chicken and vegetables among 8 tortillas. Top with the guacamole and cheese.

Caprese Portobello Pizzas SERVES 4

Portobello mushroom caps make a darn good, easy, low-carb pizza "crust." And you can top them with just about any pizza fixin's you can dream up. In this recipe, I top the caps with pesto, mozzarella, and cherry tomatoes, then finish with a balsamic drizzle. The pine nuts on top are optional, but I highly recommend them for some added texture.

Olive oil spray (I like my Misto or Bertolli)

4 large portobello mushroom caps (3 ounces each), stems discarded

Kosher salt

¼ cup prepared pesto

4 ounces part-skim mozzarella cheese, sliced

12 cherry tomatoes, sliced

6 cups (4 ounces) baby arugula

2 tablespoons shredded Parmesan cheese

Pinch of red pepper flakes

Freshly ground black pepper

6 fresh basil leaves, chopped

4 teaspoons balsamic glaze (I like DeLallo)

2 teaspoons finely chopped toasted pine nuts (optional)

PER SERVING	1 pizza
CALORIES	202
FAT	13 g
SATURATED FAT	4.5 g
CHOLESTEROL	22 mg
CARBOHYDRATE	11 g
FIBER	2.5 g
PROTEIN	12 g
SUGARS	6.5 g
SODIUM	507 mg

SKINNY SCOOP

Portobello mushroom caps should be kept dry in paper towels and refrigerated until ready to use; they will keep for up to a week. Look for mushrooms with deep, unbroken sides to keep the cheese from oozing out.

Preheat the oven to 375°F. Spray an 18 x 13-inch sheet pan with oil.

With a small metal spoon, carefully scrape the gills out of each mushroom cap and discard. Place the mushrooms on the prepared sheet pan, round side up. Spray each with oil and sprinkle with a pinch of salt. Bake for 5 minutes.

Remove the pan from the oven and flip the mushrooms over. Layer each cap with 1 tablespoon of the pesto, 1 ounce mozzarella cheese, and one-quarter of the sliced tomatoes. Return to the oven and bake until the mushrooms are tender and the cheese is melted, 20 more minutes.

Meanwhile, divide the arugula among 4 shallow bowls or plates (about 1½ cups each).

Top the arugula with the pizzas. Sprinkle each pizza with ½ tablespoon of the Parmesan, the pepper flakes, black pepper to taste, a pinch of salt, and one-quarter of the basil. Drizzle with the balsamic glaze, top with the pine nuts (if using), and serve.

(recipe continues)

SHEET PAN & BAKING DISH

Tandoori Chicken with Vegetables SERVES 4

Tandoori chicken is traditionally made in a clay oven, but guess what? It's just as tasty in a regular oven! Add some vegetables to your pan and you have an easy, wonderful, Indian-inspired dinner.

CHICKEN

¼ cup whole-milk yogurt (not Greek)

2 tablespoons fresh lemon juice

¼ cup chopped onion

3 garlic cloves, minced

2 teaspoons grated fresh ginger

2 teaspoons garam masala*

¼ teaspoon ground turmeric

¼ teaspoon cayenne pepper

¼ teaspoon smoked paprika

½ teaspoon kosher salt

8 boneless, skinless chicken thighs (3½ ounces each), trimmed of fat

Olive oil spray

VEGETABLES

5 large rainbow carrots (about 1½ pounds), halved lengthwise and cut crosswise into 1½-inch pieces

4 cups medium cauliflower florets, (about 1 pound)

1 tablespoon olive oil

1 teaspoon garam masala*

1 teaspoon kosher salt

Freshly ground black pepper

YOGURT SAUCE

½ cup whole-milk yogurt (not Greek)

1 teaspoon fresh lemon juice

1 garlic clove, minced

1 tablespoon chopped fresh cilantro, plus more for garnish

⅛ teaspoon kosher salt

*Read the label to be sure this product is gluten-free.

PER SERVING	2 thighs + 1¼ cups vegetables + 2 tablespoons sauce
CALORIES	402
FAT	13.5 g
SATURATED FAT	3.5 g
CHOLESTEROL	6 mg
CARBOHYDRATE	26 g
FIBER	7.5 g
PROTEIN	45 g
SUGARS	13 g
SODIUM	616 mg

For the chicken: In a small bowl, combine the yogurt, lemon juice, onion, garlic, ginger, garam masala, turmeric, cayenne, smoked paprika, and salt. Place the chicken thighs in a large zip-top plastic bag, add the marinade, and refrigerate for at least 1 hour or up to overnight.

When ready to cook, adjust an oven rack in the center and another 4 to 6 inches from the broiler. Preheat the oven to 425°F. Spray a large rimmed sheet pan with oil.

For the vegetables: In a large bowl, combine the carrots, cauliflower, and olive oil. Toss to coat. Add the garam masala, salt, and pepper to taste and toss to coat . Spread the vegetables onto the pan. Remove the chicken from the marinade, scrape off any excess, and nestle the chicken among the vegetables. Spray the chicken with oil.

Roast on the center rack until the vegetables are tender and the chicken is cooked through, about 30 minutes.

Meanwhile, for the yogurt sauce: In a small bowl, combine the yogurt, lemon juice, garlic, cilantro, and salt.

Switch the oven to broil. Move the pan to the higher rack and broil until the chicken and vegetables are slightly charred, 3 to 5 minutes. Sprinkle with chopped cilantro and serve with the yogurt sauce on the side.

Honey-Mustard Chicken Bake SERVES 4

Savory and sweet, these boneless chicken thighs are seasoned with a zesty homemade honey-mustard sauce and served over rainbow-colored veggies. If you use juicy thighs instead of breasts, you won't be disappointed. After testing this several times, I found that reserving half of the honey-mustard sauce and adding it at the end, just before broiling everything for a few minutes to caramelize the top, makes for the most delicious dish!

4 large boneless, skinless chicken thighs (6 ounces each)

1 teaspoon kosher salt

¼ cup honey

¼ cup Dijon mustard

3 teaspoons fresh thyme leaves

1 pound asparagus, trimmed and cut into 1-inch pieces

1½ cups cauliflower florets

1 medium red onion, cut into 1-inch pieces, layers separated

1 large red bell pepper, cut into 1-inch pieces

1 tablespoon olive oil

PER SERVING	1 thigh + 1 cup vegetables
CALORIES	383
FAT	12 g
SATURATED FAT	2.5 g
CHOLESTEROL	162 mg
CARBOHYDRATE	29 g
FIBER	5 g
PROTEIN	37 g
SUGARS	23 g
SODIUM	824 mg

Adjust an oven rack in the center and another 6 inches from the broiler and preheat the oven to 400°F.

Season both sides of the chicken with ½ teaspoon of the salt. Transfer to a plate.

In a small bowl, combine the honey, mustard, and 1 teaspoon of the thyme.

In a 9 x 13-inch baking dish, toss together the vegetables, olive oil, remaining ½ teaspoon salt, and remaining 2 teaspoons thyme.

Roast on the center rack for 10 minutes, then remove the dish from the oven. Toss the vegetables and place the chicken over the vegetables. Spoon or brush half of the honey-mustard sauce over the chicken. Return to the center rack and roast until the vegetables are tender and the chicken is cooked through, about 30 minutes.

Spoon or brush the remaining honey-mustard sauce over the chicken. Switch the oven to broil, move the dish to the upper rack, and broil until the chicken begins to brown, 3 to 5 minutes. Serve immediately.

Roasted Sausage, Peppers, and Potatoes SERVES 4

I've been making this fuss-free dish for years—my family loves it and it couldn't be any easier to whip together! You can use whatever sausage your family enjoys. I usually use sweet Italian chicken sausage links, but if you prefer hot sausage or kielbasa, go ahead and make the swap! The potatoes take the longest to cook, so it's best to cut them into small pieces for even cooking. A crisp, green salad on the side is the perfect complement.

Olive oil spray (I like my Misto or Bertolli)

1½ pounds russet potatoes (about 3 large), cut into ½-inch cubes

1 medium onion, halved and quartered, layers separated

2 red bell peppers, cut into 1-inch pieces

1 tablespoon extra-virgin olive oil

3 sprigs of fresh rosemary

½ teaspoon garlic powder

¾ teaspoon kosher salt

Freshly ground black pepper

14 ounces uncooked sweet Italian chicken sausage links*

*Read the label to be sure this product is gluten-free.

PER SERVING	1½ cups
CALORIES	336
FAT	11.5 g
SATURATED FAT	2.5 g
CHOLESTEROL	76 mg
CARBOHYDRATE	39 g
FIBER	4 g
PROTEIN	21 g
SUGARS	5 g
SODIUM	731 mg

Preheat the oven to 400°F. Spray a large rimmed sheet pan with oil.

In a large bowl, combine the potatoes, onion, bell peppers, olive oil, rosemary, garlic powder, salt, and black pepper to taste. Stir to coat the vegetables. Spread in a single layer on the prepared sheet pan.

Roast for 25 minutes. Remove from the oven, give the vegetables a stir, and add the sausage to the sheet pan. Roast, stirring the vegetables once or twice, until the potatoes are tender and the sausage is cooked through, 25 to 30 minutes. Remove the sausage and cut into ½-inch-thick slices. Return the sausage to the sheet pan and toss together with the vegetables. Remove the rosemary sprigs, divide among 4 plates, and serve immediately.

Ginger-Lime Chicken with Broccoli and Carrots SERVES 4

The zesty ginger-lime sauce in this dish has wonderful fresh flavors that are bright and gingery, which gives plain ol' chicken breasts a burst of flavor. Chicken breasts are thicker on one end, so to make sure they cook evenly, I lightly pound them out so that they are even in thickness.

Olive oil spray (I like my Misto or Bertolli)

Juice of 1 small lime

2 tablespoons olive oil

2 scallions, chopped, white and green parts kept separate

1 small fresh jalapeño pepper, seeded and minced

2 garlic cloves, minced

1 teaspoon grated fresh ginger

3 tablespoons chopped fresh cilantro

1¼ teaspoons kosher salt

Freshly ground black pepper

2 cups diagonally sliced carrots (¼ inch thick)

4 cups broccoli florets

4 boneless, skinless chicken breasts (8 ounces each)

¼ teaspoon sweet paprika

½ teaspoon onion powder

½ teaspoon garlic powder

PER SERVING	1 chicken breast + ¾ cup vegetables
CALORIES	387
FAT	13 g
SATURATED FAT	2 g
CHOLESTEROL	145 mg
CARBOHYDRATE	15 g
FIBER	4.5 g
PROTEIN	52 g
SUGARS	5 g
SODIUM	690 mg

Preheat the oven to 400°F. Line a large rimmed sheet pan with foil and spray it with oil.

In a small bowl, combine the lime juice, olive oil, scallion whites, jalapeño, garlic, ginger, 2 tablespoons of the cilantro, ½ teaspoon of the salt, and black pepper to taste.

In a large bowl, toss the carrots with 1 tablespoon of the ginger-lime sauce. Transfer to the prepared pan. Roast until partially cooked, about 10 minutes.

Meanwhile, in a large bowl, toss the broccoli with 2 tablespoons of the ginger-lime sauce.

One at a time, place a chicken breast between two sheets of plastic wrap and use a meat tenderizer or rolling pin to gently pound to an even thickness across the breast (they don't need to be thin, just even). Sprinkle the chicken with the paprika, onion powder, garlic powder, ½ teaspoon of the salt, and pepper to taste. Add the chicken breasts and broccoli to the pan of carrots.

Roast, tossing the vegetables halfway, until the chicken is cooked through and the vegetables are tender, 25 to 28 minutes.

Season the vegetables with the remaining ¼ teaspoon salt. Drizzle the remaining ginger-lime sauce over everything. Garnish with the remaining 1 tablespoon cilantro and the scallion greens.

Spinach, Bacon, and Cheddar Hasselback Chicken SERVES 4

You may have heard of Hasselback potatoes, a popular Swedish side dish that originated in a Stockholm restaurant. The potatoes are thinly sliced about three-quarters of the way through, allowing the toppings to seep into every bite. Well, I've discovered that you can do this with chicken breasts, too! You can stuff them with just about anything you can think up. This spinach, bacon, and cheddar combination is sure to become a new favorite in your house.

Cooking spray (I like my Misto or Bertolli)

2 cups frozen chopped spinach, thawed and squeezed dry

3 slices center-cut bacon, chopped

¼ cup plus 2 tablespoons shredded sharp cheddar cheese*

4 boneless, skinless chicken breasts (8 ounces each)

¾ teaspoon kosher salt

Freshly ground black pepper

*Read the label to be sure this product is gluten-free.

PER SERVING	1 chicken breast
CALORIES	346
FAT	11 g
SATURATED FAT	4 g
CHOLESTEROL	158 mg
CARBOHYDRATE	3 g
FIBER	2.5 g
PROTEIN	56 g
SUGARS	0.5 g
SODIUM	675 mg

Adjust an oven rack in the center and another 4 to 6 inches from the broiler and preheat the oven to 425°F. Line a rimmed sheet pan with foil and spray it with oil.

In a medium bowl, combine the spinach, chopped bacon, and ¼ cup of the cheddar.

Place the chicken breasts on the prepared pan. Using a sharp knife, cut slits across the top of each chicken breast that are about ½ inch apart and about three-quarters of the way through, being careful not to cut all the way through. Sprinkle with the salt and pepper to taste. Stuff each slit with the spinach mixture. Sprinkle the remaining 2 tablespoons cheddar on the tops of the chicken breasts.

Bake on the center rack until the chicken is cooked through, about 20 minutes. Switch the oven to high broil. Move the pan to the higher rack and broil until the tops are golden, about 2 minutes. Serve hot.

Giant Turkey Meatball Parmesan SERVES 4

I'm *obsessed* with this meatball recipe. That's because this isn't just any meatball . . . nope. It's *huge*, smothered with marinara and cheese, and baked in the oven like a meatloaf. My husband, Tommy—who's not nearly as concerned about eating light as I am—requested that I make this special meatball, and since I love a challenge, I knew I had to make it Skinnytaste style. And now this fun creation is one of the most popular recipes on the blog! We serve it with Italian bread and a simple green salad. For extra decadence, Tommy tops his meatball with a dollop of ricotta.

Olive oil spray (I like my Misto or Bertolli)

1 pound 93% lean ground turkey

1/3 cup seasoned wheat or gluten-free bread crumbs

3 tablespoons freshly grated Pecorino Romano cheese (I like Locatelli)

1 large egg, beaten

1 garlic clove, minced

2 teaspoons tomato paste

1½ tablespoons minced fresh parsley, plus more for garnish

½ teaspoon kosher salt

1/3 cup jarred marinara sauce, plus more (optional) for serving

¼ cup (1 ounce) shredded mozzarella cheese*

*Read the label to be sure this product is gluten-free.

PER SERVING	one-quarter meatball
CALORIES	264
FAT	13.5 g
SATURATED FAT	4.5 g
CHOLESTEROL	138 mg
CARBOHYDRATE	8 g
FIBER	1 g
PROTEIN	28 g
SUGARS	1 g
SODIUM	541 mg

Preheat the oven to 350°F. Line a rimmed sheet pan with foil or spray it with oil.

In a medium bowl, combine the turkey, bread crumbs, pecorino, egg, garlic, tomato paste, parsley, and salt. Mix gently to combine. Transfer the mixture to the prepared pan and, using your hands, form it into an oval or round loaf. Slightly flatten the top so the sauce and cheese won't roll off.

Bake until cooked through in the center and a thermometer inserted in the middle registers 160°F, 50 to 55 minutes. Remove the pan from the oven. Top the meatball with the marinara and mozzarella and bake until the sauce is hot and the cheese is melted, 3 to 5 minutes.

Garnish with the parsley, cut into 4 pieces, and serve with more warmed sauce on the side, if desired.

Petite Meatloaf Dinner SERVES 4

Meatloaf nights happen once a month in my home—it's tough to beat classic American comfort food at its finest. But I'm a big fan of making it on a *sheet pan*. These petite turkey meatloaves cook with the vegetables—everything all at once—so the whole meal is ready in just 30 minutes. Winner, winner, meatloaf sheet-pan dinner!

MEATLOAF

Cooking spray

1 pound 93% lean ground turkey

⅓ cup quick-cooking oats*

6 tablespoons ketchup

¼ cup finely chopped onion

1 large egg

1 teaspoon dried marjoram

¾ teaspoon kosher salt

2 teaspoons Worcestershire sauce*

VEGETABLES

¾ pound green beans, trimmed

12 small heirloom carrots (about 10 ounces), trimmed

2 tablespoons olive oil

¾ teaspoon kosher salt

½ teaspoon garlic powder

Freshly ground black pepper

*Read the label to be sure this product is gluten-free.

PER SERVING	1 meatloaf + 3 carrots + ½ cup green beans
CALORIES	358
FAT	18 g
SATURATED FAT	4 g
CHOLESTEROL	130 mg
CARBOHYDRATE	25 g
FIBER	6 g
PROTEIN	27 g
SUGARS	11 g
SODIUM	849 mg

For the meatloaf: Preheat the oven to 450°F. Spray an 18 x 13-inch rimmed sheet pan with oil.

In a medium bowl, combine the ground turkey, oats, 3 tablespoons of the ketchup, the onion, egg, marjoram, and salt. Mix well. Divide the mixture into 4 equal portions. On one side of the prepared pan, shape each portion into a 4 x 2½-inch freeform loaf.

In a small bowl, combine the Worcestershire sauce and the remaining 3 tablespoons ketchup and brush over the loaves.

For the vegetables: In a large bowl, combine the green beans, carrots, olive oil, salt, garlic powder, and pepper to taste. Spread the vegetables out in a single layer on the open half of the pan.

Bake for 12 minutes. Turn the vegetables and bake until the loaves are no longer pink in the center and the vegetables are tender, 12 to 15 more minutes. Serve hot.

Garlic-Dijon Roasted Pork Tenderloin with Potatoes and Green Beans SERVES 4

Pork tenderloin is one of my favorite meats to cook for weeknight dinners because it's lean and happens to be the perfect size to feed my family of four. It's also one of the most tender cuts of meat on the animal, which means it can be cooked quickly and easily. Combined with roasted potatoes and charred green beans, this dinner is always a hit in my home.

PORK

Olive oil spray (I like my Misto or Bertolli)

1 tablespoon fresh lemon juice

1½ tablespoons Dijon mustard

½ teaspoon olive oil

3 garlic cloves, minced

½ tablespoons chopped fresh rosemary

¾ teaspoon kosher salt

Freshly ground black pepper

1½ pounds pork tenderloin

VEGETABLES

1 pound baby gold or red potatoes (about 12), quartered

1 tablespoon plus 1 teaspoon olive oil

½ tablespoon chopped fresh rosemary

½ teaspoon garlic powder

1 teaspoon kosher salt

Freshly ground black pepper

4 ounces green beans, cut into thirds (about 1 cup)

PER SERVING	2 slices pork + about ⅔ cup vegetables
CALORIES	335
FAT	9.5 g
SATURATED FAT	2 g
CHOLESTEROL	111 mg
CARBOHYDRATE	21 g
FIBER	3 g
PROTEIN	39 g
SUGARS	2 g
SODIUM	746 mg

SKINNY SCOOP

Pork tenderloin is often sold in individual packages in the meat section of the grocery store; they may also be sold packaged in a marinade, but I personally avoid these because I prefer to season the meat myself.

For the pork: Preheat the oven to 425°F. Spray a 9 x 13-inch baking dish or large oval casserole with oil.

In a large bowl, combine the lemon juice, mustard, olive oil, garlic, rosemary, salt, and pepper to taste. Place the tenderloin in the bowl, turning to coat all sides evenly.

For the vegetables: In a large bowl, toss together the potatoes, 1 tablespoon of the oil, the rosemary, garlic powder, ¾ teaspoon of the salt, and pepper to taste. Transfer to the prepared baking dish. In the same bowl, toss the green beans with the remaining 1 teaspoon olive oil and ¼ teaspoon salt. Transfer to the dish with the potatoes.

Roast the vegetables, tossing halfway through, for 30 minutes. Remove the dish from the oven, stir the vegetables, and push them to the sides to make room in the center for the pork.

Put the pork in the baking dish and roast for 15 minutes. Remove the dish from the oven, flip the pork, and stir the vegetables. Roast until the pork reaches an internal temperature of 140°F to 145°F for medium, and the potatoes are browned and fork-tender, 15 to 20 more minutes.

Transfer the pork to a cutting board, tent it with foil, and let it rest for 5 minutes before slicing. Slice the pork into 8 medallions, spoon the pan drippings over the pork, and serve with the potatoes and green beans.

Dad's Czech Meat Patties with Potatoes and Cucumber Salad SERVES 4

When my father passed away this year, the only way I found comfort was to cook his signature dishes, as it made me feel closer to him. This is a slimmed-down spin on one of my favorite meals that my dad used to make when I was growing up. *Karbanátky* are Czech ground beef and cabbage patties that are breaded and fried. Dad always served them with fried potatoes and a simple cucumber salad. I've lightened up the patties using a half turkey/half beef mixture, and I bake the meat and potatoes all on one sheet pan. The results are wonderful—just as good as Dad's without all the grease.

PATTIES

Olive oil spray (I like my Misto or Bertolli)

½ cup bread crumbs, regular or gluten-free

½ small head savoy cabbage

½ pound 93% lean ground beef

½ pound 93% lean ground turkey

½ small onion, chopped

1 garlic clove, minced

1 large egg, beaten

1 teaspoon kosher salt

POTATOES

12 baby gold or red potatoes (about 1 pound), halved

1 tablespoon olive oil

½ teaspoon garlic powder

¾ teaspoon kosher salt

CUCUMBER SALAD

1 medium cucumber, peeled and very thinly sliced

¼ cup light sour cream

¼ teaspoon kosher salt

Chopped fresh parsley, for garnish

PER SERVING	2 meat patties + 6 potato halves + ⅓ cup cucumber salad
CALORIES	393
FAT	16 g
SATURATED FAT	5 g
CHOLESTEROL	129 mg
CARBOHYDRATE	34 g
FIBER	4 g
PROTEIN	30 g
SUGARS	4 g
SODIUM	797 mg

For the patties: Preheat the oven to 425°F. Spray a large rimmed sheet pan with oil.

Put ¼ cup of the bread crumbs on a plate.

Finely chop the cabbage in a food processor. Transfer it to a large bowl and add the beef, turkey, onion, garlic, egg, salt, and the remaining ¼ cup bread crumbs. Using your hands, mix well. Form into 8 balls and flatten them slightly into patties. Coat the patties with bread crumbs on both sides, then transfer to the prepared pan. Spray with oil.

For the potatoes: In another large bowl, toss together the potatoes, olive oil, garlic powder, and salt. Arrange on the sheet pan around the patties.

Roast, tossing the potatoes and flipping the patties halfway through, until golden and tender, about 30 minutes.

Meanwhile, for the cucumber salad: In a medium bowl, combine the cucumber, sour cream, and salt. Refrigerate until ready to eat.

Transfer 2 meat patties to each plate. Toss the potatoes with the parsley and serve alongside with the cucumber salad.

Carne Asada Fries SERVES 2

Forget nachos! These South of the Border-flavored fries—a San Diego invention—are piled high with steak, cheese, and pico de gallo, almost as if a steak burrito exploded on a bed of fries. Typically, these fries will set you back an entire day's worth of calories, but I lightened them up so you can eat them with no regret. Cheap, filling, and messy, they are totally addicting.

BEEF

Olive oil spray (I like my Misto or Bertolli)

1 (8-ounce) lean sirloin steak, ½ inch thick

½ teaspoon kosher salt

½ teaspoon ground cumin

¼ teaspoon garlic powder

Freshly ground black pepper

FRIES

Olive oil spray (I like my Misto or Bertolli)

11 ounces russet potatoes (2 small)

2 teaspoons olive oil

½ teaspoon kosher salt

¼ teaspoon garlic powder

TOPPINGS

½ cup (2 ounces) shredded cheddar cheese* or queso fresco

½ cup pico de gallo, homemade (see Skinny Scoop) or store-bought

*Read the label to be sure this product is gluten-free.

PER SERVING	2 cups
CALORIES	456
FAT	19 g
SATURATED FAT	8 g
CHOLESTEROL	108 mg
CARBOHYDRATE	36 g
FIBER	4 g
PROTEIN	38 g
SUGARS	3 g
SODIUM	966 mg

SKINNY SCOOP

To make pico de gallo: Combine 1 cup chopped tomato, ¼ cup chopped scallions, ¼ cup chopped fresh cilantro, ½ jalapeño (minced), 2 tablespoons fresh lime juice, and ¼ teaspoon kosher salt.

For the beef: Adjust oven racks in the top and bottom third of the oven. Preheat the broiler to high. Spray a large rimmed sheet pan lightly with oil.

Season the steak with the salt, cumin, garlic powder, and pepper to taste. Arrange on the prepared pan. Broil on the top rack for about 4 minutes. Flip the pieces of steak and broil for 2 more minutes. Remove the pan from the oven, transfer the steak to a plate, and tent it with foil (the meat will continue cooking).

Meanwhile, for the fries: Turn the oven to the bake setting and preheat to 450°F. Spray the pan with oil.

Cut the potatoes lengthwise into ¼-inch-thick slabs, then cut each slab lengthwise into ¼-inch-wide fries. Arrange the fries in a single layer on the prepared pan, drizzle with the oil, sprinkle with the salt and garlic powder, and toss well to coat.

Roast in the bottom third of the oven until browned on the bottom, about 10 minutes. Flip the fries and roast until crisp and browned, 8 to 10 more minutes. Remove the pan from the oven.

Meanwhile, slice the beef into thin strips across the grain, then chop the strips into small pieces. When the fries are done, top with the steak and cheddar. Return the pan to the oven to melt the cheese, about 2 minutes.

Top with the pico de gallo and serve immediately.

Garlic-Turmeric Salmon with Rainbow Carrots, Cauliflower, and Lemon SERVES 2

I cook salmon at least once a week, not only because I love it, but since I know it's one of the best ways to increase my intake of omega-3 fatty acids. Five ounces of baked salmon contains at least 1,000 milligrams of omega-3 fats—more than the average American adult gets from all food sources over the course of several days. Turmeric adds great flavor, nutrition, and anti-inflammatory properties to this already nutrient-rich, veggie-loaded dish. Go fish!

Olive oil spray (I like my Misto or Bertolli)

¾ teaspoon kosher salt

½ teaspoon ground turmeric

¼ teaspoon ground ginger

2 skinless wild-caught salmon fillets, 1 inch thick (6 ounces each)

1 garlic clove, minced

1 pound baby rainbow carrots

2 cups cauliflower florets

1½ tablespoons olive oil

Pinch of crushed red pepper flakes

Juice of ½ lemon

Chopped fresh cilantro, for garnish

PER SERVING	1 salmon fillet + 2 cups vegetables
CALORIES	443
FAT	21.5 g
SATURATED FAT	3 g
CHOLESTEROL	94 mg
CARBOHYDRATE	26 g
FIBER	9.5 g
PROTEIN	38 g
SUGARS	14 g
SODIUM	703 mg

Preheat the oven to 425°F. Spray a rimmed sheet pan with oil.

In a small bowl, combine ¼ teaspoon of the salt, ¼ teaspoon of the turmeric, and ⅛ teaspoon of the ground ginger.

Spray the fish with oil, then rub each fillet with the garlic and spice mixture. Transfer to a plate.

Arrange the carrots and cauliflower on the prepared pan, drizzle with the olive oil, and season with the pepper flakes, ¼ teaspoon of the salt, and the remaining ¼ teaspoon turmeric and ⅛ teaspoon ground ginger. Toss to coat evenly and spread in a single layer.

Roast, stirring once halfway, until almost done, about 25 minutes. Push the vegetables to one side of the pan and add the salmon to the other side. Roast until the salmon flakes easily with a fork and the vegetables are crisp-tender, 8 to 10 minutes. To serve, sprinkle everything with the remaining ¼ teaspoon salt and the lemon juice, and garnish with the cilantro.

Lemon-Roasted Fish and Cauli-Rice SERVES 2

This fantastic sheet-pan dish is fast, light, and delicious! Roasting the "riced" cauliflower—which is available precut in most supermarkets—gives it a nutty taste and a pretty golden color. The flavor and texture is the perfect complement for this fish.

Olive oil spray (I like my Misto or Bertolli)

16 ounces (3¾ cups) fresh riced cauliflower

1 tablespoon olive oil

3 garlic cloves, chopped

¾ teaspoon kosher salt

2 skinless sea bass or red snapper fillets (6 ounces each)

Freshly ground black pepper

½ tablespoon unsalted butter, melted

4 thin lemon slices, plus 4 wedges, for serving

2 teaspoons chopped fresh parsley

PER SERVING	1 fish fillet + 1½ cups cauliflower
CALORIES	322
FAT	13.5 g
SATURATED FAT	3.5 g
CHOLESTEROL	77 mg
CARBOHYDRATE	16 g
FIBER	6.5 g
PROTEIN	37 g
SUGARS	6 g
SODIUM	631 mg

Preheat the oven to 425°F. Spray a large rimmed sheet pan with oil.

Combine the riced cauliflower, olive oil, garlic, and ½ teaspoon of the salt on the prepared pan. Spread the mixture out in a single layer. Roast, stirring 2 or 3 times, until the cauliflower is golden, about 20 minutes.

Arrange the fish on top of the cauliflower, season it with the remaining ¼ teaspoon salt and pepper to taste, then drizzle the melted butter over the top. Place the lemon slices over the fish.

Roast until the fish is opaque and flakes easily, 8 to 10 minutes. Remove the pan from the oven and discard the lemon slices. Sprinkle the fish with the parsley and serve with the lemon wedges.

SKINNY SCOOP

To rice cauliflower yourself, remove and discard the core of a whole cauliflower, then cut it into florets. Working in batches, pulse the florets in a food processor, 3 to 4 times, until the cauliflower resembles grains of rice (don't overprocess or it will get mushy).

Miso Black Cod with Shiitakes and Bok Choy SERVES 2

Black cod (also known as sablefish) is one of my favorite fish because it has such a high—but healthy—fat content. Every luscious bite provides texture and flavor that's vastly different from the leaner Atlantic cod. For maximum flavor, it's best to marinate the fish 2 to 3 days in advance, although overnight would be fine if you're pressed for time. Once marinated, this dish comes together in less than 15 minutes. Your only problem will be finding something to do with all the time you saved!

¼ cup mirin

2 tablespoons white miso*
(I like Miso Master Organic)

2 garlic cloves, minced

1½ teaspoons grated
fresh ginger

1 tablespoon light brown sugar

2 skinless wild-caught Alaskan
black cod or salmon fillets
(5 ounces each)

Cooking spray (I like my Misto or
Bertolli)

8 ounces baby bok choy

5 ounces shiitake mushrooms,
stemmed and sliced

1 tablespoon reduced-sodium
soy sauce*

1 teaspoon toasted sesame oil

¼ teaspoon black sesame seeds

¼ teaspoon white sesame seeds

1 scallion, sliced

*Read the label to be sure this
product is gluten-free.

PER SERVING	1 fish fillet + 1 cup vegetables
CALORIES	447
FAT	25 g
SATURATED FAT	5 g
CHOLESTEROL	70 mg
CARBOHYDRATE	23 g
FIBER	3.5 g
PROTEIN	23 g
SUGARS	10 g
SODIUM	836 mg

FOOD FACTS: BLACK COD

Because black cod lives in deep, cold waters, it accumulates more fat—and more of the good-for-your-heart omega-3 fatty acids, EPA and DHA—than most other fish, making it wonderfully tasty *and* incredibly healthy. In fact, it has even more omega-3s than wild salmon (except king salmon)!

In a small bowl, combine the mirin, miso, half of the garlic, 1 teaspoon of the ginger, and the brown sugar. Place the fish in a shallow container, pour the marinade over the top, and cover with plastic wrap. Refrigerate overnight or for up to 3 days (the longer the better).

When ready to cook, adjust an oven rack in the center and another 4 to 6 inches from the broiler and preheat the oven to 425°F. Spray a large rimmed sheet pan with oil.

Reserving 2 teaspoons of the marinade (discard the rest), place the fish on the prepared pan.

Rinse the bok choy well and slice into 1½-inch pieces. Put the slightly wet bok choy into a large bowl and add the mushrooms, soy sauce, sesame oil, reserved marinade, and the remaining garlic clove and ½ teaspoon ginger. Toss well, then arrange the vegetables on the pan around the fish.

Bake on the center rack until the fish is just cooked through, 8 to 10 minutes. Switch the oven to high broil, move the pan to the higher rack, and broil until the fish is golden brown, 3 to 4 minutes.

Divide the vegetables between 2 plates and place a piece of fish on top of each. Sprinkle with both sesame seeds and the scallion, and serve immediately.

Pesce Primavera SERVES 4

Baked fish with lots of fresh vegetables is my go-to for a fast and healthy meal. This dish is so versatile that you can use any combination of vegetables you happen to have in your fridge—cauliflower, bell peppers, zucchini, red onions, or whatever you like. For best results, however, try to keep it colorful!

Olive oil spray (I like my Misto or Bertolli)

2 cups bite-size pieces broccoli florets

2 cups 1-inch pieces asparagus (about 8 ounces)

2 cups halved cherry tomatoes

1 cup shredded carrots

2 garlic cloves, minced

1½ tablespoons extra-virgin olive oil

1 teaspoon kosher salt

Freshly ground black pepper

4 skinless fish fillets (5 ounces each), such as sole or flounder

2 tablespoons fresh lemon juice

¼ cup freshly grated Pecorino Romano cheese (I like Locatelli)

2 tablespoons chopped fresh basil

PER SERVING	1 fillet + 1¼ cups vegetables
CALORIES	233
FAT	10.5 g
SATURATED FAT	2.5 g
CHOLESTEROL	70 mg
CARBOHYDRATE	13 g
FIBER	4.5 g
PROTEIN	24 g
SUGARS	6 g
SODIUM	848 mg

SKINNY SCOOP

When it comes to buying fish, always choose whatever's freshest and local, and whenever possible try to make sure it's also sustainable.

Preheat the oven to 400°F. Spray a 9 x 13-inch baking dish with oil.

In a large bowl, combine the broccoli, asparagus, tomatoes, carrots, garlic, 1 tablespoon of the olive oil, ½ teaspoon of the salt, and pepper to taste. Transfer the vegetables to the prepared baking dish and roast until the vegetables begin to soften, about 10 minutes.

Meanwhile, season one side of the fish fillets with ¼ teaspoon of the salt and pepper to taste. Roll up the fillets and place them seam side down on a plate. Season the tops with the remaining ¼ teaspoon salt and pepper to taste.

Toss the vegetables, then place the fish seam side down on top. Drizzle the fish with the remaining ½ tablespoon olive oil and the lemon juice.

Roast until the fish is cooked through in the center and the vegetables are tender and cooked, about 20 minutes.

Top everything with the pecorino and fresh basil and serve immediately.

Crab-Stuffed Shrimp SERVES 4

On Long Island, where I live, we have tons of seafood restaurants. But I'm often disappointed when I order this dish out because the stuffing never has enough crabmeat—it's usually all breading. Problem solved: I made them myself with tons of lump crab. Now, I'll never order them out again! I love these shrimp with a big green salad on the side, or, if you don't mind using two sheet pans, you can roast some asparagus or broccoli alongside them.

Olive oil spray (I like my Misto or Bertolli)

32 peeled and deveined tail-on jumbo shrimp (about 1¼ pounds)

⅓ cup panko bread crumbs, regular or gluten-free

1 tablespoon fresh lemon juice

1 tablespoon mayonnaise

1 teaspoon Dijon mustard

1 large egg, beaten

1 large egg white

2 tablespoons chopped fresh parsley

½ teaspoon Old Bay Seasoning

⅛ teaspoon paprika

Freshly ground black pepper

9 ounces lump crabmeat, picked over for bits of shell

1½ tablespoons unsalted butter, melted

Lemon wedges, for serving

PER SERVING	8 stuffed shrimp
CALORIES	298
FAT	10 g
SATURATED FAT	3.5 g
CHOLESTEROL	292 mg
CARBOHYDRATE	6 g
FIBER	0.5 g
PROTEIN	41 g
SUGARS	0 g
SODIUM	909 mg

Adjust one rack in the center of the oven and another 6 inches from the broiler. Preheat the oven to 350°F. Spray a rimmed sheet pan with oil.

Butterfly the shrimp by cutting a slit down the back of the shrimp, slicing about three-quarters of the way through. Flatten with a knife.

In a large bowl, combine the panko, lemon juice, mayonnaise, mustard, whole egg, egg white, parsley, Old Bay, paprika, and pepper to taste. Stir well, then fold in the crabmeat, being careful not to overmix. Place 1 tablespoon of the crab mixture onto each shrimp and transfer to the prepared pan. Brush the melted butter over the top of each.

Bake on the center rack until the shrimp are opaque, about 8 minutes. Switch the oven to broil, move the sheet pan to the top rack, and broil until golden, about 2 minutes. Serve with the lemon wedges.

Lemon Parmesan Shrimp with Broccoli and Cauliflower   SERVES 4

One of the easiest, tastiest ways to prepare shrimp is to roast them. Add some vegetables to the pan, finish it all with fresh lemon juice and Parmesan cheese, and you have yourself a quick and complete meal. This dish is loaded with vegetables—in fact, it may seem like there isn't enough space for the shrimp at first! But the vegetables shrink as they are roasted, leaving plenty of room to nestle in the shrimp.

Olive oil spray (I like my Misto or Bertolli)

1 pound peeled and deveined large shrimp

2 tablespoons plus 2 teaspoons olive oil

2 garlic cloves, minced

2 tablespoons finely chopped shallot

1 teaspoon Italian seasoning

1 teaspoon kosher salt

Freshly ground black pepper

6 cups bite-size pieces cauliflower florets (1 pound)

6 cups bite-size pieces broccoli florets (1 pound)

3 tablespoons freshly grated Parmesan cheese

2 tablespoons chopped fresh parsley

2 tablespoons toasted pine nuts

Juice of 1 lemon, plus ½ lemon, cut into wedges

PER SERVING	2 cups shrimp and vegetables
CALORIES	300
FAT	14 g
SATURATED FAT	2 g
CHOLESTEROL	138 mg
CARBOHYDRATE	18 g
FIBER	6.5 g
PROTEIN	28 g
SUGARS	6 g
SODIUM	695 mg

Preheat the oven to 400°F. Spray a large rimmed sheet pan with oil.

Pat the shrimp dry and place in a medium bowl. Add 2 teaspoons of the olive oil, the garlic, shallot, Italian seasoning, ½ teaspoon of the salt, and pepper to taste. Toss gently to coat and set aside.

Put the cauliflower and broccoli on the prepared sheet pan and toss with the remaining 2 tablespoons olive oil, ½ teaspoon salt, and pepper to taste. Spread the vegetables out in an even layer. Roast, tossing halfway through, until tender, about 20 minutes. Remove the pan from the oven and nestle the shrimp evenly among the vegetables. Roast until the shrimp are opaque and cooked through, about 8 minutes.

Top everything with the Parmesan, parsley, pine nuts, and lemon juice. Toss gently and serve with the lemon wedges on the side.

Curry-Roasted Vegetables and Chickpeas with Mint-Cilantro Chutney SERVES 4

This is a wonderful vegetarian meal to prepare in advance if you like cooking ahead for the week. These curry-infused roasted veggies and chickpeas are seasoned with turmeric, garam masala, and other spices, and then finished with a spicy lime-infused mint and cilantro chutney. Sounds fancy, but it couldn't be any easier because everything cooks at the same time. While it cooks, the chutney comes together in minutes and will last several days stored in an airtight jar.

VEGETABLES

Olive oil spray (I like my Misto or Bertolli)

1 small head cauliflower, cut into 1-inch florets

4 medium carrots (12 ounces), cut on an angle into ¼-inch-thick slices

1 (15-ounce) can chickpeas,* rinsed and drained

¼ medium red onion, cut into ½-inch-thick slices

3 garlic cloves, smashed with the side of a knife

3 tablespoons extra-virgin olive oil

1 teaspoon curry powder*

½ teaspoon ground turmeric

¼ teaspoon ground cumin

¼ teaspoon garam masala*

1 teaspoon kosher salt

Freshly ground black pepper

CHUTNEY

1½ tablespoons fresh lime juice

¼ cup chopped fresh cilantro

¼ cup chopped fresh mint

½ fresh jalapeño pepper, including seeds, chopped

¼ teaspoon kosher salt

*Read the label to be sure this product is gluten-free.

PER SERVING	1½ cups vegetables + chickpeas with 1 tablespoon chutney
CALORIES	241
FAT	12 g
SATURATED FAT	1.5 g
CHOLESTEROL	0 mg
CARBOHYDRATE	29 g
FIBER	5 g
PROTEIN	7 g
SUGARS	6 g
SODIUM	566 mg

For the vegetables: Preheat the oven to 425°F.

Spray an 18 x 13-inch rimmed sheet pan with oil and add the cauliflower, carrots, chickpeas, onion, and garlic. Drizzle with the olive oil and toss well.

In a small bowl, combine the curry powder, turmeric, cumin, garam masala, salt, and pepper to taste. Sprinkle the spice mixture over the vegetables, toss well, and spread in a single layer. Roast, stirring halfway, until the vegetables are crisp-tender and slightly charred, 30 to 35 minutes.

Meanwhile, for the chutney: In a small food processor or blender, combine the lime juice, cilantro, mint, jalapeño, and salt. Pulse until chopped but not completely smooth, adding a little water if needed.

Top the vegetables with the chutney and serve right away.

Cacio e Pepe Roasted Spaghetti Squash SERVES 2

Cacio e pepe means "cheese and pepper" in Italian. Those are two of the five ingredients in this super simple dish, which traditionally involves tossing pasta with olive oil, Pecorino Romano cheese, and plenty of black pepper. I've made it low-carb and lighter by swapping out the pasta for spaghetti squash. Fast, simple, and delicious.

1 medium spaghetti squash (2¾ pounds)

Kosher salt and freshly ground black pepper

1½ tablespoons extra-virgin olive oil

½ cup finely grated Pecorino Romano cheese (I like Locatelli)

PER SERVING	1½ cups
CALORIES	478
FAT	18 g
SATURATED FAT	6 g
CHOLESTEROL	22 mg
CARBOHYDRATE	74 g
FIBER	12.5 g
PROTEIN	16 g
SUGARS	14 g
SODIUM	442 mg

Preheat the oven to 400°F. Line an 18 x 13-inch rimmed sheet pan with foil.

Halve the squash lengthwise and use a spoon to scrape out the seeds and stringy yellow strands, then discard. Season the flesh with a pinch of salt and pepper to taste and place the squash cut side down on the prepared pan.

Bake until the flesh can be easily pierced with a fork, 55 to 60 minutes. Remove the pan from the oven and let cool for 10 minutes.

Using a fork, scrape out the squash flesh into a bowl; it will separate into spaghetti-like strands. Add the olive oil, Pecorino Romano, and ½ teaspoon pepper. Toss well and serve immediately.

Pressure Cooker

Colombian Chicken and Potato Soup SERVES 6

In Colombia, this soup is called *ajiaco*, and it is a staple dish in the region of Bogotá. This is my aunt's specialty, and she always makes it for me because she knows how much I love it. Together we created a lightened-up version that cooks in a pressure cooker so it's ready fast, too! Typically, in Colombia, it's made with three different types of potatoes, but to simplify the dish and use ingredients readily available in the States, we used a combo of russet and Yukon Gold. My favorite part of this soup is the toppings: Capers give it a delicious tang, while the avocado and cream make it creamy and delicious. It's heaven!

2 medium ears corn, husked

1½ pounds Yukon Gold potatoes (4 to 5), cut into ¼-inch-thick slices

¾ pound russet potatoes (about 2 medium), peeled and cut into ¼-inch-thick slices

1 pound boneless, skinless chicken breasts, cubed

2 medium scallions, chopped

2 tablespoons chicken bouillon* (I like Better Than Bouillon)

FOR SERVING

6 ounces diced avocado (from 1 large Hass)

¼ cup crème fraîche or heavy cream

3 tablespoons capers, drained, plus (optional) 6 teaspoons brine

*Read the label to be sure this product is gluten-free.

PER SERVING	1²/₃ cups soup + 1 piece of corn + toppings
CALORIES	327
FAT	10.5 g
SATURATED FAT	3.5 g
CHOLESTEROL	62 mg
CARBOHYDRATE	41 g
FIBER	5.5 g
PROTEIN	23 g
SUGARS	2.5 g
SODIUM	935 mg

Using a sharp knife, cut each ear of corn into 3 pieces (about 2½ inches long). Set aside on a plate.

In an electric pressure cooker, combine 5½ cups water, the potatoes, chicken, scallions, and chicken bouillon. Seal and cook on high pressure for 6 minutes, until the potatoes are tender. Natural release, then open when the pressure subsides. Press the sauté button. Add the corn and cook, uncovered, until the corn is tender, 5 more minutes.

To serve, place a piece of corn in each of 6 bowls, then ladle about 1²/₃ cups of soup into each. Top the bowls with 1 ounce avocado, 2 teaspoons crème fraîche, and ½ tablespoon of the capers. If desired, add 1 teaspoon of the caper brine to each bowl.

NO PRESSURE COOKER? NO PROBLEM!

To make this in a large pot or Dutch oven, increase the water to 6 cups. Bring to a boil, then cook, covered, for 20 to 25 minutes on medium-low heat, until the potatoes are tender, then add the corn and cook an additional 5 minutes.

Arroz con Pollo SERVES 4

Growing up with a Latin mom, I had rice with just about every meal. So it's no surprise that one of my favorite dishes from childhood was arroz con pollo. In fact, I still request it when I have dinner at my mom's. It's pure comfort food to me. To make it a bit healthier, I use brown rice in place of white, and I cook it in my Instant Pot with fabulous results! Serve this dish with some sliced tomatoes and cucumbers for a quick and simple side salad.

4 large bone-in chicken thighs (6½ ounces each), skin removed and fat trimmed

½ teaspoon apple cider vinegar

1 teaspoon sazón seasoning, homemade (see page 127) or store-bought (I like Badia Sazón Tropical)

½ teaspoon garlic powder

½ teaspoon kosher salt

3 teaspoons olive oil

⅓ cup chopped onion

½ cup chopped red bell pepper

¼ cup chopped scallions

¼ cup chopped fresh cilantro, plus more (optional) for garnish

2 garlic cloves, minced

1¼ cups uncooked long-grain brown rice (I like Carolina)

¾ cup frozen mixed vegetables (peas, carrots, corn, and green beans)

¼ cup canned tomato sauce

¼ cup pitted green Spanish olives plus ½ tablespoon brine

1 teaspoon chicken bouillon* (I like Better Than Bouillon)

Cayenne pepper sauce (I like Cholula), for serving (optional)

*Read the label to be sure this product is gluten-free.

PER SERVING	1 thigh + 1 cup rice
CALORIES	511
FAT	14 g
SATURATED FAT	3 g
CHOLESTEROL	175 mg
CARBOHYDRATE	52 g
FIBER	4 g
PROTEIN	41 g
SUGARS	3 g
SODIUM	788 mg

SKINNY SCOOP

If you have a different brand of electric pressure cooker, or if you use a different type of brown rice, the time and liquid amount might differ slightly.

Season the chicken with the vinegar, ½ teaspoon of the sazón, the garlic powder, and the salt.

Press the sauté button on an electric pressure cooker. When hot, add 2 teaspoons of the oil and cook the chicken until browned, 1 to 2 minutes per side. Transfer to a plate.

To the pressure cooker (still on sauté), add the remaining 1 teaspoon oil, the onion, bell pepper, scallions, cilantro, and garlic and cook, stirring, until softened, about 2 minutes. Add the rice, ¾ cup plus 2 tablespoons water, the frozen mixed vegetables, tomato sauce, olives, olive brine, remaining ½ teaspoon sazón, and the bouillon. Stir well. Return the chicken to the pot.

Seal and cook on high pressure for 27 minutes, until the liquid is absorbed and the chicken and rice are cooked. Quick or natural release, then open when the pressure subsides.

To serve, place 1 cup rice on each plate, top with 1 chicken thigh, and garnish with the cilantro, if desired. If you like spice, top with the hot sauce (it's a must for me).

Chicken and Lentil Soup SERVES 8

This nourishing soup is a staple in my home—the kind of meal I love to whip up on a cold night because it fills you up and is so cozy. It also makes plenty of servings so you can enjoy it for lunch the next day and then freeze the leftovers for future meals! Plus, lentils are inexpensive, which means this dish is easy on the wallet, too. I prefer to use chicken thighs, but chicken breasts would also work.

1 pound dried green or brown lentils

¾ pound boneless, skinless chicken thighs (about 3), trimmed of fat

2 tablespoons chicken bouillon* (I like Better Than Bouillon)

1 small onion, chopped

1 medium tomato, chopped

2 scallions, chopped

3 garlic cloves, chopped

¼ cup chopped fresh cilantro

1 teaspoon garlic powder

1 teaspoon ground cumin

¼ teaspoon dried oregano

½ teaspoon sazón seasoning with annatto, homemade (recipe below) or store-bought (I like Badia Sazón Tropical)

½ teaspoon kosher salt

*Read the label to be sure this product is gluten-free.

PER SERVING	1⅓ cups
CALORIES	273
FAT	2.5 g
SATURATED FAT	0.5 g
CHOLESTEROL	0 mg
CARBOHYDRATE	40 g
FIBER	18 g
PROTEIN	25 g
SUGARS	4 g
SODIUM	623 mg

In an electric pressure cooker, combine the lentils, chicken, bouillon, onion, tomato, scallions, garlic, cilantro, garlic powder, cumin, oregano, sazón, and salt. Stir in 7 cups water. Seal and cook on high pressure for 30 minutes. Natural release, then open when the pressure subsides. Shred the chicken (do this in the pot), stir, and serve.

NO PRESSURE COOKER? NO PROBLEM!

To make this in a large pot or Dutch oven, increase the water to 8 cups. Bring to a boil, then cook, covered, over medium-low heat for 45 to 50 minutes, adding more water if needed. Shred the chicken and serve.

SAZÓN SEASONING
Makes 6 tablespoons

1 tablespoon ground coriander

1 tablespoon ground cumin

1 tablespoon ground annatto seeds (achiote) or turmeric

1 tablespoon garlic powder

1 tablespoon kosher salt

2 teaspoons dried oregano

1 teaspoon freshly ground black pepper

In a small bowl, combine the coriander, cumin, annatto, garlic powder, salt, oregano, and pepper and mix well. The sazón will keep in an airtight container at room temperature for up to 6 months.

PER SERVING	1 teaspoon	CARBOHYDRATE	1 g
CALORIES	6	FIBER	0 g
FAT	0 g	PROTEIN	0 g
SATURATED FAT	0 g	SUGARS	0 g
CHOLESTEROL	0 mg	SODIUM	188 mg

Coq au Vin SERVES 6

Coq au vin is a classic French recipe of chicken stewed with bacon, mushrooms, and wine. Braising chicken in wine is an age-old tradition, and for good reason: after hours of simmering, you end up with very tender meat in a richly flavored sauce. A pressure cooker cuts the cooking time almost in half while still creating fork-tender chicken and vegetables. Leftovers taste even better!

4 slices center-cut bacon, chopped

10 ounces (4 medium) carrots, cut into ½-inch pieces

4 celery stalks, cut into ½-inch pieces

1 medium onion, chopped

12 ounces cremini or button mushrooms, quartered

6 baby red potatoes (about 8 ounces), quartered

4 garlic cloves, minced

2 small shallots, minced

2 teaspoons tomato paste

3 sprigs of fresh thyme

2 teaspoons kosher salt

Freshly ground black pepper

1 tablespoon all-purpose flour, wheat or gluten-free

2 tablespoons unsalted butter

6 bone-in chicken thighs (32 ounces total), skin removed and fat trimmed

6 chicken drumsticks (28 ounces total), skin removed

2 cups good dry red wine (Pinot Noir, Chianti, or Burgundy)

2½ cups low-sodium chicken broth*

2 bay leaves

Chopped fresh parsley, for garnish

*Read the label to be sure this product is gluten-free.

PER SERVING	1 thigh + 1 drumstick + 1½ cups vegetables and sauce
CALORIES	574
FAT	17.5 g
SATURATED FAT	6 g
CHOLESTEROL	292 mg
CARBOHYDRATE	23 g
FIBER	4 g
PROTEIN	64 g
SUGARS	6 g
SODIUM	867 mg

Press the sauté button on an electric pressure cooker. When hot, add the bacon and cook, stirring, until crisp, 5 to 6 minutes. Using a slotted spoon, transfer the bacon to paper towels to drain.

To the pressure cooker (still on sauté), add the carrots, celery, onion, mushrooms, potatoes, garlic, shallots, tomato paste, thyme, 1 teaspoon of the salt, and pepper to taste. Cook, stirring, until softened, about 8 minutes. Sprinkle the flour over the vegetables and cook, stirring, for 30 seconds to cook the raw flour. Transfer the vegetables to a large bowl.

In the pressure cooker, melt ½ tablespoon of the butter. Add 3 chicken thighs. Cook until browned on one side, about 3 minutes, then flip and cook until the second side is browned, about 2 minutes. Transfer to a plate. Add another ½ tablespoon of the butter to the pot and repeat with the remaining 3 thighs. Repeat with the remaining butter and drumsticks, cooking 2 minutes per side. Transfer to the plate with the others.

Add the wine to the pot and scrape up any browned bits stuck to the bottom. Stir in the broth, bay leaves, the remaining 1 teaspoon salt, and pepper to taste. Return half of the vegetables to the pot, followed by all the chicken, then the remaining vegetables. Stir well.

Seal and cook on high pressure for 15 minutes, until the chicken and vegetables are tender and cooked. Natural release, then open when the pressure subsides. Discard the thyme sprigs and bay leaves. Serve, topped with the cooked bacon and parsley.

NO PRESSURE COOKER? NO PROBLEM!

To make this in a large pot or Dutch oven, sauté over medium-high heat in steps 1 to 3. For step 4, bring to a boil, then cook, covered, over medium-low heat until the chicken and vegetables are tender, about 40 minutes.

NO PRESSURE COOKER? NO PROBLEM!

To make this in a large pot or Dutch oven, follow the recipe through step 1, but increase the chicken broth by ¼ cup. Bring to a boil over high heat. Reduce the heat to low, cover, and cook until the chicken is tender, about 35 minutes. Continue the recipe at step 2, beginning with transferring the chicken to a plate.

Shortcut Vietnamese Chicken Pho SERVES 4

A few years ago, I tasted my very first bowl of pho, a Vietnamese noodle soup, and immediately became addicted. The problem was, I would have to drive at least forty minutes to get a decent bowl of it any time a craving struck. So naturally, I learned how to create it myself.

Pho is notoriously difficult to make from scratch, since it involves a lot of ingredients and time spent cooking. But I figured out a quick and easy version that uses a pressure cooker and canned broth as a shortcut, as well as bone-in chicken to add depth of flavor to the broth. The fish sauce and aromatic herbs give the broth its trademark balance of savory and fresh. You can double this recipe if you want extra for leftovers.

PHO BROTH

2 teaspoons avocado oil or olive oil

3-inch piece fresh ginger, peeled and halved lengthwise

1 large yellow onion, peeled and halved

4 cups low-sodium chicken broth*

2 tablespoons fish sauce

4 bone-in chicken thighs (5 ounces each), skin removed and fat trimmed

½ small bunch fresh cilantro

½ tablespoon coriander seeds

½ tablespoon raw sugar

BOWLS

5 ounces rice stick noodles

1 cup bean sprouts

2 large scallions, sliced

¼ cup fresh cilantro leaves

1 fresh jalapeño pepper, thinly sliced

Handful fresh mint leaves, for garnish

Handful fresh Thai basil leaves, for garnish

1 lime, cut into wedges

Sriracha sauce (optional)

*Read the label to be sure this product is gluten-free.

PER SERVING	1 bowl
CALORIES	385
FAT	9 g
SATURATED FAT	2 g
CHOLESTEROL	135 mg
CARBOHYDRATE	42 g
FIBER	3 g
PROTEIN	32 g
SUGARS	5 g
SODIUM	965 mg

For the pho broth: Press the sauté button on an electric pressure cooker. When hot, add the oil and ginger, and place the onion halves in the bottom of the pressure cooker cut side down. Cook, without moving, until they are both charred, 4 to 5 minutes. Stir in 1 cup water, the broth, fish sauce, chicken thighs, cilantro, coriander seeds, and sugar.

Seal and cook on high pressure for 18 minutes, until the chicken is tender. Quick release, then open when the pressure subsides. Transfer the chicken to a plate. Strain the broth and discard the solids.

For the bowls: Return the broth to the pot. Press the sauté button and bring the broth to a boil. Add the noodles and cook until pliable and opaque, 3 to 4 minutes.

Remove the chicken from the bone, slice, and transfer to 4 shallow bowls. Divide the noodles among the bowls (about 3½ ounces each). Top each bowl with ¼ cup bean sprouts and equal amounts of the scallions and cilantro.

Pour 1 cup of the broth over each bowl and serve topped with the jalapeño, mint, basil, and lime wedges. If you like spice, top with the Sriracha as well.

White Chicken Chili with Hominy SERVES 6

I'm a huge fan of white chilis, and I always prefer them over traditional red chilis made with tomatoes and beef. This version is hearty, healthy, and ready in under 30 minutes! I'm in the camp that likes beans in chili; I especially love smaller beans such as navy or Great Northern, but you can also use cannellini here. This meal is freezer-friendly, so make a double batch and freeze half for another night!

1 pound boneless, skinless chicken breasts

2 (15-ounce) cans low-sodium small white beans,* not drained

1 (15-ounce) can hominy,* rinsed and drained

2 (4.25-ounce) cans chopped green chiles

1 tablespoon chicken bouillon* (I like Better Than Bouillon)

2 large scallions, roughly chopped

10 sprigs of fresh cilantro, leaves and stems roughly chopped

6 garlic cloves, peeled

½ teaspoon ground cumin

½ teaspoon chili powder*

¼ teaspoon crushed red pepper flakes (optional)

1 bay leaf

TOPPINGS

6 ounces diced avocado (from 1 large Hass)

¼ cup chopped red onion

Chopped fresh cilantro

Lime wedges, for serving (optional)

*Read the label to be sure this product is gluten-free.

PER SERVING	1⅓ cups + 1 ounce avocado
CALORIES	323
FAT	7 g
SATURATED FAT	1 g
CHOLESTEROL	49 mg
CARBOHYDRATE	41 g
FIBER	11.5 g
PROTEIN	27 g
SUGARS	2 g
SODIUM	906 mg

In an electric pressure cooker, combine the chicken, white beans (including liquid), hominy, and green chiles.

In a blender, combine 1 cup water, the chicken bouillon, scallions, cilantro, and garlic and puree until smooth. Pour the puree into the pressure cooker, then stir in the cumin and chili powder. Add the pepper flakes (if using) and bay leaf.

Seal and cook on high pressure for 20 minutes, until the chicken is tender and cooked. Quick or natural release, then open when the pressure subsides. Discard the bay leaf, shred the chicken well with two forks (do this in the pot), and stir well.

Divide the chili among 6 bowls. Top each with equal amounts of the avocado, red onion, and cilantro. Serve with the lime wedges on the side, if desired.

NO PRESSURE COOKER? NO PROBLEM!

To make this in a slow cooker, simply toss all of the ingredients except the toppings into the cooker and cook on low for 6 to 8 hours. Continue the recipe at step 3, beginning with discarding the bay leaf. To make this in a large pot on the stovetop, add an additional ¼ cup water to the pot of ingredients (minus the toppings) before cooking. Cover and bring to a boil. Reduce the heat to low and cook for 40 minutes. Continue the recipe at step 3, beginning with discarding the bay leaf.

SKINNYTASTE ONE & DONE

NO PRESSURE COOKER? NO PROBLEM!

To make this in a large pot or Dutch oven, sauté over medium-high heat in step 2. Increase the water to ¾ cup. Bring to a boil, then cook, covered, over medium-low heat until the chicken is mostly cooked, about 30 minutes. Add the squash and cook until tender, about 15 minutes. Stir in the coconut milk and serve.

Coconut Chicken and Butternut Curry in a Hurry SERVES 4

When I want curry on the dinner table in 30 minutes, I use my electric pressure cooker. I love the savory and sweet flavors in this stew-like chicken dish. Although this recipe is perfect on its own, you can serve it with flatbread, such as naan or roti, on the side. The sauce is so good, you'll want something for sopping up every last drop!

4 large bone-in chicken thighs (6½ ounces each), skin removed and fat trimmed

1¼ teaspoons kosher salt

½ tablespoon olive oil

½ medium onion, finely chopped

5 garlic cloves, minced

½ teaspoon ground cumin

1½ teaspoons garam masala*

2 teaspoons curry powder*

1 (14.5-ounce) can petite diced tomatoes

2 tablespoons chopped fresh cilantro, plus more for garnish

3 cups peeled and cubed (½-inch) butternut squash

½ cup canned full-fat coconut milk, plus more (optional) for drizzling

*Read the label to be sure this product is gluten-free.

PER SERVING	1 chicken thigh + 1¼ cups vegetables and sauce
CALORIES	405
FAT	13.5 g
SATURATED FAT	3.5 g
CHOLESTEROL	195 mg
CARBOHYDRATE	28 g
FIBER	8 g
PROTEIN	44 g
SUGARS	14 g
SODIUM	806 mg

Season the chicken with 1 teaspoon of the salt.

Press the sauté button on an electric pressure cooker. When hot, add the oil, onion, and garlic and cook, stirring, until softened, about 1 minute. Stir in the cumin, garam masala, and curry powder and cook until fragrant, about 1 minute. Add the chicken, tomatoes, cilantro, and ½ cup water and stir well.

Seal and cook on high pressure for 20 minutes, until the chicken is cooked through. Quick release, then open when the pressure subsides. Add the butternut and the remaining ¼ teaspoon salt. Seal and cook on high pressure for 5 minutes, until the squash is tender. Quick release, then open when the pressure subsides. Stir in the coconut milk.

Divide among 4 bowls. Garnish with the cilantro and more coconut milk, if desired, and serve.

SKINNY SCOOP

Kabocha squash can be used in place of butternut, if desired.

Chicken Tortilla Soup SERVES 8

My kids love my tortilla soup because it delivers just a little bit of kick and they can mix and match their toppings as they wish. And *I* love it because it's easy to make. I cut half of the tortillas into strips and sauté them in a little oil to serve as a crunchy topping, then cook the other half right in the soup to thicken it. If your family likes less spice, you can adjust spices to their taste.

8 (6-inch) corn tortillas

2½ teaspoons olive oil

4 garlic cloves, minced

4 cups reduced-sodium chicken broth*

3 cups canned tomato sauce

1 pound boneless, skinless chicken breasts

1 (15-ounce) can black beans,* rinsed and drained

1½ cups fresh or frozen corn kernels

2 tablespoons chopped chipotle peppers in adobo sauce

1 teaspoon ground cumin

¾ teaspoon chili powder,* hot Mexican-style or regular

½ teaspoon kosher salt

Freshly ground black pepper

TOPPINGS

8 ounces sliced avocado (from 2 small Hass)

Chopped red onion (optional)

Chopped fresh cilantro

8 lime wedges, for serving

*Read the label to be sure this product is gluten-free.

PER SERVING	1½ cups + toppings
CALORIES	**286**
FAT	**8.5 g**
SATURATED FAT	**1.5 g**
CHOLESTEROL	**36 mg**
CARBOHYDRATE	**38 g**
FIBER	**10 g**
PROTEIN	**20 g**
SUGARS	**5 g**
SODIUM	**923 mg**

Cut 4 of the tortillas into ¼-inch-wide strips. Roughly chop the remaining 4 tortillas.

Press the sauté button on an electric pressure cooker. When hot, add 1 teaspoon of the oil and half of the tortilla strips. Cook, stirring occasionally, until crisp, 10 to 12 minutes. Transfer to paper towels. Repeat with 1 teaspoon of the oil and the remaining tortilla strips.

To the pressure cooker (still on sauté), add the remaining ½ teaspoon oil and the garlic. Cook, stirring, until fragrant, about 1 minute. Add the chopped tortillas, chicken broth, tomato sauce, chicken, beans, corn, chipotle peppers, cumin, chili powder, salt, and black pepper to taste.

Seal and cook on high pressure for 20 minutes, until the chicken is tender and cooked. Quick or natural release, then open when the pressure subsides. Shred the chicken well with two forks (do this in the pot).

Ladle 1½ cups of soup into each serving bowl. Divide the tortilla strips, avocado, red onion (if using), and cilantro among the bowls to serve. Squeeze 1 lime wedge over the soup before eating.

NO PRESSURE COOKER? NO PROBLEM!

To make this in a large pot or Dutch oven, cook the tortillas and sauté the garlic over medium-high heat. For step 4, bring to a boil, then cook over low heat, until the chicken and vegetables are tender, about 40 minutes.

Turkey Breast with Sweet Potatoes, Green Beans, and Gravy SERVES 4

This is the easiest turkey dinner I've ever made—seriously. The entire dish, including the gravy, cooks in a pressure cooker. The turkey comes out juicy, while the sweet potatoes and green beans are tender, but the best part is the gravy! It's so rich and tasty, and you get a generous serving. Serve this with cranberry sauce or relish on the side for a dinner your family is sure to be thankful for.

1 (1¾-pound) boneless, skin-on turkey breast half

1 teaspoon kosher salt

Freshly ground black pepper

Olive oil spray (I like my Misto or Bertolli)

1½ tablespoons unsalted butter

1 medium onion, chopped

1 medium celery stalk, chopped

6 garlic cloves, minced

⅓ cup all-purpose flour

2¼ cups low-sodium chicken broth

1 large carrot, cut into 1-inch pieces

2 tablespoons chopped fresh sage

2 bay leaves

4 medium sweet potatoes (5 ounces each), peeled and sliced into 1-inch-thick rounds

10 ounces green beans, trimmed and halved

PER SERVING	4 ounces turkey + 1 sweet potato + ½ cup green beans + ⅔ cup gravy
CALORIES	571
FAT	19 g
SATURATED FAT	6.5 g
CHOLESTEROL	140 mg
CARBOHYDRATE	49 g
FIBER	8.5 g
PROTEIN	49 g
SUGARS	9 g
SODIUM	567 mg

SKINNY SCOOP

I like my sweet potatoes on the softer side, but if you like them firmer, you can use the quick release at the end of the cooking cycle.

Season the turkey breast with the salt and pepper to taste.

Press the sauté button on an electric pressure cooker (6- or 8-quart is the ideal size). Spray the pot with oil. When hot, add the turkey breast and cook until browned, 2 to 3 minutes per side. Transfer to a plate.

Add the butter to the pot and let it melt. Add the onion, celery, and garlic and cook, stirring, until the onion is softened, 4 to 5 minutes. Stir in the flour and cook, stirring, until the mixture is golden, 30 to 60 seconds. Stir in 1 cup of the broth, using a wooden spoon to scrape up any browned bits and smooth out any lumps. Add the remaining 1¼ cups broth, 1 cup water, the carrot, sage, and bay leaves. Return the turkey to the pressure cooker.

Seal and cook on high pressure for 10 minutes. Quick release, then open when the pressure subsides. Arrange the sweet potatoes on top, cover, and cook on high pressure for 10 minutes, until tender. Let the pressure release naturally for 10 minutes, then quick release. Open when the pressure subsides.

Transfer the turkey breast to a cutting board. Using a slotted spoon, transfer the sweet potatoes to a serving platter. Loosely tent each with foil. Discard the bay leaves.

Press the sauté button. When hot, add the green beans and cook, stirring occasionally, until crisp-tender, about 8 minutes.

Discard the skin of the turkey, slice, and arrange it alongside the sweet potatoes. Spoon the green beans and gravy onto the platter and serve.

Turkey Cheeseburger Soup SERVES 6

Cheeseburger soup is always a hit with my family! It's the kind of soup you crave on a cold night—thick and cheesy, with turkey and chunks of potatoes in every bite. To get it creamy without using any cream, I add a large piece of cauliflower to the pot, then, once it's cooked, I puree it in a blender with some of the broth. The results are rich, velvety, and so, so good.

½ pound 93% lean ground turkey

1 tablespoon unsalted butter

1 medium onion, chopped

2 medium carrots, chopped

2 celery stalks, chopped

2 garlic cloves, minced

2 tablespoons all-purpose flour, wheat or gluten-free

½ teaspoon kosher salt

Freshly ground black pepper

3½ cups low-sodium chicken broth*

10 ounces Yukon Gold potatoes (2 medium), peeled and finely diced

1 (12-ounce) wedge cauliflower (¼ of a large head), stem attached

1¾ cups shredded reduced-fat sharp cheddar cheese*

2 tablespoons chopped scallions, for garnish

*Read the label to be sure this product is gluten-free.

PER SERVING	1½ cups
CALORIES	254
FAT	11.5 g
SATURATED FAT	6 g
CHOLESTEROL	52 mg
CARBOHYDRATE	19 g
FIBER	3.5 g
PROTEIN	20 g
SUGARS	5 g
SODIUM	670 mg

Press the sauté button on an electric pressure cooker. Add the turkey and brown the meat, using a wooden spoon to break it into small pieces as it cooks, 4 to 5 minutes. Drain the meat and transfer it to a small bowl.

In the pressure cooker (still on sauté), melt the butter. Add the onion, carrots, celery, and garlic. Cook, stirring, until softened, about 5 minutes. Add the flour, salt, and pepper to taste and cook, stirring, for 1 minute to cook the flour. Return the turkey to the pressure cooker and add the chicken broth, potatoes, and cauliflower and stir.

Seal and cook on high pressure for 10 minutes, until the potatoes are soft. Quick release, then open when the pressure subsides.

Transfer the cauliflower and 1 cup of the liquid to a blender and blend until smooth. Pour the puree into the soup and stir well. Add the cheddar and stir until melted. Serve topped with the scallions.

NO PRESSURE COOKER? NO PROBLEM!

To make this in a large pot or Dutch oven, sauté over medium-high heat in steps 1 and 2. For step 3, bring to a boil, then cook, covered, over low heat until the potatoes and cauliflower are tender, 25 to 30 minutes. Transfer 1 cup of the liquid and the whole cauliflower to the blender, and blend until smooth. Stir the puree into the soup, add the cheddar, and serve topped with the scallions.

Instant Spaghetti and Meat Sauce SERVES 5

This recipe is one of the reasons why I adore my pressure cooker. The pasta and the sauce cook at the same time, making this the quickest and easiest way to get a meal on the table—with minimal dirty dishes—while also pleasing the whole family! And it's perfect for those busy weeknights when you need to get dinner on the table *fast*. Here, I use ground turkey, but you can also substitute ground beef. For best results, be sure to use a brand of marinara you love—DeLallo Pomodoro Fresco is my pick.

1 pound 93% lean ground turkey

¾ teaspoon kosher salt

¼ cup chopped onion

1 garlic clove, minced

1 (25.25-ounce) jar marinara sauce

8 ounces spaghetti, wheat or gluten-free, broken in half

Freshly grated Parmesan cheese, for serving (optional)

PER SERVING	1½ cups
CALORIES	401
FAT	15 g
SATURATED FAT	3 g
CHOLESTEROL	67 mg
CARBOHYDRATE	44 g
FIBER	2.5 g
PROTEIN	25 g
SUGARS	6 g
SODIUM	704 mg

Press the sauté button on an electric pressure cooker. When hot, add the ground turkey and salt and brown the meat, using a wooden spoon to break it into small pieces as it cooks, about 3 minutes. Add the onion and garlic and cook until softened, 3 to 4 minutes. Add the marinara sauce, 2 cups water, and the spaghetti, making sure the liquid covers everything. Do not stir, as space will be tight.

Seal and cook on high pressure for 9 minutes, until the pasta and sauce is cooked. Quick release, then open when the pressure subsides. Serve right away, topped with Parmesan, if desired.

NO PRESSURE COOKER? NO PROBLEM!

To make this in a large pot or Dutch oven, sauté over medium-high heat in step 1. Add ¼ cup more water. Bring to a boil, then cook, covered, over medium-low heat until the liquid is absorbed and the pasta is cooked, about 17 minutes, before topping with Parmesan and serving.

Navy Bean, Bacon, and Spinach Soup SERVES 6

Bacon makes everything better, especially in this hearty white bean soup. It's yummy, inexpensive, and easy to make—and, bonus, leftovers are even more delicious the next day! This soup is perfect to enjoy during cooler weather and uses pantry staples, such as canned beans and broth. If you don't eat pork, turkey bacon works great, too. To thicken the soup, I puree some of the soup and beans and leave the rest a little chunky for texture.

3 (15-ounce) cans navy beans,*
rinsed and drained

4 slices center-cut bacon,
chopped

1 medium onion, chopped

1 large carrot, chopped

1 large celery stalk, chopped

2 tablespoons tomato paste

4 cups reduced-sodium
chicken broth*

1 sprig of fresh rosemary

2 bay leaves

3 cups (about 2 ounces)
baby spinach

*Read the label to be sure this
 product is gluten-free.

PER SERVING	1¹⁄₃ cups
CALORIES	207
FAT	3 g
SATURATED FAT	0.5 g
CHOLESTEROL	2 mg
CARBOHYDRATE	39 g
FIBER	17.5 g
PROTEIN	15 g
SUGARS	3 g
SODIUM	815 mg

In a blender, blend 1 can of the beans with 1 cup water.

Press the sauté button on an electric pressure cooker. When hot, add the bacon and cook, stirring, until crisp, 4 to 5 minutes. Using a slotted spoon, transfer the bacon to paper towels to drain.

To the pressure cooker (still on sauté), add the onion, carrot, and celery. Cook, stirring, until softened, about 5 minutes. Stir in the tomato paste until incorporated. Stir in the pureed beans, remaining whole beans, broth, rosemary, and bay leaves.

Seal and cook on high pressure for 15 minutes. Natural release, then open when the pressure subsides. Discard the rosemary and bay leaves. Place 2 cups of the soup in a blender and puree until smooth. Stir the puree back into the soup along with the spinach. Stir until the spinach is wilted.

To serve, ladle into 6 bowls and top with the cooked bacon.

NO PRESSURE COOKER? NO PROBLEM!

To make this in a large pot or Dutch oven, sauté over medium-high heat in steps 2 and 3. Bring to a boil, then cook the soup, covered, on low heat until the vegetables are tender, 25 to 30 minutes.

Quickest Gnocchi Bolognese SERVES 6

The gnocchi and the Bolognese in this recipe are made in one pot, which means one less pan to clean! And the meat sauce tastes like it was simmering for hours on the stove, but, thanks to the pressure cooker, it's ready in less than 30 minutes. A speedy sensation! This dish is a favorite of my husband, Tommy. He loves it topped with fresh basil and plenty of freshly grated Pecorino Romano.

2 ounces pancetta, chopped

1 teaspoon unsalted butter

1 medium onion, chopped

2/3 cup chopped celery

2/3 cup chopped carrot

1 garlic clove, minced

1 pound 93% lean ground beef

3/4 teaspoon kosher salt

Freshly ground black pepper

1/4 cup dry white wine, such as Pinot Grigio

1/2 cup fat-free milk

1 pound dried potato gnocchi (I like DeLallo)

1/8 teaspoon grated nutmeg

2 1/2 cups canned crushed tomatoes (I like Tuttorosso)

1 bay leaf

6 tablespoons part-skim ricotta cheese

2 tablespoons chopped fresh parsley or basil

Freshly grated Pecorino Romano cheese (I like Locatelli), for serving (optional)

PER SERVING	1 generous cup + garnish
CALORIES	401
FAT	12 g
SATURATED FAT	4.5 g
CHOLESTEROL	77 mg
CARBOHYDRATE	42 g
FIBER	3.5 g
PROTEIN	31 g
SUGARS	8 g
SODIUM	815 mg

Press the sauté button on an electric pressure cooker. When hot, add the pancetta and cook, stirring, until the fat is rendered, about 1 1/2 minutes. Add the butter, onion, celery, carrot, and garlic and cook, stirring, until softened, 5 to 7 minutes. Add the ground beef, 1/2 teaspoon of the salt, and pepper to taste. Brown the meat, using a wooden spoon to break it into small pieces as it cooks, 4 to 5 minutes. Add the wine and cook, stirring, until it reduces, 1 to 2 minutes. Stir in the milk, gnocchi, and nutmeg. Add the crushed tomatoes, 1/2 cup water, the bay leaf, the remaining 1/4 teaspoon salt, and pepper to taste.

Seal and cook on high pressure for 6 minutes, until the gnocchi are tender. Quick or natural release, then open when the pressure subsides. If the gnocchi are not done, press the sauté button and cook for 2 to 3 more minutes. Discard the bay leaf.

Serve topped with the ricotta, parsley, and pecorino (if using).

NO PRESSURE COOKER? NO PROBLEM!

To make a quick stovetop version of the sauce in a large pot or Dutch oven, sauté over medium-high heat in step 1. Omit the 1/2 cup water. Bring to a boil, then cook, covered, over medium low heat, about 35 minutes, stirring occasionally. Cook the gnocchi separately according to the package directions.

Caldo de Papa (Potato and Short Rib Soup) SERVES 6

I grew up eating this hearty Colombian soup—popular in the Andean region, where the altitude is high and the climate is cool—for dinner. But on a recent vacation to Bogotá, I was surprised to find it served for breakfast with arepas (a type of corn pancake) and hot chocolate. Turns out, it's popular as a hangover remedy after a night of drinking. It's the kind of dish that sticks to your ribs on a cold day, no matter what time you enjoy it. The fresh cilantro and scallions on top are a must, so don't skip them!

SOUP

¾ pound bone-in beef short ribs (about 4), fat trimmed

1 (8-ounce) beef marrowbone

1 celery stalk, left whole

4 teaspoons kosher salt

¼ bunch fresh cilantro with stems, plus ½ cup chopped fresh cilantro

5 large scallions

3 garlic cloves

1¼ pounds Yukon Gold potatoes (5 or 6), peeled, halved, and cut into ½-inch-thick slices

FOR SERVING

2 tablespoons finely chopped fresh cilantro

2 tablespoons finely chopped scallion

6 ounces sliced avocado (from 1 large Hass)

PER SERVING	generous 1¾ cups + 1 ounce avocado
CALORIES	225
FAT	10 g
SATURATED FAT	3 g
CHOLESTEROL	34 mg
CARBOHYDRATE	21 g
FIBER	4.5 g
PROTEIN	14 g
SUGARS	1 g
SODIUM	802 mg

For the soup: In an electric pressure cooker, combine the ribs, marrowbone, 7 cups water, the celery, and salt. Use kitchen string to tie together the ¼ bunch cilantro and 2 of the scallions, then add to the pressure cooker.

Seal and cook on high pressure for 30 minutes, until the ribs are tender. Natural release, then open when the pressure subsides. Discard the cilantro, scallions, and celery stalk. Measure out ½ cup of the broth and transfer it to a blender.

Roughly chop the remaining 3 scallions. To the blender, add the garlic, chopped scallions, and the ½ cup chopped cilantro. Blend until smooth. Pour the mixture into the pressure cooker and add the potatoes. Cover and cook on high pressure for 8 minutes, until the potatoes are tender. Quick release, then open when the pressure subsides. Remove the meat from the bones and shred (do this in the pot); discard the bones.

To serve, ladle generous 1¾ cups of soup into serving bowls and top each with the chopped cilantro and scallion. Serve with the avocado slices on the side.

NO PRESSURE COOKER? NO PROBLEM!

To make this in a large pot or Dutch oven, bring the rib mixture to a boil in step 1, then cook, covered, on low heat until tender, about 1 hour. Continue with the recipe at step 2, beginning with discarding the cilantro. In step 3, to cook the potatoes, add them to the pot and cook until tender, about 20 minutes.

FOOD FACTS: BONE BROTH

Broth simmered with beef or poultry
bones gives you an extra dose of
body-boosting nourishment, including
protein and minerals such as calcium,
phosphorous, magnesium, and potassium.

Beef Stroganoff Noodle Soup SERVES 8

My definition of a successful dinner is not necessarily a fancy meal, but rather a dish that pleases everyone in my house. This soup does just that! It's an unfussy take on beef stroganoff that you eat with a spoon instead of a fork. Filled with noodles, mushrooms, and ground beef, it's comforting, as well as quick to make. My two toughest critics (Tommy and Madison) absolutely love it.

1¼ pounds 93% lean ground beef

¾ teaspoon kosher salt

¾ cup chopped onion

2 tablespoons tomato paste

8 ounces sliced cremini mushrooms

2 tablespoons all-purpose flour, wheat or gluten-free

2 sprigs of fresh thyme

1 teaspoon Worcestershire sauce*

2 tablespoons chicken bouillon* (I like Better Than Bouillon)

1 teaspoon sweet paprika

5 ounces egg noodles (I like No Yolks) or gluten-free

½ cup sour cream

1 tablespoon chopped fresh parsley, for garnish

*Read the label to be sure this product is gluten-free.

PER SERVING	1½ cups
CALORIES	259
FAT	10 g
SATURATED FAT	4 g
CHOLESTEROL	67 mg
CARBOHYDRATE	20 g
FIBER	1.5 g
PROTEIN	25 g
SUGARS	3 g
SODIUM	725 mg

Press the sauté button on an electric pressure cooker. When hot, add the ground beef and salt and brown the meat, using a wooden spoon to break it into small pieces as it cooks, about 5 minutes. Add the onion and tomato paste and cook, stirring, until the onion is softened, 4 to 5 minutes. Add the mushrooms, sprinkle with the flour, and cook, stirring, for 1 minute to cook the flour. Add the thyme, Worcestershire sauce, bouillon, paprika, and 7½ cups water.

Seal and cook on high pressure for 25 minutes, until the meat is tender. Quick release, then open when the pressure subsides. Discard the thyme and stir in the noodles. Seal and cook for 2 minutes on high pressure, until the pasta is tender and cooked. Quick release, then open when the pressure subsides. Put 1 cup of the broth into a blender, add the sour cream, and blend until smooth. Pour the puree into the soup and stir well. Garnish with parsley and serve.

NO PRESSURE COOKER? NO PROBLEM!

To make this in a large pot or Dutch oven, sauté over medium-high heat in step 1. Bring to a boil, then cook, covered, over low heat for about 40 minutes. Discard the thyme, add the noodles, and cook until tender. Put 1 cup of the broth from the pot into a blender, add the sour cream, and blend until smooth. Stir the puree into the soup. Garnish and serve.

American-Style Cheesy Beef Goulash and Macaroni SERVES 6

Everyone needs a few quick and easy family-pleasing meals in their arsenal for busy weeknights. That's where this recipe comes in. This is not the kind of Hungarian goulash I grew up eating with my European immigrant dad. This American version, which dates back to the early 1900s, is more like a cross between a healthier Hamburger Helper and mac and cheese. The macaroni cooks right in the sauce so it's super simple to make.

½ tablespoon olive oil

1 medium yellow onion, chopped

1 pound 90% lean ground beef

1¼ teaspoons sweet paprika

¾ teaspoon kosher salt

1 red or orange bell pepper, chopped

2 garlic cloves, minced

1 teaspoon Worcestershire sauce*

1 (15-ounce) can tomato sauce

1 (14.5-ounce) can petite diced tomatoes

1 (15-ounce) can low-sodium beef broth*

1 bay leaf

8 ounces elbow macaroni, whole wheat or gluten-free

¾ cup shredded cheddar cheese*

Chopped fresh parsley, for garnish (optional)

*Read the label to be sure this product is gluten-free.

PER SERVING	1½ cups
CALORIES	395
FAT	14.5 g
SATURATED FAT	6 g
CHOLESTEROL	64 mg
CARBOHYDRATE	39 g
FIBER	6.5 g
PROTEIN	23 g
SUGARS	8 g
SODIUM	865 mg

Press the sauté button on an electric pressure cooker. When hot, add the oil and onion and cook, stirring occasionally, until the onion begins to brown, about 3 minutes. Add the beef, season with the paprika and salt, and brown the meat, using a wooden spoon to break it into small pieces as it cooks, 3 to 4 minutes. Add the bell pepper, garlic, and Worcestershire sauce and cook, stirring occasionally, until fragrant and softened, 4 to 5 minutes. Add the tomato sauce, tomatoes, broth, and bay leaf. Stir in the macaroni.

Seal and cook on high pressure for 5 minutes. Quick release so the pasta stops cooking, then open when the pressure subsides. Discard the bay leaf. Top the dish with the cheddar, cover, and let sit until the cheese has melted. Garnish with parsley, if desired, and serve.

SKINNY SCOOP

You can sub in ground turkey or chicken in place of the beef. You can also use mozzarella or Parmesan in place of the cheddar, or omit the cheese altogether.

NO PRESSURE COOKER? NO PROBLEM!

To make this in a large pot or Dutch oven, sauté over medium-high heat in step 1. Bring to a boil, then cook, covered, over medium-low heat until the pasta is cooked and the liquid is absorbed, about 20 minutes.

SKINNY SCOOP

If you have picky kids who don't like chunky soups, replace the diced tomatoes with a can of crushed tomatoes.

Beef, Tomato, and Acini di Pepe Soup SERVES 6

This soup will always remind me of Helen, a friend who was like a grandmother to me and everyone in my neighborhood. One of the kindest, smartest people I knew, Helen lived well into her nineties. After attending her funeral, we stopped at a quaint deli, and maybe it was fate, but the menu featured Grandma's Soup. I ordered it, as a tribute and because I figured any soup named after someone's grandmother had to be good. Fortunately, I was right! It was so delicious that I immediately re-created it at home, and my family *devoured* it. The small bits of meat taste almost like meatballs, without the extra work of forming them. Tommy and my older daughter, Karina, topped theirs with shredded mozzarella and grated Pecorino Romano and called it pizza soup. I topped mine with only Pecorino Romano, which is *so* worth it!

1 pound 90% lean ground beef

1½ teaspoons kosher salt

½ cup chopped onion

½ cup chopped celery

½ cup chopped carrot

1 (28-ounce) can diced tomatoes

4 cups beef stock*

2 bay leaves

4 ounces acini di pepe (or any small pasta, such as orzo), wheat or gluten-free

Freshly grated Pecorino Romano cheese (I like Locatelli), for topping (optional)

*Read the label to be sure this product is gluten-free.

PER SERVING	1 generous cup
CALORIES	250
FAT	8 g
SATURATED FAT	3 g
CHOLESTEROL	50 mg
CARBOHYDRATE	22 g
FIBER	2.5 g
PROTEIN	19 g
SUGARS	6 g
SODIUM	875 mg

Press the sauté button on an electric pressure cooker. When hot, add the ground beef and salt and brown the meat, using a wooden spoon to break it into small pieces as it cooks, 4 to 5 minutes. Add the onion, celery, and carrot and cook, stirring, until softened, 3 to 4 minutes. Add the tomatoes, beef stock, and bay leaves.

Seal and cook on high pressure for 35 minutes, until the beef and vegetables are tender. Quick or natural release, then open when the pressure subsides. Stir in the pasta. Seal and cook on high pressure for 6 minutes (half of the time in the pasta package directions), until the pasta is cooked. Quick or natural release, then open when the pressure subsides. Remove the bay leaves and ladle into 6 bowls, topped with the pecorino (if using) to serve.

NO PRESSURE COOKER? NO PROBLEM!

To make this in a large pot or Dutch oven, sauté over medium-high heat in step 1. Add ¼ cup water with the stock. Bring to a boil, then cook, covered, on low heat, for double the cook time.

PRESSURE COOKER

Easy Lamb Stew with Chickpeas SERVES 4

My family, especially Madison, loves this stew because the lamb is so tender it just melts in your mouth. What kid craves lamb stew? My Madison does! It's a great fall or winter dish, since the flavor is rich and comforting, and leftovers taste even better the next day. You can replace the chickpeas with potatoes, if you'd like.

2 teaspoons olive oil

2 medium carrots, chopped

1 medium celery stalk, chopped

½ large onion, chopped

½ teaspoon kosher salt

Freshly ground black pepper

1½ pounds lean, trimmed lamb stew meat (leg), cut into 1-inch chunks

1 (8-ounce) can tomato sauce

½ tablespoon beef bouillon* (I like Better Than Bouillon)

1 (16-ounce) can chickpeas,* rinsed and drained

1 sprig of fresh thyme

2 bay leaves

*Read the label to be sure this product is gluten-free.

PER SERVING	1½ cups
CALORIES	372
FAT	13 g
SATURATED FAT	3.5 g
CHOLESTEROL	111 mg
CARBOHYDRATE	23 g
FIBER	2.5 g
PROTEIN	41 g
SUGARS	5 g
SODIUM	967 mg

Press the sauté button on an electric pressure cooker. When hot, add the oil, carrots, celery, onion, ¼ teaspoon of the salt, and pepper to taste. Cook, stirring, until softened, about 5 minutes. Add the lamb, season with the remaining ¼ teaspoon salt, and stir well. Add 1 cup water, the tomato sauce, beef bouillon, chickpeas, thyme, and bay leaves.

Seal and cook on high pressure for 35 minutes, until the lamb is tender. Natural release, then open when the pressure subsides. Discard the thyme sprig and bay leaves. Divide among 4 bowls and serve.

SKINNY SCOOP

This recipe can be doubled easily and frozen for another day. To freeze, transfer the stew to freezer-safe containers, and freeze for up to 3 months. Thaw overnight in the refrigerator before reheating.

NO PRESSURE COOKER? NO PROBLEM!

To make this in a large pot or Dutch oven, sauté over medium-high heat in step 1. Add ¼ cup more water. Bring to a boil, then cook, covered, over low heat, for double the cooking time. Discard the thyme sprig and bay leaves before serving.

Unstuffed Cabbage Bowls SERVES 4

Stuffed cabbage reminds me of my childhood—it was a staple in my home growing up—but making the dish can be a bit time-consuming. I came up with the idea to chop the cabbage and turn the dish into bowls instead, and they came out so good and were done in a fraction of the time. This recipe is a fan favorite on my website. Quick and easy stuffed cabbage, without all the work. It's a no-brainer!

In the recipe I first shared, I used cooked brown rice, but the question kept coming up if I could make the rice in the pot with the meat. I tested this out using the pot-in-pot method (see page 15), and it worked great. If you would like to omit this step, simply use 2½ cups cooked brown rice instead.

Olive oil spray (I like my Misto or Bertolli)

1 pound 93% lean ground beef

1½ teaspoons kosher salt

1 cup chopped onion

1 garlic clove, minced

1 tablespoon dried marjoram

Freshly ground black pepper

1 (8-ounce) can tomato sauce

1 cup reduced-sodium beef broth*

2 tablespoons raisins

½ teaspoon Hungarian paprika

1 cup uncooked short-grain brown rice

9 cups chopped cabbage (1 medium head)

*Read the label to be sure this product is gluten-free.

PER SERVING	1½ cups
CALORIES	491
FAT	12.5 g
SATURATED FAT	4.5 g
CHOLESTEROL	94 mg
CARBOHYDRATE	57 g
FIBER	7.5 g
PROTEIN	40 g
SUGARS	12 g
SODIUM	954 mg

SKINNY SCOOP

You'll need a heatproof glass or stainless-steel bowl you can stack inside your pressure cooker without obstructing the lid. I used a glass Pyrex bowl and the steaming rack/trivet that came with my Instant Pot.

Press the sauté button on an electric pressure cooker. Spray the pot with oil, then add the beef and 1 teaspoon of the salt. Brown the meat, using a wooden spoon to break it into small pieces as it cooks, about 5 minutes. Add the onion, garlic, marjoram, and pepper to taste. Stir in the tomato sauce, beef broth, raisins, and paprika. Turn the pressure cooker off.

Place the rice, 1¼ cups water, and the remaining ½ teaspoon salt in a heatproof bowl and stir. Set the steaming rack/trivet over the meat, then place the bowl on top of the rack.

Seal and cook on high pressure for 27 minutes, until the rice is cooked and the liquid is absorbed. Natural release for 10 minutes, then open when the pressure subsides.

Carefully remove the bowl of rice and fluff with a fork. Remove the rack and add the cabbage to the pot. Seal and cook on high pressure for 3 minutes, until the cabbage is tender. Quick release, then open when the pressure subsides. Stir ½ cup of the cooked rice into the pot. Serve over the remaining rice.

Salmon Salad with Green Beans and Egg SERVES 1

This brain-boosting, feel-good salad features wild salmon, which contains heart-healthy omega-3 fatty acids and vitamin B12, nutrients that help produce brain chemicals that affect mood. It also happens to be my favorite fish, so I try to eat it at least once a week. This dish couldn't be easier to make—it takes less than 10 minutes from start to finish because everything cooks together at the same time.

1 (5-ounce) skinless wild-caught salmon fillet, about 1 inch thick

¼ teaspoon plus ⅛ teaspoon kosher salt

Freshly ground black pepper

2 large eggs

3 ounces haricots verts or green beans (about 12), trimmed

1 tablespoon extra-virgin olive oil

2 teaspoons red wine vinegar

1 teaspoon Dijon mustard

1 cup chopped romaine lettuce

1 medium campari tomato, quartered

4 pitted Kalamata olives

PER SERVING	1 salad
CALORIES	577
FAT	37.5 g
SATURATED FAT	7 g
CHOLESTEROL	450 mg
CARBOHYDRATE	14 g
FIBER	5.5 g
PROTEIN	44 g
SUGARS	5 g
SODIUM	976 mg

FOOD FACTS: FEEL-GOOD FISH

The omega-3 fatty acids in salmon, called docosahexaenoic acid or DHA, aren't just good for your skin; they're also good for your mood! Studies show that people who eat omega-3–rich fish tend to have lower risks of depression, aggressiveness, and hostility.

Season the salmon with ¼ teaspoon of the salt and pepper to taste.

Set a steamer basket or steaming rack/trivet in the bottom of an electric pressure cooker and pour in 1 cup water. Place the fish, eggs, and beans on the rack.

Seal and cook on high pressure for 2 minutes, until the fish flakes easily and the beans are tender. Quick release, then open when the pressure subsides. Remove the salmon and beans, leaving the eggs in the pot. Quickly run the beans under cold running water and set aside. Cover the pressure cooker and cook the eggs for an additional 3 minutes, until hard-boiled. Quick release, then open when the pressure subsides. Quickly run the eggs under cold running water until they are cool enough to hold. Peel right away and slice them in half.

In a small bowl, whisk together the oil, vinegar, mustard, remaining ⅛ teaspoon salt, and pepper to taste.

Place the romaine on a plate and put the beans to one side. Flake the salmon into large chunks and put it on one side of the plate. Arrange the egg halves, tomato, and olives over the lettuce. Drizzle with the dressing and serve.

Stuffed Artichokes with Bread Crumbs and Tomato Caper Sauce SERVES 2

Every year, my BFF Gabbie and I visit a restaurant in Manhattan's Little Italy that makes the best stuffed artichokes, and naturally I was inspired to make a version at home. You can easily share one between a few people as an appetizer, or have one all to yourself as a meal. Plan on getting your hands dirty as a necessary part of enjoying them. Grabbing one leaf after another and scraping off the stuffing and meat of the artichoke with your teeth, you'll work your way toward the center, where the leaves are softer. Take a spoon and scoop out the prickly nettles that stick out from the heart—you don't want to eat that part. The heart itself is the best thing in the world to eat—a prize after all that work!

ARTICHOKES

2 artichokes (about 10 ounces each), rinsed

1 lemon wedge

STUFFING

Olive oil spray

½ cup bread crumbs, regular or gluten-free

1 garlic clove, minced

2 tablespoons freshly grated Pecorino Romano cheese (I like Locatelli)

2½ tablespoons chopped fresh parsley, plus more for garnish

SAUCE

1 teaspoon unsalted butter

4 garlic cloves, sliced

1 (14.5-ounce) can petite diced tomatoes

⅓ cup dry white wine

½ cup reduced-sodium vegetable or chicken broth

1 teaspoon fresh lemon juice

½ tablespoon capers, drained

2 tablespoons pitted and sliced Italian olives

¼ cup shredded Pecorino Romano cheese (I like Locatelli)

PER SERVING	1 stuffed artichoke + sauce + cheese topping
CALORIES	438
FAT	10.5 g
SATURATED FAT	5 g
CHOLESTEROL	13 mg
CARBOHYDRATE	63 g
FIBER	19 g
PROTEIN	22 g
SUGARS	10 g
SODIUM	1,394 mg

For the artichokes: Remove any damaged outer leaves. Using a sharp knife, carefully trim off the stem and top third of each artichoke. Rub the cut top with the lemon wedge to prevent browning.

Set a steamer basket or rack in the bottom of an electric pressure cooker. Place the artichokes on the rack and pour 1 cup of water into the pot. Seal and cook on high pressure for 15 minutes, until the outer leaves can easily be pulled off. Natural release, then open when the pressure subsides. Use tongs to remove the artichokes and set aside. Drain and dry the pot.

For the stuffing: Press the sauté button on an electric pressure cooker. Spray with oil. When hot, add the bread crumbs and garlic and cook, stirring, until the crumbs are toasted and golden, about 2 minutes. Transfer to a small bowl and stir the pecorino and chopped parsley into the crumbs. Wipe the pot clean.

For the sauce: Press the sauté button on the electric pressure cooker. Add the butter and garlic and cook, stirring, until golden, about 1 minute. Add the tomatoes and wine and cook to let the alcohol cook

out, about 3 minutes. Add the broth, ¼ cup water, lemon juice, capers, and olives and cook for 1 minute to warm through. Turn off.

Stuff the centers and leaves of the artichokes with the stuffing, then top with the shredded pecorino. Place the artichokes in the pot over the sauce. Seal and cook on high pressure for 2 minutes, until the cheese melts. Natural release, then open when the pressure subsides.

To serve, place each artichoke in a bowl and divide the sauce. Garnish with parsley.

Tomato-Spinach Tortellini Soup SERVES 8

This soup is a win-win: My family loves the flavors, and the kitchen smells amazing while it cooks. It's loaded with vegetables, but since everything gets pureed (except the spinach and tortellini), the kids don't mind it at all. Different brands of vegetable broth will be more or less salty, so be sure to taste the soup and season with more salt, if you think it needs it. It's filling on its own as a main dish, but if you wish, serve some crusty bread on the side. Pass the spoons!

1½ tablespoons unsalted butter

1 cup finely chopped celery

1 cup finely chopped carrot

1 cup finely chopped onion

4 cups reduced-sodium vegetable broth

1½ cups 2% milk

1 (28-ounce) can crushed tomatoes

¼ cup chopped fresh basil

2 bay leaves

1 (9-ounce) package three-cheese fresh tortellini (I like Buitoni)

⅓ cup freshly grated Pecorino Romano cheese (I like Locatelli), plus optional more for topping

½ teaspoon kosher salt

Freshly ground black pepper

4 cups (about 2½ ounces) baby spinach

PER SERVING	1⅓ cups
CALORIES	222
FAT	7 g
SATURATED FAT	3.5 g
CHOLESTEROL	25 mg
CARBOHYDRATE	29 g
FIBER	3 g
PROTEIN	11 g
SUGARS	11 g
SODIUM	608 mg

Press the sauté button on an electric pressure cooker. Add the butter and when it has melted, add the celery, carrot, and onion. Cook, stirring, until tender, 5 to 6 minutes. Add the broth, milk, tomatoes, basil, and bay leaves.

Seal and cook on high pressure for 20 minutes, until the vegetables are tender. Quick or natural release, then open when the pressure subsides. Discard the bay leaves and puree the soup right in the pot with an immersion blender until smooth (or in a regular blender, in batches).

Press the sauté button and bring the soup back to a boil. Stir in the tortellini, ⅓ cup of the pecorino, the salt, and pepper to taste. Cook according to the pasta package directions, adding the spinach in the last minute. To serve, ladle into 8 bowls and top with pecorino, if desired.

NO PRESSURE COOKER? NO PROBLEM!

To make this in a large pot or Dutch oven, sauté over medium-high heat in step 1. Add ¼ cup water with the broth. Bring to a boil, then cook, covered, on low heat, and double the cook time. Add the tortellini at the end, cooking according to package directions.

**NO PRESSURE COOKER?
NO PROBLEM!**

To make this in a large pot or Dutch
oven, sauté over medium-high heat
in step 2. Add ¼ cup more water in
step 3. Bring to a boil, then cook,
covered, on low heat, and double
the cook time, stirring in the onion
mixture after 90 minutes.

Mexican Pinto Beans with Queso SERVES 8

Every time I'm in California, I go on a quest to find all the best Mexican taco spots. While I was having tacos in Berkeley, California, what really caught my attention wasn't the tacos, but the pinto beans! They were topped with tomatoes, cilantro, avocado, and—my favorite part—chunks of Oaxaca cheese. I re-created them for Tommy, and I think he fell in love with me all over again. (Mozzarella cheese is a perfect swap for Oaxaca, if you can't find it or prefer to substitute.) Serve the beans as soup with tortillas on the side, or as a side dish over rice.

1 pound dried pinto beans

1 teaspoon olive oil

1 small yellow onion, chopped, plus ½ medium yellow onion left whole

3 garlic cloves, minced

¼ cup chopped fresh cilantro

1 (4.24-ounce) can chopped green chiles

1 fresh jalapeño pepper

2 tablespoons chicken or vegetable bouillon* (I like Better Than Bouillon)

2 bay leaves

1 teaspoon kosher salt

TOPPINGS

2 medium tomatoes, seeded and chopped

¼ medium red onion, chopped

2 scallions, chopped

¼ cup chopped fresh cilantro

3 ounces queso Oaxaca or mozzarella cheese, crumbled or cut into ¼-inch cubes

8 ounces sliced avocado (from 2 small Hass)

FOR SERVING

Lime wedges

Tortillas (optional)

*Read the label to be sure this product is gluten-free.

PER SERVING	1 generous cup + toppings
CALORIES	308
FAT	8.5 g
SATURATED FAT	3 g
CHOLESTEROL	11 mg
CARBOHYDRATE	45 g
FIBER	12 g
PROTEIN	17 g
SUGARS	4 g
SODIUM	807 mg

Rinse the beans and put them in a medium bowl. Cover with water by 2 inches and let soak overnight. Drain and discard the water.

Press the sauté button on an electric pressure cooker. When hot, add the oil and chopped onion and cook, stirring, until softened, 3 to 4 minutes. Add the garlic and cilantro and cook, stirring, until fragrant, about 1 minute. Transfer to a bowl.

In the pressure cooker, combine the soaked beans, green chiles, jalapeño, onion half, bouillon, bay leaves, and 6 cups water. Seal and cook on high pressure for 45 minutes, until the beans are tender. Natural release, then open when the pressure subsides. Discard the bay leaves, jalapeño, and onion half.

Press the sauté button on the pressure cooker. Stir in the reserved sautéed onion mixture and the salt. Cook the beans, stirring occasionally, until thickened, about 30 minutes.

Meanwhile, for the toppings: In a small bowl, combine the tomatoes, red onion, scallions, and cilantro.

Ladle the beans into serving bowls and top with the tomato mixture, cheese, and avocado. Serve with lime wedges and tortillas, if desired.

Pot-in-Pot Puerto Rican Rice and Beans SERVES 4

Thanks to the pot-in-pot cooking method that works so well with electric pressure cookers such as the Instant Pot, this is hands-down the quickest rice and beans recipe you'll ever make. On nights when I don't have much in the fridge, this is my go-to meal, since it uses pantry staples I always have on hand. It's also Tommy's favorite Puerto Rican meal, and he doesn't mind skipping the meat when this is on the menu—although he typically has more than one serving! This dish is also great topped with a fried egg.

SOFRITO

½ small onion

½ cubanelle pepper, seeded

3 garlic cloves

¼ cup chopped fresh cilantro

BEANS

1 teaspoon olive oil

1 (15.5-ounce) can pink or red kidney beans,* undrained (I like Goya)

½ cup canned tomato sauce

1 medium (5-ounce) all-purpose or russet potato, peeled and cut into ¼-inch cubes

½ tablespoon sazón seasoning, homemade (see page 127) or store-bought (I like Badia Sazón Tropical)

1 bay leaf

⅛ teaspoon dried oregano

¼ teaspoon kosher salt

Freshly ground black pepper

RICE

1 cup uncooked white basmati rice

¾ teaspoon kosher salt

TOPPINGS

5 ounces sliced avocado (from 1 medium Hass)

1 large tomato, halved and sliced

Hot sauce, for serving (optional)

*Read the label to be sure this product is gluten-free.

PER SERVING	1½ cups + ¼ avocado
CALORIES	376
FAT	7 g
SATURATED FAT	1 g
CHOLESTEROL	0 mg
CARBOHYDRATE	68 g
FIBER	11 g
PROTEIN	12 g
SUGARS	6 g
SODIUM	845 mg

SKINNY SCOOP

You'll need a heatproof glass or stainless-steel bowl you can stack inside your electric pressure cooker without obstructing the lid. I used a glass Pyrex bowl and the steaming rack/trivet that came with my Instant Pot.

For the sofrito: In a small food processor, finely chop the onion, cubanelle, garlic, and cilantro.

For the beans: Press the sauté button on an electric pressure cooker. When hot, add the oil and sofrito and cook, stirring, until softened, about 2 minutes. Add the beans (not drained) to the pot, along with ¾ cup water, the tomato sauce, potato, sazón, bay leaf, oregano, salt, and black pepper to taste.

For the rice: In a heatproof bowl that will fit in the pressure cooker, stir together 1¼ cups water, the rice, and salt. Place the steaming rack/trivet over the beans, then place the bowl on top of the rack.

Seal and cook on high pressure for 12 minutes, until the rice is cooked and can easily be fluffed with a fork. Natural release for 10 minutes.

Carefully take the bowl of rice out of the pressure cooker and fluff with a fork. Remove the rack from the pressure cooker. Discard the bay leaf and serve the beans over the rice, topped with the avocado, tomato, and hot sauce, if desired.

Air Fryer

SKINNY SCOOP

When preparing kale, be sure to cut out and discard the tough, fibrous center ribs before chopping the leaves.

Buffalo Drumsticks with Creamy Cabbage and Kale Slaw SERVES 4

Fried chicken is my weakness—especially the drumsticks! An overnight bath in a brine made of buttermilk and hot sauce makes this air-fried chicken moist and juicy, and infuses so much flavor into every bite. The breading is a mildly spiced seasoned crumb mixture that comes out super crispy.

CHICKEN

8 chicken drumsticks (3½ ounces each), skin removed

½ teaspoon poultry seasoning

¼ teaspoon garlic powder

¼ teaspoon kosher salt

1 cup low-fat (1%) buttermilk

¼ cup Frank's RedHot Sauce

2 sprigs of fresh thyme

Cooking spray

CRUMBS

⅔ cup panko bread crumbs, regular or gluten-free

½ cup crushed cornflakes, regular or gluten-free

1½ teaspoons kosher salt

1½ teaspoons sweet paprika

1 teaspoon chili powder*

½ teaspoon garlic powder

SLAW

1 tablespoon minced shallot

1½ tablespoons apple cider vinegar

¼ cup low-fat (1%) buttermilk

½ tablespoon olive oil

½ teaspoon kosher salt

Freshly ground black pepper

3 cups thinly sliced green cabbage

1 cup packed thinly sliced lacinato kale

*Read the label to be sure this product is gluten-free.

PER SERVING	2 drumsticks + 1 cup slaw
CALORIES	383
FAT	10 g
SATURATED FAT	2.5 g
CHOLESTEROL	179 mg
CARBOHYDRATE	16 g
FIBER	2.5 g
PROTEIN	41 g
SUGARS	3 g
SODIUM	810 mg

NO AIR FRYER? NO PROBLEM!

To make this in the oven, bake on a rack on a large baking sheet in a 400°F oven until golden brown and cooked through, 40 to 45 minutes.

For the chicken: Season the chicken with the poultry seasoning, garlic powder, and salt and toss to coat well. Pour the buttermilk and hot sauce into a large bowl, stir well, and add the thyme and chicken. Refrigerate for about 6 hours or up to overnight.

Preheat an air fryer to 360°F.

For the crumbs: In a shallow bowl, combine the panko, cornflakes, salt, paprika, chili powder, and garlic powder. Stir well.

Line a sheet pan with wax paper. Remove the chicken from the buttermilk, dredge each piece in the crumb mixture, and place them on the lined sheet pan. Spray both sides of the chicken with oil.

Place 4 of the drumsticks in the air fryer basket in a single layer and cook for 22 to 24 minutes, turning halfway, until the crust is golden and the chicken is cooked through in the center. Transfer to a plate and repeat with the remaining 4 drumsticks. Return all of the chicken to the air fryer and cook for 1 minute to heat through.

For the slaw: In a large bowl, whisk together the shallots and vinegar. Whisk in the buttermilk, olive oil, salt, and pepper to taste. Add the cabbage and kale and toss well. Serve alongside each drumstick.

Chicken Katsu with Sesame-Pineapple Slaw SERVES 4

I'm pretty sure every country has its own version of fried chicken cutlets. In Japan, it's *katsu*, a crispy deep-fried chicken dish that's served with tonkatsu sauce, a Japanese condiment similar to BBQ sauce. This air-fryer version will not disappoint. The chicken comes out crispy on the outside and juicy on the inside, and uses only a few spritzes of oil. It pairs wonderfully with a simple sesame-pineapple slaw.

SLAW

1½ tablespoons pineapple juice

½ tablespoon toasted sesame oil

½ tablespoon Dijon mustard

Pinch of kosher salt

Freshly ground black pepper

1¾ cups shredded green cabbage

1¾ cups shredded red cabbage

¾ cup diced pineapple, canned or fresh

1 teaspoon black sesame seeds

TONKATSU SAUCE

¼ cup ketchup (I like Sir Kensington)

¼ cup unsweetened applesauce

2 tablespoons Worcestershire sauce*

1 tablespoon reduced-sodium soy sauce*

1 teaspoon grated fresh ginger

1 garlic clove, minced

CHICKEN

2 tablespoons all-purpose flour, wheat or gluten-free

1 large egg, lightly beaten

1 cup panko bread crumbs, regular or gluten-free

¾ teaspoon kosher salt

Freshly ground black pepper

2 boneless, skinless chicken breasts (8 ounces each), halved horizontally to make 4 cutlets total

Olive oil spray (I like my Misto or Bertolli)

1 medium scallion, sliced, for garnish

*Read the label to be sure this product is gluten-free.

PER SERVING	1 chicken cutlet + 2 tablespoons sauce + 1 cup slaw
CALORIES	313
FAT	6.5 g
SATURATED FAT	1.5 g
CHOLESTEROL	119 mg
CARBOHYDRATE	33 g
FIBER	3 g
PROTEIN	30 g
SUGARS	12 g
SODIUM	859 mg

For the slaw: In a large bowl, whisk together the pineapple juice, sesame oil, mustard, salt, and pepper to taste. Add the green and red cabbage and the pineapple, toss to combine, and garnish with the sesame seeds.

For the tonkatsu sauce: In a small blender or food processor, combine the ketchup, applesauce, Worcestershire, soy sauce, ginger, and garlic. Blend until well combined and smooth.

For the chicken: Preheat an air fryer to 400°F.

Place the flour on a plate and place the egg in a shallow bowl. On another plate, combine the panko, ¼ teaspoon of the salt, and pepper to taste.

Season the chicken cutlets with the remaining ½ teaspoon salt and pepper to taste. Dredge each cutlet first in the flour, then in the egg, and finally in the panko mixture, shaking off any excess as you go. Spray both sides of each chicken cutlet with oil.

Place 2 of the cutlets in the air fryer basket in a single layer and cook for 8 minutes, turning halfway, until golden and crisp. Set aside and repeat with the remaining 2 pieces. Return the first batch to the air fryer, setting the cutlets on top of the other chicken pieces, and cook for 1 minute, until everything is hot.

To serve, place 1 cup of the slaw and 1 chicken cutlet on each of 4 plates. Top the chicken with 2 tablespoons of the tonkatsu sauce and

NO AIR FRYER? NO PROBLEM!

To make this in the oven, bake the chicken on a sheet pan in a 425°F oven for 15 minutes, then broil for

SKINNY SCOOP

To make this mild and
kid-friendly, omit the
cayenne and jalapeño.

Spicy Fried Chicken Sandwiches SERVES 4

If fried chicken sandwiches were healthy for you, I'd eat one every day because I *love* them! That being said, I think I've nailed all the required characteristics of a sublime one: chicken that has a crispy exterior and moist, juicy interior, finished with a fresh, tangy slaw. If you grew up eating fried chicken sandwiches from Wendy's or Chick-fil-A, you'll find this version a tastier and slimmer step up from the fast-food kind.

2 boneless, skinless chicken breasts (8 ounces each)

2 cups low-fat (1%) buttermilk

1½ teaspoons plus ⅛ teaspoon kosher salt

Freshly ground black pepper

2 teaspoons red wine vinegar

2 teaspoons olive oil

1 teaspoon Dijon mustard

¼ small red onion, thinly sliced

1¾ cups thinly sliced green cabbage

1 fresh jalapeño pepper, seeded and thinly sliced

2 tablespoons finely chopped fresh parsley

1 cup panko bread crumbs, regular or gluten-free

½ teaspoon cayenne pepper

Olive oil spray (I like my Misto or Bertolli)

4 tablespoons light mayonnaise

4 potato rolls, whole wheat (I like Martin's) or gluten-free

PER SERVING	1 sandwich
CALORIES	377
FAT	12.5 g
SATURATED FAT	2 g
CHOLESTEROL	79 mg
CARBOHYDRATE	34 g
FIBER	4.5 g
PROTEIN	34 g
SUGARS	8 g
SODIUM	712 mg

NO AIR FRYER? NO PROBLEM!

To make this in the oven, bake on a rack on a large sheet pan in a 425°F oven until golden brown and cooked through, 20 to 25 minutes, turning halfway.

Pound out the thicker end of the chicken breasts so that they are evenly thick (about ½ inch). Cut each breast in half so you have 4 thick pieces.

In a medium bowl, whisk together the buttermilk, 1 teaspoon of the salt, and pepper to taste. Add the chicken and turn to coat. Cover with plastic wrap and refrigerate for at least 1 hour.

When ready to cook, in a large bowl, whisk together the vinegar, olive oil, mustard, ⅛ teaspoon of the salt, and pepper to taste. Add the onion, cabbage, jalapeño, and parsley and toss to combine. Cover and refrigerate until ready to assemble the sandwiches.

Preheat an air fryer to 375°F.

In a shallow bowl, combine the panko, cayenne, remaining ½ teaspoon salt, and black pepper to taste. Dredge the chicken in the panko mixture, shaking off any excess.

Place 2 pieces of the coated chicken in the air fryer basket in a single layer and spray the tops with oil. Cook the chicken for 14 to 16 minutes (depending on the thickness), turning halfway. Spray the other side with oil and cook until golden and cooked through (a thermometer inserted in the thickest part of the breast should read 165°F). Repeat with the remaining 2 pieces of chicken.

To assemble the sandwiches, spread the mayo on the bottoms of the rolls. Top with the chicken, then pile ½ cup of the slaw on the chicken. Put the tops of the rolls on the slaw and serve.

Everything (but the) Bagel Chicken Roll-Ups SERVES 4

I absolutely love "everything" bagels. Not surprisingly, when I decided to coat my chicken in the "everything" seasoning that tops those bagels, a new favorite chicken dish was born! Even better, I stuffed it with my favorite bagel topping: cream cheese and scallions, plus some cheddar and spinach. You can find "everything" bagel seasoning in most grocery stores or online; it has a lot of salt, so I decreased the amount of it that I used, and added more sesame seeds to bring down the sodium. A crisp green salad would be perfect on the side.

¼ cup "everything" bagel seasoning

½ cup sesame seeds

2 egg whites, beaten

½ cup (3 ounces) whipped cream cheese

½ cup (2 ounces) shredded reduced-fat cheddar cheese*

¼ cup chopped scallions

8 thin-sliced chicken breast cutlets (4 ounces each)

½ cup chopped baby spinach

Olive oil spray (I like my Misto or Bertolli)

*Read the label to be sure this product is gluten-free.

PER SERVING	2 roll-ups
CALORIES	527
FAT	22 g
SATURATED FAT	7 g
CHOLESTEROL	168 mg
CARBOHYDRATE	11 g
FIBER	6 g
PROTEIN	61 g
SUGARS	1 g
SODIUM	976 mg

SKINNY SCOOP

To make your own "everything" bagel seasoning, in a small bowl, combine 2 tablespoons dried minced onion, 2 tablespoons dried minced garlic, 2 tablespoons poppy seeds, 1 tablespoon white sesame seeds, 1 tablespoon black sesame seeds, and 2 teaspoons coarse salt.

In a shallow bowl, combine the bagel seasoning and sesame seeds. Place the egg whites in another bowl.

Preheat an air fryer to 375°F.

In a small bowl, combine the cream cheese, cheddar, and scallions.

Place the chicken cutlets on a cutting board. Spread 1½ tablespoons of the cheese mixture on each cutlet, then put 1 tablespoon spinach leaves in the center of each. Roll up the chicken and place seam side down.

Dredge each roll-up in the egg whites, then in the seasoning mixture, shaking off any excess as you go.

Transfer in batches to the air fryer basket and spray the tops with oil. Cook for 15 minutes, turning halfway, until golden and crisp on the outside and cooked through in the center.

Transfer the roll-ups to plates and serve.

NO AIR FRYER? NO PROBLEM!

To make this dish in the oven, bake the chicken on a sheet pan in a 425°F oven for 25 minutes.

Glazed Korean BBQ Chicken Wings SERVES 4

My family loves chicken wings—and not just as an appetizer. They are great for weeknight dinners when I want something fast and easy. I pair them with a salad or some cucumber wedges, and dinner is done. *Gochujang* is a fermented Korean chile paste that's so delicious. You can find it in most grocery stores and it's worth buying, since I find lots of uses for it. If you can't find drumettes in the supermarket, you can make them yourself: Cut off the wing tips of the chicken wings and freeze them to make stock. You'll be left with the drumette portion that looks like a mini drumstick.

3 garlic cloves

1-inch piece fresh ginger, peeled

¼ cup chopped onion

4 tablespoons reduced-sodium soy sauce*

¼ cup unsweetened applesauce

2 tablespoons gochujang*

2 tablespoons honey

1 tablespoon unseasoned rice vinegar

20 chicken wing drumettes, skinned (3 pounds total)

Olive oil spray (I like my Misto or Bertolli)

1 teaspoon toasted sesame oil

1 scallion, chopped

1 teaspoon sesame seeds

*Read the label to be sure this product is gluten-free.

PER SERVING	5 drumettes
CALORIES	431
FAT	12 g
SATURATED FAT	3 g
CHOLESTEROL	161 mg
CARBOHYDRATE	13 g
FIBER	1 g
PROTEIN	63 g
SUGARS	11 g
SODIUM	655 mg

SKINNY SCOOP

You can make this with other chicken pieces besides drumettes—swap them for 8 skinless drumsticks or thighs. Note that the cooking time will vary with different cuts.

In a small blender, combine the garlic, ginger, onion, 3 tablespoons of the soy sauce, the applesauce, 1 tablespoon of the gochujang, 1 tablespoon of the honey, and the vinegar. Process until smooth. Pour the sauce into a large zip-top plastic bag and add the chicken. Massage the marinade into the chicken, making sure all the wings are coated evenly. Refrigerate the chicken for at least 1 hour or up to overnight.

When ready to cook, preheat an air fryer to 400°F. Spray the basket with oil.

In a small bowl, combine the remaining 1 tablespoon soy sauce, 1 tablespoon gochujang, 1 tablespoon honey, and the sesame oil.

Remove the chicken from the marinade and discard the excess marinade. Place half of the chicken drumettes in the air fryer basket in a single layer and cook for 16 to 18 minutes, shaking halfway, until the chicken is no longer pink in the center of the thickest part. Brush half of the sauce onto the wings and cook for 2 more minutes, until golden. Transfer to a plate and repeat with the remaining wings and sauce. Once all the wings are cooked, return the first batch to the air fryer and cook for 1 minute so that everything is hot.

Serve topped with the scallions and sesame seeds.

NO AIR FRYER? NO PROBLEM!

To make this in the oven, bake at 425°F for 45 minutes, turning halfway. Brush with the soy-gochujang sauce and cook for 2 more minutes.

Chicken, Pesto, and Cheese Stromboli SERVES 4

Stromboli is basically pizza dough that's filled with deli meats and cheese, rolled up, and baked in the oven. But guess what? You can fill it with anything your heart desires! Use some cut-up steak, peppers, and onions for a Philly cheesesteak version, or roasted vegetables and cheese to make it meatless. This chicken, pesto, spinach, and mozzarella combo is delicious *and* healthy, and it's perfect served with a green salad on the side. I used my Greek yogurt pizza dough recipe to make this lighter and higher in protein, but to save time, just use store-bought pizza dough.

Simplest Pizza Dough (page 210) or 14 ounces refrigerated store-bought pizza dough

All-purpose flour, for sprinkling

1 pound boneless, skinless chicken breasts

1 teaspoon dried oregano

1 teaspoon kosher salt

Freshly ground black pepper

Olive oil spray (I like my Misto or Bertolli)

4 teaspoons store-bought pesto

1 cup (4 ounces) shredded mozzarella cheese

32 baby spinach leaves

1 large egg, beaten

1 teaspoon Italian seasoning

PER SERVING	1 stromboli
CALORIES	402
FAT	13 g
SATURATED FAT	5 g
CHOLESTEROL	145 mg
CARBOHYDRATE	28 g
FIBER	1 g
PROTEIN	41 g
SUGARS	3 g
SODIUM	995 mg

Divide the dough into 4 equal balls (about 3½ ounces each). Sprinkle a work surface and rolling pin with a little flour and roll out each ball of dough into a thin 10-inch round.

Preheat an air fryer to 360°F.

Line a plate with paper towels. Season the chicken with the oregano, salt, and pepper to taste. Spray the chicken with oil. Place the chicken in the basket and cook for 15 minutes, turning halfway, until cooked through. Transfer the chicken to a cutting board and thinly slice it crosswise. Transfer to the prepared plate to soak up any moisture (to prevent the crust from getting soggy).

Spread 1 teaspoon of the pesto down the center of each dough round. Sprinkle ¼ cup of the mozzarella down the center of each round, over the pesto. Top the mozzarella with 8 baby spinach leaves and one-quarter of the chicken slices. Fold the sides of the dough over the filling, firmly overlapping each other, and place seam side down on the work surface. Repeat with the remaining ingredients. Brush the tops of the stromboli with the egg and sprinkle with the Italian seasoning.

Working in batches, cook the stromboli in the air fryer for 8 to 10 minutes, turning halfway, until puffed and golden. Serve hot.

Nuggets Three Ways   SERVES 4

What's more kid-friendly than chicken nuggets!? Even the pickiest children devour them, and adults love them, too. You can serve the Classic Chicken Nuggets with ketchup, BBQ sauce, ranch-style dressing (for homemade, see page 31), or the dip of your choice. Personally, I like them simply sprinkled with lemon juice and, on the side, a crisp green salad or veggie sticks, like cut-up carrots and cucumbers. I've also included spicier Buffalo Chicken Nuggets—they pair perfectly with blue cheese dressing—and vegetarian Breaded Cauliflower Nuggets. The cauliflower ones were inspired by the fried cauliflower my dad used to make, which was my favorite way to eat cauliflower as a kid. This version is much healthier, and delicious spritzed with fresh lemon juice.

CLASSIC CHICKEN NUGGETS
Makes 32 nuggets | Serves 4

PER SERVING	8 nuggets
CALORIES	197
FAT	5.5 g
SATURATED FAT	1.5 g
CHOLESTEROL	121 mg
CARBOHYDRATE	7 g
FIBER	1 g
PROTEIN	28 g
SUGARS	0.5 g
SODIUM	504 mg

NO AIR FRYER? NO PROBLEM!

To make this in the oven, bake at 425°F for 8 to 10 minutes, turn, then cook 4 to 5 minutes, until golden brown and cooked through.

1 large egg, beaten

6 tablespoons Italian-seasoned whole wheat bread crumbs

2 tablespoons panko bread crumbs

2 tablespoons freshly grated Parmesan cheese

1 pound boneless, skinless chicken breasts, cut into 32 (1-inch) pieces

½ teaspoon kosher salt

Freshly ground black pepper

Olive oil spray (I like my Misto or Bertolli)

Lemon wedges, for serving (optional)

Preheat an air fryer to 400°F.

Put the egg in a shallow bowl. In a separate shallow bowl, combine the bread crumbs, panko, and Parmesan.

Sprinkle the chicken pieces with the salt and pepper to taste. Working in batches, dredge the pieces first in the egg, then in the bread-crumb mixture, shaking off any excess. Put them on a work surface and spray all over with oil.

Add just enough chicken to the air fryer basket to make a single layer without overcrowding the basket and cook for 6 to 8 minutes, turning halfway, until golden. Repeat with more batches of the remaining chicken. Serve hot with the lemon wedges, if desired.

BUFFALO CHICKEN NUGGETS

Makes 32 nuggets | Serves 4

If you want to make these even spicier, substitute cayenne pepper for the chili powder.

PER SERVING	8 nuggets
CALORIES	266
FAT	4 g
SATURATED FAT	1 g
CHOLESTEROL	96 mg
CARBOHYDRATE	10 g
FIBER	1 g
PROTEIN	27 g
SUGARS	1 g
SODIUM	681 mg

NO AIR FRYER? NO PROBLEM!

To make this in the oven, bake at 425°F for 8 to 10 minutes, turn, then cook 4 to 5 minutes, until golden brown and cooked through.

1 large egg, beaten

3 tablespoons Frank's RedHot Sauce

6 tablespoons Italian-seasoned whole wheat bread crumbs

¼ cup panko bread crumbs

½ teaspoon garlic powder

½ teaspoon sweet paprika

½ teaspoon chili powder

Freshly ground black pepper

1 pound boneless, skinless chicken breasts, cut into 32 (1-inch) pieces

½ teaspoon kosher salt

Olive oil spray (I like my Misto or Bertolli)

Preheat an air fryer to 400°F.

In a shallow bowl, combine the egg and hot sauce. In a separate shallow bowl, combine the bread crumbs, panko, garlic powder, paprika, chili powder, and ⅛ teaspoon black pepper.

Sprinkle the chicken pieces with the salt and black pepper to taste. Working in batches, dredge the pieces first in the egg mixture, then in the bread-crumb mixture, shaking off any excess. Put them on a work surface and spray all over with oil.

Add just enough chicken to the air fryer basket to make a single layer without overcrowding the basket and cook for 6 to 8 minutes, turning halfway, until golden. Repeat with more batches of the remaining chicken. Serve hot.

BREADED CAULIFLOWER NUGGETS

Makes 28 nuggets | Serves 4

PER SERVING	7 pieces
CALORIES	134
FAT	5 g
SATURATED FAT	2 g
CHOLESTEROL	142 mg
CARBOHYDRATE	14 g
FIBER	4 g
PROTEIN	9 g
SUGARS	4 g
SODIUM	479 mg

NO AIR FRYER? NO PROBLEM!

To make this in the oven, bake at 425°F for 20 to 25 minutes, turning halfway, until golden brown and tender when pierced with a fork.

28 bite-size (about 1½ inches) cauliflower florets (1 pound total)

3 large eggs, beaten

½ teaspoon kosher salt

Freshly ground black pepper

½ cup plus 2 tablespoons Italian-seasoned whole wheat bread crumbs

3 tablespoons seasoned panko bread crumbs

2 tablespoons freshly grated Parmesan cheese

Olive oil spray (I like my Misto or Bertolli)

Lemon wedges, for serving (optional)

Preheat an air fryer to 375°F.

Place the cauliflower in a microwave-safe bowl. Microwave on high for 2 minutes, until crisp-tender.

In a shallow bowl, combine the eggs, salt, and pepper to taste. In a separate shallow bowl, combine the bread crumbs, panko, and Parmesan.

Dredge the cauliflower florets first in the egg, then in the bread-crumb mixture, shaking off any excess. Put them on a work surface and spray all over with oil.

Add just enough cauliflower to the air fryer basket to make a single layer without overcrowding the basket and cook for 8 minutes, turning halfway, until golden. Repeat with more batches of the remaining cauliflower. Serve hot, with lemon wedges, if desired.

Cheesy Jalapeño Popper Stuffed Chicken SERVES 4

What happens when you combine jalapeño poppers with chicken? Pure awesomeness! Stuffed with diced jalapeño, cream cheese, a blend of Mexican cheese, scallions, and bacon, this chicken dish will blow you away. It has a mild kick, but if you'd like more, leave the seeds in the jalapeños. And you can use this recipe as a template for so many other stuffing variations. Try spinach, sun-dried tomatoes, and feta; or ham and Swiss; or broccoli and cheddar . . . just to name a few! You can also skip the bread crumbs to make it lower in carbs. A fresh salad or sliced tomatoes and cucumbers on the side is perfect to make this a meal.

8 thin-sliced chicken breast cutlets (4 ounces each)

¾ teaspoon kosher salt

Freshly ground black pepper

2 slices center-cut bacon

3 ounces ⅓-less-fat cream cheese, at room temperature

1 cup (4 ounces) shredded reduced-fat Mexican cheese blend* (I like Sargento)

3 fresh jalapeño peppers, seeded and chopped

2 tablespoons chopped scallions

½ cup plus 2 tablespoons Italian-seasoned bread crumbs, whole wheat or gluten-free

1 tablespoon olive oil

Juice of 1½ limes

Olive oil spray (I like my Misto or Bertolli)

*Read the label to be sure this product is gluten-free.

PER SERVING	2 stuffed cutlets
CALORIES	479
FAT	20.5 g
SATURATED FAT	8 g
CHOLESTEROL	176 mg
CARBOHYDRATE	13 g
FIBER	1.5 g
PROTEIN	61 g
SUGARS	3 g
SODIUM	992 mg

Sprinkle the chicken with the salt and black pepper to taste.

Preheat an air fryer to 400°F.

Cut the bacon to fit in the air fryer and cook for 6 to 8 minutes, turning halfway, until crisp. Remove and when cool enough to handle, crumble.

In a medium bowl, combine the cream cheese, Mexican cheese blend, jalapeños, scallions, and cooked bacon.

Lay the chicken cutlets on a work surface and spread 3 heaping tablespoons of the cream cheese mixture on each. Roll each one up and place seam side down on a work surface. Close the ends with toothpicks so the cheese doesn't ooze out.

Place the bread crumbs in a shallow bowl. In a second shallow bowl, combine the olive oil and lime juice. Dredge the chicken first in the lime-oil mixture, then in the bread crumbs, shaking off any excess. Place seam side down on a work surface and spray all over with oil.

Preheat an air fryer once again to 400°F.

Working in batches, put the chicken rolls into the air fryer basket in a single layer and cook for 12 minutes, turning halfway, until golden on the outside and cooked through in the center. Repeat with the remaining chicken rolls. Remove the toothpicks and serve hot.

NO AIR FRYER?
NO PROBLEM!

To make this in the oven,
bake on a sheet pan at
450°F for 22 to 25 minutes.

Italian Sausage and Pepper Calzones SERVES 4

Whether served with Italian bread, as a pizza topping, or in a calzone, sausage and peppers are a winning combo in my home. Calzones, which are similar to stromboli (see page 180) but shaped like half-moons, are usually stuffed with ricotta cheese. Here, however, I skipped the ricotta altogether and used mozzarella instead, which was a perfect match for the sausage and peppers. Provolone would also work well. I like to serve this with a green salad on the side.

Simplest Pizza Dough (page 210)

All-purpose flour, for sprinkling

4 Italian chicken sausage links, sweet or hot

1 medium onion, cut into ¼-inch-thick slices

1 red bell pepper, cut into ¼-inch-thick slices

Olive oil spray (I like my Misto or Bertolli)

¼ teaspoon kosher salt

½ teaspoon dried thyme

Freshly ground black pepper

1 cup (4 ounces) shredded part-skim mozzarella cheese

1 large egg, lightly beaten

Store-bought marinara sauce, warmed, for serving (optional)

PER SERVING	1 calzone
CALORIES	380
FAT	13.5 g
SATURATED FAT	5.5 g
CHOLESTEROL	125 mg
CARBOHYDRATE	33 g
FIBER	2 g
PROTEIN	31 g
SUGARS	5 g
SODIUM	983 mg

NO AIR FRYER? NO PROBLEM!

To make this in the oven, put the sausage, onion, and peppers in a baking dish and bake in a 425°F oven until cooked through and tender, about 20 minutes. Then stuff into the dough and bake until golden on both sides, 15 to 20 minutes.

Divide the dough into 4 equal balls (about 3½ ounces each). Lightly sprinkle a work surface and rolling pin with flour and roll the dough out into thin 9-inch rounds.

Preheat an air fryer to 370°F.

Place the sausage in the air fryer and cook for 2 minutes. Spray the onion and bell pepper with oil and sprinkle with the salt, thyme, and pepper to taste. Add to the air fryer basket with the sausage. Cook for 8 minutes, turning the sausage halfway and tossing the vegetables, until the vegetables are tender and slightly golden on the edges and the sausage is cooked through. Transfer to a cutting board. Very thinly slice the sausage.

Divide the sausage, pepper, and onion among the dough rounds, arranging the filling evenly over the bottom half of each, 1 inch from the edge. Top each with ¼ cup of the mozzarella. Brush the borders with half the beaten egg and fold the top of the dough over the filling to make a half-moon, leaving a ½-inch border uncovered at the bottom. Seal the edges by pinching the layers together or crimping with a fork. Brush the tops with the remaining beaten egg.

Working in batches, place the calzones in the air fryer in a single layer and cook for 10 minutes, turning halfway, until golden. Repeat with the remaining calzones. Serve hot, with the marinara on the side, if desired.

Crispy Breaded Pork Chops SERVES 6

When I was a kid, our family friend Debbie rented an apartment on the second floor of our home, and she would often invite my brother and me up for dinner. We loved going to Debbie's because, unlike my parents who made everything from scratch, Debbie opened our eyes to the world of Shake 'n Bake pork chops with Rice-A-Roni from a box. We loved it! These homemade Shake 'n Bake-inspired pork chops taste a whole lot better than the boxed variety. They're crispy, juicy, and flavorful and, of course, they're a lot less processed and a lot better for you. Serve them with a simple garden salad of chopped romaine, cucumbers, and tomato.

Olive oil spray (I like my Misto or Bertolli)

6 boneless or bone-in center-cut pork loin chops, ¾ inch thick (5 ounces each for boneless; 6 ounces each for bone-in), fat trimmed

½ teaspoon plus ¾ teaspoon kosher salt

1 large egg, beaten

½ cup panko bread crumbs, regular or gluten-free

⅓ cup crushed cornflake crumbs, regular or gluten-free

2 tablespoons freshly grated Parmesan cheese

1¼ teaspoons sweet paprika

½ teaspoon garlic powder

½ teaspoon onion powder

¼ teaspoon chili powder*

⅛ teaspoon freshly ground black pepper

*Read the label to be sure this product is gluten-free.

PER SERVING	1 pork chop
CALORIES	263
FAT	10.5 g
SATURATED FAT	3.5 g
CHOLESTEROL	110 mg
CARBOHYDRATE	6 g
FIBER	0.5 g
PROTEIN	33 g
SUGARS	0.5 g
SODIUM	359 mg

Preheat an air fryer to 400°F. Lightly spray the basket with oil.

Season the pork chops on both sides with ½ teaspoon of the salt.

Put the egg in a medium shallow bowl. In a large shallow bowl, combine the panko, cornflake crumbs, Parmesan, paprika, garlic powder, onion powder, chili powder, pepper, and remaining ¾ teaspoon salt. Dredge the pork first in the egg, then in the panko mixture, shaking off any excess. Spray both sides with oil.

Place 3 of the chops in the air fryer basket in a single layer and cook for 12 minutes, turning halfway, until golden and crisp and no longer pink in the center. Repeat with the remaining 3 chops. Return all of the chops to the air fryer and cook for 1 minute to heat through. Serve hot.

NO AIR FRYER? NO PROBLEM!

Although they come out much crispier in the air fryer, you can also make these in the oven by baking at 425°F for 20 to 25 minutes.

Philly Cheesesteak Egg Rolls SERVES 4

Q

Cheesesteaks remind me of my teenage years when my mom owned a luncheonette, eponymously named Marlene's Kitchen. I went to vocational school a few blocks away, and I would often stop by the luncheonette and have Mom make my favorite sandwich: a Philly-style steak and cheese. Those were the good old days when I could eat whatever I wanted and not gain a pound! These baked egg rolls are stuffed full of the same delicious flavors that I still love about that sandwich, though without much of the fat and calories. Nice and crisp on the outside, they satisfy a craving in a healthier way, while conjuring up those childhood memories at the same time.

½ pound sirloin steak

½ teaspoon kosher salt

Freshly ground black pepper

Olive oil spray (I like my Misto or Bertolli)

1 medium onion, cut into ½-inch-thick slices

1 green bell pepper, cut into ¼-inch-wide slices

1 red bell pepper, cut into ¼-inch-wide slices

1 cup (4 ounces) shredded sharp cheddar cheese

12 egg roll wrappers (I like Nasoya)

PER SERVING	3 egg rolls
CALORIES	387
FAT	13.5 g
SATURATED FAT	7 g
CHOLESTEROL	78 mg
CARBOHYDRATE	41 g
FIBER	2.5 g
PROTEIN	27 g
SUGARS	4 g
SODIUM	760 mg

SKINNY SCOOP

You can serve this with a light ranch-style dressing (see page 31), either for dipping or drizzled over 4 wedges of iceberg lettuce.

Preheat an air fryer to 400°F.

Sprinkle both sides of the steak with ¼ teaspoon of the salt and black pepper to taste. Spray both sides of the steak with oil and place in the air fryer basket. Cook for 2 minutes, until cooked to medium. Transfer to a cutting board and thinly slice across the grain. Transfer the slices to a medium bowl.

Reduce the air fryer temperature to 370°F.

Place the onion and bell peppers in a medium bowl, spritz them with olive oil, and season with the remaining ¼ teaspoon salt and black pepper to taste. Put the mixture in the air fryer basket and cook for 4 to 5 minutes, shaking the basket halfway, until the vegetables are tender and slightly golden on the edges. Transfer to a cutting board. Finely chop and transfer the vegetables to the bowl with the steak. Stir in the cheddar.

Place an egg roll wrapper on a work surface with the points facing top and bottom like a diamond. Spoon ¼ cup of the steak mixture on the bottom third of the wrapper. Fold the bottom corner up over the mixture snugly, then roll to the center of the wrapper. Fold in the left and right corners snugly to form an envelope. Roll up, leaving the top corner open. Wet the top edges with water, then roll tightly to seal. Repeat with the remaining ingredients. Spray each roll evenly with oil on all sides.

Working in batches, put the egg rolls in the air fryer basket in a single layer and cook for 5 minutes, turning halfway, until the rolls are crisp and golden brown. Working in batches, repeat with the remaining egg rolls. Return all of the batches to the basket and cook for 1 minute to heat them all up. Serve immediately.

London Broil with Tomatoes, Red Onion, and Balsamic SERVES 4

Every year we plant more tomatoes than we can possibly use, and at the end of each summer we agree that the following year we'll buy fewer tomato plants. Never happens. One of my favorite ways to use the surplus of tomatoes is as a simple salad over a juicy steak. London broil gets a bad rap because most people marinate it in too much acid and overcook it until it's tough. If you treat it more like a filet and season it simply with salt and cook it to medium-rare, it's delicious. It's also inexpensive and lean. The trick is to thinly slice it across the grain before serving. This dish is also great cooked on the grill: 8 to 10 minutes over medium-high heat, turning halfway; an instant thermometer will register 125°F for medium-rare doneness when it's ready.

1½ pounds top round for London broil, 1 inch thick

1 garlic clove, halved

1¾ teaspoons kosher salt

Freshly ground black pepper

⅓ cup chopped red onion

1 tablespoon extra-virgin olive oil

2 tablespoons balsamic vinegar

3½ cups chopped beefsteak tomatoes (2 to 3 large)

1 tablespoon chopped fresh herbs, such as basil or oregano

PER SERVING	4½ ounces steak + ¾ cup salad
CALORIES	310
FAT	12 g
SATURATED FAT	3.5 g
CHOLESTEROL	107 mg
CARBOHYDRATE	9 g
FIBER	2 g
PROTEIN	40 g
SUGARS	6 g
SODIUM	527 mg

Let the steak stand at room temperature for at least 10 minutes or up to 30. If the steak is too large for your air fryer, cut it into two pieces. Rub the steak all over with the garlic halves and sprinkle with 1¼ teaspoons of the salt and pepper to taste.

Preheat an air fryer to 390°F.

Working in batches, add the steak to the air fryer basket and cook for 10 to 12 minutes, turning halfway, until it is charred and a thermometer registers 125°F for medium-rare. Let it rest for 5 to 10 minutes before thinly slicing across the grain.

Meanwhile, in a large bowl, combine the onion, olive oil, vinegar, the remaining ½ teaspoon salt, and pepper to taste. Let sit for 5 minutes to mellow. Add the tomatoes and herbs and toss gently.

To serve, divide the steak among 4 serving plates and top with the tomato salad.

SKINNY SCOOP

To heat the tortillas, place them one at a time directly over a low flame on a gas stove until slightly charred, 20 to 30 seconds per side. Set aside on a plate, covered with a towel, to keep them warm while you cook the fish.

Crispy Beach Fish Tacos SERVES 4

Fish tacos are one of those things we just can't pass up after a long day at the beach. If the menu has fish tacos on it, there's a 95 percent chance that we're ordering them, along with a refreshing watermelon *agua fresca*. That being said, those hard-to-resist tacos are typically battered and deep fried—not a great combination for your health or waistline. A slimmer solution: air-frying for the same crispy texture. It works great, and, bonus, it doesn't heat up your kitchen.

WATERMELON AGUA FRESCA

6 cups seedless watermelon cubes

4 thin lime slices, for garnish

4 fresh mint sprigs, for garnish

GUACAMOLE

5 ounces avocado (from 1 medium Hass)

2 tablespoons chopped tomato

2 tablespoons chopped fresh cilantro

Juice of ½ lime

¼ teaspoon kosher salt

FISH STRIPS

Olive oil spray (I like my Misto or Bertolli)

1 pound cod or halibut fillets, cut crosswise into 16 strips 2 inches long

1 teaspoon kosher salt

1 large egg, beaten

1 cup panko bread crumbs, wheat or gluten-free

¼ teaspoon ground cumin

¼ teaspoon garlic powder

¼ teaspoon cayenne pepper

TACOS

8 (6-inch) corn tortillas, warmed

1 cup shredded red cabbage

1 radish, thinly sliced

1 tablespoon chopped fresh cilantro

8 lime wedges, for serving

PER SERVING	2 tacos + 1 cup agua fresca
CALORIES	418
FAT	9 g
SATURATED FAT	1.5 g
CHOLESTEROL	95 mg
CARBOHYDRATE	60 g
FIBER	8 g
PROTEIN	29 g
SUGARS	17 g
SODIUM	495 mg

NO AIR FRYER? NO PROBLEM!

To make this in the oven, bake at 425°F for 10 minutes.

For the agua fresca: In a blender, combine the watermelon and ¾ cup water. Puree until smooth. Refrigerate until ready to drink. To serve, divide among 4 glasses. Garnish each with a lime slice and a sprig of mint.

For the guacamole: In a small bowl, mash the avocado with a fork. Add the tomato, cilantro, lime juice, and salt. Stir well, cover, and set aside.

For the fish strips: Preheat an air fryer to 400°F.

Line a cutting board or sheet pan with parchment or wax paper. Season the fish with ½ teaspoon of the salt. Place the egg in a shallow bowl. On another plate, combine the panko, cumin, garlic powder, cayenne, and remaining ½ teaspoon salt. Dredge the fish pieces first in the egg, then in the panko mixture, shaking off any excess as you go. Place on the prepared cutting board or sheet pan. Spray both sides of the fish with oil.

Add just enough fish strips to the air fryer basket to make a single layer and cook for 4 minutes. Turn the fish and cook for 2 minutes longer, until golden and crisp. Repeat with more batches of the remaining fish strips.

For the tacos: Place 2 strips of fish on each tortilla. Top with 2 tablespoons shredded cabbage, 2 tablespoons guacamole, the radish slices, and ⅛ tablespoon cilantro. Serve with the lime wedges and the agua fresca.

Wild Salmon with Avocado-Basil Salad SERVES 4

The air fryer does so much more than make deliciously crispy fries, breaded nuggets, and fried chicken. You'll be surprised to know that salmon comes out juicy and mouthwatering—and in half the time it takes to bake! This is such a quick and healthy dish, packed with beneficial omega-3 fatty acids. The key to the best-tasting fish is to always shop at a reliable fishmonger, and buy wild-caught when possible. The avocado and tomato salad is the perfect fresh and healthy complement.

AVOCADO SALAD

¼ cup chopped red onion

1 tablespoon extra-virgin olive oil

1 tablespoon balsamic vinegar

¼ teaspoon plus ⅛ teaspoon kosher salt

Freshly ground black pepper

2 medium tomatoes, chopped

2 small garlic cloves, minced

2 tablespoons chopped fresh basil

5 ounces diced avocado (from 1 medium Hass)

SALMON

4 pieces skin-on wild-caught salmon fillet, about 1 inch thick (6 ounces each)

½ teaspoon kosher salt

PER SERVING	1 fillet + ½ cup salad
CALORIES	349
FAT	19.5 g
SATURATED FAT	3 g
CHOLESTEROL	94 mg
CARBOHYDRATE	8 g
FIBER	3.5 g
PROTEIN	35 g
SUGARS	3 g
SODIUM	327 mg

For the avocado salad: In a large bowl, combine the red onion, olive oil, vinegar, ¼ teaspoon of the salt, and pepper to taste. Let sit for 5 minutes.

To the onion mixture, add the tomatoes, garlic, basil, avocado, remaining ⅛ teaspoon salt, and pepper to taste.

For the salmon: Preheat an air fryer 400°F.

Season the salmon with the salt. Working in batches, place the fish in the air fryer basket skin side down. Cook for 5 minutes (or longer if your fish is thick), until the salmon flakes easily with a fork.

Divide the fish among 4 plates. Top with the avocado salad, and serve.

NO AIR FRYER? NO PROBLEM!

To make this in the oven, bake at 425°F for 10 minutes.

FOOD FACTS: WILD-CAUGHT VS. FARM-RAISED SALMON

Wild salmon are caught in the wild, whereas farm-raised salmon are harvested on farms located either on land (in ponds, pools, or tanks) or in the ocean (in nets or mesh cages). By choosing wild-caught salmon over farm-raised, you'll get a higher quality *and* better tasting fish with fewer contaminants and toxins.

Crispy Salmon Fish Sticks with Lime-Dill Dipping Sauce SERVES 4

These fish sticks get their zing from Tajín, a chile-lime seasoning salt that's available in most supermarkets. And since dill, lime, and salmon just belong together (you can trust me on this!), the yogurt dipping sauce transforms this dish into something really special. My cousin Kathy came up with this recipe while trying to find creative ways to get her daughter to eat more fish. So even if your family isn't a huge fan of fish, give these a try—they're famous for winning over even the pickiest eaters!

DIPPING SAUCE

¼ cup 0% Greek yogurt

3 tablespoons light mayonnaise

Juice of ½ lime

2 teaspoons finely chopped fresh dill

½ teaspoon chile-lime seasoning salt (I like Tajín Clásico)

⅛ teaspoon kosher salt

FISH STICKS

1¾ pounds skinless wild-caught salmon fillets, about 1 inch thick

2 teaspoons chile-lime seasoning salt (I like Tajín Clásico)

2 teaspoons finely chopped fresh dill

2 large egg whites, lightly beaten

1 cup plus 2 tablespoons panko bread crumbs, regular or gluten-free

PER SERVING	4 sticks + scant 2 tablespoons sauce
CALORIES	409
FAT	16.5 g
SATURATED FAT	2.5 g
CHOLESTEROL	114 mg
CARBOHYDRATE	17 g
FIBER	0.5 g
PROTEIN	45 g
SUGARS	2 g
SODIUM	730 mg

For the dipping sauce: In a small bowl, combine the yogurt, mayonnaise, lime juice, dill, chile-lime salt, and kosher salt. Set aside.

For the fish sticks: Cut the salmon into 16 sticks that are about 4 x 1 inch. Season the fish with 1 teaspoon of the chile-lime salt and all the dill.

Place the egg whites in a shallow bowl. In a second shallow bowl, combine the panko and remaining 1 teaspoon chile-lime salt. Dredge each piece of fish first in the egg whites, then in the panko mixture, shaking off any excess as you go.

Preheat an air fryer to 400°F.

Add just enough breaded fish sticks to the air fryer basket to make a single layer without crowding the basket. Cook for 8 minutes, turning halfway, until golden and crisp. Repeat with more batches of the remaining fish sticks.

Serve hot with the dipping sauce on the side.

SKINNY SCOOP

Tajín is also great sprinkled over fresh grilled corn, guacamole, mango, edamame, or anywhere you want a little punch of flavor.

NO AIR FRYER? NO PROBLEM!

To make this in the oven, bake at 425°F for 10 minutes.

Breaded Popcorn Shrimp with Tartar Sauce SERVES 4

What's better than breaded and fried shrimp dipped in a tangy tartar sauce? Not much, in my opinion! For this recipe, I put the air fryer to the ultimate test to find out if it's possible to create "fried" shrimp without all the oil. Turns out it's not only possible, it's air-frying perfection!

This winning combo of buttermilk and both panko and regular bread crumbs (skipping the flour altogether, which gave it a chalky taste) creates light, crisp, and perfectly cooked shrimp. If you can't find small shrimp, you can cut extra-large or jumbos into small pieces.

TARTAR SAUCE

¼ cup light sour cream

3 tablespoons light mayonnaise

1 teaspoon fresh lemon juice

⅓ cup finely chopped dill pickles

1 tablespoon chopped fresh dill

⅛ teaspoon kosher salt

⅛ teaspoon freshly ground black pepper

SHRIMP

88 peeled and deveined tiny shrimp (1¼ pounds)

1 teaspoon sweet paprika

½ teaspoon garlic powder

¼ teaspoon kosher salt

1 cup low-fat (1%) buttermilk

⅔ cup seasoned panko bread crumbs

½ cup seasoned whole wheat bread crumbs

1 teaspoon dried parsley flakes

Olive oil spray (I like my Misto or Bertolli)

FOR SERVING

1 head butter lettuce, leaves separated

Lemon wedges

PER SERVING	22 shrimp + 3 tablespoons sauce
CALORIES	308
FAT	8 g
SATURATED FAT	2.5 g
CHOLESTEROL	181 mg
CARBOHYDRATE	25 g
FIBER	3 g
PROTEIN	32 g
SUGARS	6 g
SODIUM	1,083 mg

NO AIR FRYER? NO PROBLEM!

To make this in the oven, bake at 425°F for 10 minutes, turning halfway.

For the tartar sauce: In a small bowl, combine the sour cream, mayonnaise, lemon juice, pickles, dill, salt, and pepper. Refrigerate until ready to serve.

For the shrimp: Preheat an air fryer to 400°F. Season the shrimp with the paprika, garlic powder, and salt. Place the buttermilk in a shallow bowl. In a second shallow bowl, combine the panko, bread crumbs, and parsley.

Put the shrimp in the buttermilk. Using a fork, transfer the shrimp one at a time to the bread-crumb mixture, toss to coat, then transfer to a plate, arranging them in a single layer. Spray the tops of the shrimp generously with oil.

Add just enough shrimp oil side down to the air fryer basket to make a single layer. Spray the second sides with oil. Cook for 4 minutes. Shake the basket, then cook for 2 minutes, until golden. Repeat with more batches of the remaining shrimp.

To serve, divide the lettuce among 4 plates. Arrange the shrimp over the lettuce and serve with the lemon wedges and tartar sauce on the side.

Shrimp and Pork Spring Rolls with Carrot-Cabbage Slaw SERVES 4

In the Philippines, there's a version of spring rolls called *lumpia*. Typically deep-fried, they're delicious, but greasy! My skinny version is air-fried to completely sidestep all the extra oil. And honestly, though they are usually served as an appetizer, I don't see why you can't have them for lunch or dinner with a big salad on the side! There's no need to precook the filling, since it cooks right in the wrapper all at the same time.

LUMPIA

½ pound peeled and deveined extra-large shrimp, minced

½ pound ground pork

½ cup thinly sliced green cabbage

⅓ cup finely chopped red onion

¼ cup finely chopped celery

¼ cup finely chopped carrot

2 garlic cloves, minced

2 tablespoons reduced-sodium soy sauce

¼ teaspoon freshly ground black pepper

24 (5-inch) square spring roll wrappers

1 egg, beaten

Canola oil spray (I like my Misto)

SLAW

5 cups thinly sliced green cabbage

1 cup shredded carrots

¼ small red onion, sliced

¼ cup apple cider vinegar

2 tablespoons extra-virgin olive oil

¼ teaspoon kosher salt

½ cup Thai sweet chili sauce, for dipping (optional)

PER SERVING	6 rolls + 1 cup slaw
CALORIES	455
FAT	20.5 g
SATURATED FAT	6 g
CHOLESTEROL	155 mg
CARBOHYDRATE	31 g
FIBER	4 g
PROTEIN	30 g
SUGARS	20 g
SODIUM	849 mg

NO AIR FRYER? NO PROBLEM!

To make this in the oven, bake at 425°F for 12 to 14 minutes, turning halfway.

For the lumpia: In a medium bowl, combine the minced shrimp, pork, cabbage, onion, celery, carrot, garlic, soy sauce, and black pepper by hand until evenly combined.

To roll the lumpia, position 1 spring roll wrapper in front of you like a diamond (one point is facing you) and place 2 tablespoons of the filling on the bottom third of the wrapper. Lift the point nearest you and wrap it around the filling. Fold the left and right corners in toward the center, brush the top point with some of the beaten egg, and continue rolling into a tight cylinder. Transfer to a platter or sheet pan and cover with a damp towel. Repeat with the remaining wrappers and filling.

Preheat an air fryer to 370°F.

Working in batches, place the lumpia in the air fryer basket in a single layer. Spray both sides with oil. Cook for 10 minutes, turning halfway, until golden brown and the filling is fully cooked. Repeat with the remaining lumpia.

For the slaw: In a large bowl, toss together the cabbage, carrots, red onion, vinegar, oil, and salt.

Divide the lumpia and slaw among 4 plates. Serve with the sweet chili sauce on the side for dipping, if desired.

Spicy Shrimp Tempura Roll Bowls SERVES 4

Shrimp tempura rolls satisfied my sushi craving when I was pregnant with my daughter Madison. And while I still enjoy them occasionally these days, I don't have them as often as I'd like to because the shrimp are deep-fried (and calorie heavy). That is, until now! Thanks to the air fryer, I'm able to get the same crispy texture for the shrimp without all the grease; and rather than making rolls, I simply pile all of the sushi elements into a bowl for a quick and easy weeknight dish.

SPICY MAYO

2 tablespoons light mayonnaise

5 teaspoons Sriracha sauce

ASIAN VINAIGRETTE

2 tablespoons reduced-sodium soy sauce*

2 tablespoons unseasoned rice vinegar

1 tablespoon toasted sesame oil

1 teaspoon grated fresh ginger

SHRIMP TEMPURA

16 peeled and deveined extra jumbo shrimp (½ pound)

⅛ teaspoon kosher salt

⅛ teaspoon freshly ground black pepper

1 large egg white

1 tablespoon fat-free milk

¾ cups panko bread crumbs, regular or gluten-free

Olive oil spray (I like my Misto or Bertolli)

FOR ASSEMBLY

3 cups cooked short-grain brown rice, warm

2 Persian (mini) cucumbers, seeded and julienned

5 ounces thinly sliced avocado (from 1 medium Hass)

4 nori snack sheets, thinly sliced

1 teaspoon black sesame seeds

1 tablespoon chopped fresh chives

*Read the label to be sure this product is gluten-free.

PER SERVING	1 bowl
CALORIES	405
FAT	13 g
SATURATED FAT	2 g
CHOLESTEROL	70 mg
CARBOHYDRATE	54 g
FIBER	6 g
PROTEIN	18 g
SUGARS	4 g
SODIUM	641 mg

Preheat an air fryer to 400°F.

For the spicy mayo: In a small bowl, combine the mayonnaise, Sriracha, and 1 teaspoon water.

For the Asian vinaigrette: In a small bowl, whisk together the soy sauce, vinegar, sesame oil, and ginger.

For the shrimp tempura: Season the shrimp with the salt and pepper. In a shallow bowl, combine the egg white and milk. Place the panko in a second shallow bowl.

Dredge the shrimp first in the egg mixture, then in the panko, shaking off any excess as you go.

Place 8 of the shrimp in the air fryer basket. Spray the shrimp with oil. Cook for 5 minutes, until the shrimp turn pink and the coating is golden brown. Repeat with the remaining 8 shrimp.

To assemble the bowls, divide the rice, cucumbers, and avocado among 4 bowls. Top with 4 shrimp, then drizzle the vinaigrette and spicy mayo over each bowl. Garnish with the nori, black sesame seeds, and chives.

NO AIR FRYER? NO PROBLEM!

To make this in the oven, bake the shrimp on a sheet pan in a 400°F oven, turning halfway, until the shrimp turn pink and the coating is golden brown, 8 to 9 minutes.

Crispy Codfish Cakes
with Horseradish Cream SERVES 4

I'm always looking for exciting new ways to get my family to eat fish. Here, I place codfish cakes on a bed of lettuce and squeeze lots of lemon over everything, then I serve them with a delicious horseradish cream on the side for dipping. If you're like my husband, Tommy, who just loves a fish fillet sandwich, you can serve these fish cakes on a bun.

HORSERADISH CREAM
½ cup light sour cream

4 teaspoons prepared horseradish

¼ teaspoon Dijon mustard

CODFISH CAKES
1 pound skinless cod fillets

½ cup plus ⅓ cup seasoned whole wheat or gluten-free bread crumbs

2 tablespoons light mayonnaise

2 tablespoons fresh lemon juice

2 large eggs

¼ cup finely chopped fresh parsley

2 scallions, green parts only, finely chopped

½ teaspoon Old Bay Seasoning

½ teaspoon kosher salt

Freshly ground black pepper

Olive oil spray (I like my Misto or Bertolli)

FOR SERVING
1 head Boston lettuce, leaves separated

9 ounces cherry tomatoes, halved

Lemon wedges

PER SERVING	2 cakes + 2½ tablespoons cream + salad
CALORIES	276
FAT	10 g
SATURATED FAT	3.5 g
CHOLESTEROL	155 mg
CARBOHYDRATE	18 g
FIBER	3 g
PROTEIN	28 g
SUGARS	4 g
SODIUM	726 mg

NO AIR FRYER? NO PROBLEM!

To make this in the oven, bake the fish at 425°F for 10 minutes, then form patties and bake for 10 more minutes, turning halfway.

For the horseradish cream: In a small bowl, whisk together 2 tablespoons water, the sour cream, horseradish, and Dijon mustard. Refrigerate until ready to use.

For the codfish cakes: Preheat an air fryer to 400°F. Place the fish in the air fryer and cook for 8 to 10 minutes, turning halfway, until it is cooked through and easily flakes with a fork. Transfer to a large bowl, let cool, and flake into small pieces.

To the cod, add ⅓ cup of the bread crumbs, the mayonnaise, lemon juice, 1 of the eggs, the parsley, scallions, Old Bay, salt, and pepper to taste. Stir well. Divide into 8 portions, about ¼ cup each, and form into patties.

In a shallow bowl, whisk the remaining egg. Put the remaining ½ cup bread crumbs in a second shallow bowl. Dredge each patty first in the egg, then in the bread crumbs, shaking off any excess as you go. Spray both sides of the cakes with olive oil.

Preheat the air fryer to 400°F once again.

Working in batches, cook the patties, turning halfway, until golden brown and crisp, about 8 minutes.

To serve, divide the lettuce and tomatoes among 4 plates. Top each with 2 fish cakes, dollop the horseradish cream on the side, and serve with the lemon wedges.

Margherita Pizzas SERVES 4

Making homemade pizza from scratch in the air fryer is easy, no pizza stone needed! We love making our own pizza at home, and when we do, we keep our toppings simple—mozzarella and fresh basil—but you can absolutely play around and add your own favorite toppings! For instance, try Italian chicken sausage, pepperoni, bell peppers, onions, mushrooms, spinach . . . the possibilities are endless.

Simplest Pizza Dough (recipe follows)

All-purpose flour, wheat or gluten-free, for dusting

4 tablespoons store-bought pizza sauce (I like DeLallo or Rao's)

1 cup (4 ounces) shredded mozzarella cheese*

Fresh basil leaves, torn

*Read the label to be sure this product is gluten-free.

PER SERVING	1 pizza
CALORIES	242
FAT	6 g
SATURATED FAT	3.5 g
CHOLESTEROL	19 mg
CARBOHYDRATE	29 g
FIBER	1 g
PROTEIN	17 g
SUGARS	3 g
SODIUM	524 mg

Preheat an air fryer to 400°F.

Divide the dough into 4 equal balls (about 3½ ounces each). Dust a work surface and rolling pin with a little flour and roll each ball into thin 7-inch rounds. Prick the center of the dough 5 to 6 times with a fork to help prevent any bubbles from forming.

Place 1 round of dough in the air fryer basket and cook for 5 to 6 minutes, turning halfway, until firm and golden. Repeat with the remaining dough rounds. Transfer to a plate.

Spread 1 tablespoon of the pizza sauce over each crust. Top each with ¼ cup of the cheese. One at a time, return the pizzas to the air fryer and cook for 3 minutes, until the cheese is melted and bubbling. Top with fresh basil and eat right away.

SKINNY SCOOP

You can make the dough ahead of time, wrap it in plastic, and refrigerate it for 2 to 3 days. Be sure to let it return to room temperature before baking or the crust will blow up like a balloon. If you'd like to make the crust gluten-free, I recommend Bob's Red Mill 1 to 1 Baking Flour.

NO AIR FRYER? NO PROBLEM!

To make this in the oven, bake the dough on a sheet pan lined with a silicone mat (or sprayed with oil) in a 450°F oven for 5 to 6 minutes. Flip the crusts, top with the sauce and cheese, and bake until the cheese is bubbling, 5 to 6 more minutes.

(recipe continues)

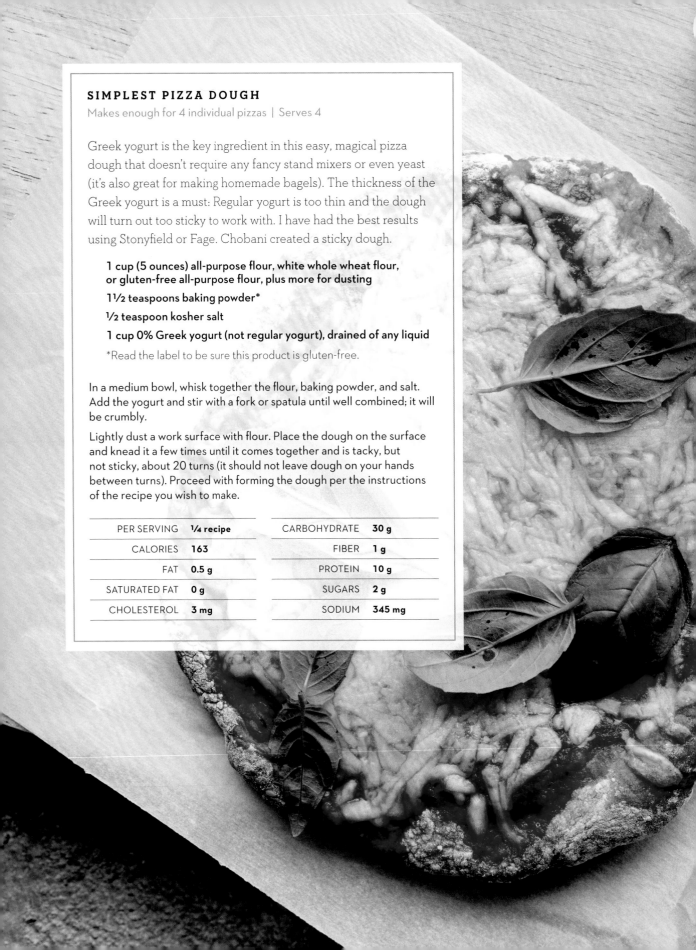

SIMPLEST PIZZA DOUGH
Makes enough for 4 individual pizzas | Serves 4

Greek yogurt is the key ingredient in this easy, magical pizza dough that doesn't require any fancy stand mixers or even yeast (it's also great for making homemade bagels). The thickness of the Greek yogurt is a must: Regular yogurt is too thin and the dough will turn out too sticky to work with. I have had the best results using Stonyfield or Fage. Chobani created a sticky dough.

> 1 cup (5 ounces) all-purpose flour, white whole wheat flour, or gluten-free all-purpose flour, plus more for dusting
>
> 1½ teaspoons baking powder*
>
> ½ teaspoon kosher salt
>
> 1 cup 0% Greek yogurt (not regular yogurt), drained of any liquid
>
> *Read the label to be sure this product is gluten-free.

In a medium bowl, whisk together the flour, baking powder, and salt. Add the yogurt and stir with a fork or spatula until well combined; it will be crumbly.

Lightly dust a work surface with flour. Place the dough on the surface and knead it a few times until it comes together and is tacky, but not sticky, about 20 turns (it should not leave dough on your hands between turns). Proceed with forming the dough per the instructions of the recipe you wish to make.

PER SERVING	¼ recipe	CARBOHYDRATE	30 g
CALORIES	163	FIBER	1 g
FAT	0.5 g	PROTEIN	10 g
SATURATED FAT	0 g	SUGARS	2 g
CHOLESTEROL	3 mg	SODIUM	345 mg

Dutch Oven

Creamy Butternut Pasta with Spicy Sausage and Spinach SERVES 5

This is the ideal winter dish: It's comforting and hearty, without any guilt. The butternut squash creates a decadent and dreamy pasta sauce that's creamy, though there isn't any cream. Even if you don't think you like butternut squash, I guarantee this dish will change your mind! A popular dish on Skinnytaste.com, it's wonderfully savory with the spicy chicken sausage and Parmesan cheese. One reviewer even called it "restaurant quality"!

Kosher salt

1 pound butternut squash, peeled and chopped

10 ounces casarecce or penne pasta, wheat or gluten-free

11 ounces (4 links) spicy Italian chicken sausage*, casings removed

1 tablespoon whipped butter

¼ cup minced shallots

3 garlic cloves, minced

Freshly ground black pepper

2 cups roughly chopped baby spinach

2 tablespoons freshly shaved Parmesan cheese, plus more (optional) for serving

4 fresh sage leaves, thinly sliced

*Read the label to be sure this product is gluten-free.

PER SERVING	1⅓ cups
CALORIES	373
FAT	8 g
SATURATED FAT	2.5 g
CHOLESTEROL	54 mg
CARBOHYDRATE	56 g
FIBER	4.5 g
PROTEIN	20 g
SUGARS	4 g
SODIUM	445 mg

Bring a large pot of salted water to a boil. Add the butternut squash and cook until tender, 18 to 20 minutes. Using a slotted spoon, transfer the squash to a blender with ¼ cup of the cooking water and blend until smooth.

Return the pot of water to a boil. Add the pasta and cook according to the package directions to al dente. Reserving 1 cup of the pasta water, drain the pasta in a colander.

Set the pot over medium heat. Add the sausage and brown, using a wooden spoon to break it into small pieces as it cooks, 4 to 5 minutes. Transfer to a plate.

Reduce the heat to medium-low and melt the butter. Add the shallots and garlic and cook, stirring, until soft and golden, 5 to 6 minutes. Pour the pureed butternut squash into the pot, and season with ¼ teaspoon salt and pepper to taste. Stir in ¾ cup of the reserved pasta water to thin out the sauce, adding more if needed. Stir in the spinach, Parmesan, and sage. Add the cooked pasta and sausage and toss until combined.

Serve with additional Parmesan on the side, if desired.

Gnocchi with Sausage and Garlicky Broccoli Rabe SERVES 5

The combination of broccoli rabe and sausage (plus garlic and cheese) makes my taste buds do a happy dance! If you've never tried broccoli rabe—which has a slightly bold, earthy flavor—step out of your comfort zone and give it a shot. My daughter Karina shares my love for it, so I always save this recipe for when I know she'll be around. I typically enjoy the sausage and broccoli rabe combo with pasta, but light, pillowy gnocchi takes this dish to the next level.

1 bunch (1¼ pounds) broccoli rabe

Kosher salt

1 pound fresh or frozen gnocchi, gluten-free*

1 teaspoon olive oil

1 pound sweet Italian chicken sausage links,* (5½ ounces each) casings removed

3 garlic cloves, sliced

¼ teaspoon crushed red pepper flakes (optional)

Freshly ground black pepper

¼ cup freshly grated Pecorino Romano cheese (I like Locatelli), plus more (optional) for serving

*Read the label to be sure this product is gluten-free.

PER SERVING	1½ cups
CALORIES	341
FAT	10 g
SATURATED FAT	3 g
CHOLESTEROL	74 mg
CARBOHYDRATE	40 g
FIBER	4.5 g
PROTEIN	25 g
SUGARS	0.5 g
SODIUM	897 mg

Trim all of the stems off the broccoli rabe and discard; cut the rest into 2-inch pieces.

Bring a large heavy pot of salted water to a boil over high heat. Add the gnocchi and cook according to the package directions. Using a slotted spoon, transfer the gnocchi to a colander in the sink. Add the broccoli rabe to the boiling water and cook until wilted and tender, about 3 minutes. Reserving 1 cup of the cooking liquid, drain the broccoli rabe in a colander.

Return the pot to medium heat. Add the oil and sausage and brown, using a wooden spoon to break it into small pieces as it cooks, 4 to 5 minutes. Add the garlic and cook, stirring, until fragrant, about 2 minutes. Stir in the broccoli rabe and ¾ cup of the reserved cooking liquid. Add the pepper flakes (if using) and black pepper to taste. Stir in the gnocchi. Stir in the pecorino until well combined, adding the remaining ¼ cup cooking liquid if dry.

Serve immediately, with more cheese on the side for sprinkling, if desired.

Chicken Fajita Pasta   SERVES 5

Chicken fajitas meet pasta night in this one-dish dinner! No, that's not a typo. This Mexican-inspired dish has become a regular in my recipe rotation, and it's very popular on the Skinnytaste website, too. Tommy, my chicken fajita-loving husband, is obsessed with this dish and gets the credit for adding avocado to it. This meal easily comes together in 30 minutes once you have your veggies prepped, which makes it the perfect recipe for weeknight cooking. Speedy and scrumptious!

1 pound boneless, skinless chicken breasts, cut into ¾-inch pieces

1½ teaspoons ground cumin

1 teaspoon sweet paprika

½ teaspoon chili powder*

½ teaspoon garlic powder

1 teaspoon kosher salt

2 teaspoons olive oil

1 large white onion, chopped

1 large red bell pepper, chopped

1 large yellow bell pepper, chopped

3 garlic cloves, minced

2 cups reduced-sodium chicken broth*

1 (10-ounce) can diced tomatoes with green chiles (I like Rotel)

7 ounces cavatappi or other corkscrew pasta, wheat or gluten-free

½ cup light sour cream

4 ounces diced avocado (from 1 small Hass)

1 scallion, chopped

2 tablespoons chopped fresh cilantro

*Read the label to be sure this product is gluten-free.

PER SERVING	1½ cups
CALORIES	390
FAT	11.5 g
SATURATED FAT	3 g
CHOLESTEROL	67 mg
CARBOHYDRATE	42 g
FIBER	6 g
PROTEIN	28 g
SUGARS	7 g
SODIUM	760 mg

In a large bowl, combine the chicken with 1 teaspoon of the cumin, ½ teaspoon of the paprika, ¼ teaspoon of the chili powder, ¼ teaspoon of the garlic powder, and ¾ teaspoon of the salt and toss to coat.

In a Dutch oven or large pot, heat 1 teaspoon of the olive oil over high heat. When the oil is very hot, add the chicken and cook, stirring, until browned and cooked through, 5 to 6 minutes. Transfer to a plate.

Reduce the heat to medium and add the remaining 1 teaspoon olive oil. When the oil is hot, add the onion, bell peppers, and remaining ½ teaspoon cumin, ½ teaspoon paprika, ¼ teaspoon chili powder, ¼ teaspoon garlic powder, and ¼ teaspoon salt. Cook, stirring occasionally, until softened, about 10 minutes. Add the garlic and cook, stirring, until fragrant and well combined, about 30 seconds. Transfer to the plate of chicken.

In the same pot, combine the broth, tomatoes, and uncooked pasta. Stir well and bring to a boil. Cover, reduce the heat to medium-low, and cook until the pasta is tender and most of the liquid is absorbed, about 15 minutes. Return the chicken and vegetables to the pot, stir well, and cook until heated through, about 2 minutes. Remove the pot from the heat and stir in the sour cream.

To serve, spoon 1½ cups into bowls and top each with the avocado, scallion, and cilantro.

Mini Turkey Meatball Vegetable Soup SERVES 7

This kid-friendly recipe is a fan favorite on the Skinnytaste blog, because—hello!?—who doesn't love mini meatballs in their soup! Loaded with tomatoes, zucchini, carrots, and spinach, this soup is flavored with my secret ingredient: a Parmesan cheese rind. I always keep the rinds in my freezer just for making soup, so don't throw them out! This soup is also great to prep for lunches during the week because it freezes and reheats well.

MEATBALLS

1⅓ pounds 93% lean ground turkey breast

¼ cup seasoned bread crumbs, whole wheat or gluten-free

¼ cup freshly grated Parmesan cheese

¼ cup finely chopped fresh parsley

¼ cup finely chopped onion

1 large egg, beaten

1 garlic clove, minced

¼ teaspoon kosher salt

Cooking spray

SOUP

2 teaspoons olive oil

1 cup chopped carrot

½ cup chopped celery

½ cup chopped onion

2 garlic cloves, minced

4 cups reduced-sodium chicken broth*

2 (14.5-ounce) cans no-salt-added petite diced tomatoes

Parmesan cheese rind (optional)

1 sprig of fresh rosemary

2 bay leaves

¼ cup chopped fresh parsley

2 tablespoons chopped fresh basil

½ teaspoon kosher salt

Freshly ground black pepper

8 ounces zucchini (from 1 medium), cut into ½-inch cubes

2 cups chopped baby spinach

Freshly grated Parmesan cheese, for garnish (optional)

*Read the label to be sure this product is gluten-free.

PER SERVING	1½ cups
CALORIES	244
FAT	10.5 g
SATURATED FAT	3 g
CHOLESTEROL	92 mg
CARBOHYDRATE	14 g
FIBER	4 g
PROTEIN	23 g
SUGARS	8 g
SODIUM	949 mg

For the meatballs: In a large bowl, combine the ground turkey, bread crumbs, Parmesan, parsley, onion, egg, garlic, and salt. Using clean hands, gently mix well. Form 42 small meatballs that are about 1 tablespoon each.

Heat a Dutch oven or large pot over medium-high heat. Spray it with oil. Working in 3 or 4 batches, cook the meatballs until browned on one side, 2 to 3 minutes. Turn and brown the other side, 2 to 3 minutes. Transfer to a plate.

For the soup: To the pot, add the oil, carrot, celery, onion, and garlic. Cook, stirring, until the vegetables are softened, 10 to 12 minutes. Add the broth, tomatoes, Parmesan rind (if using), rosemary, bay leaves, parsley, basil, salt, and pepper to taste. Bring to a boil. Reduce the heat to low, cover, and cook until the vegetables are soft and the flavors meld, 30 to 40 minutes.

Discard the bay leaves, rosemary sprig, and Parmesan rind. Drop the meatballs in, along with the zucchini and spinach. Cover and simmer until the zucchini is tender and the meatballs are cooked through, 8 to 10 minutes. Serve with grated Parmesan on top, if desired.

Cheesy Turkey Taco Chili Mac SERVES 8

This dish is truly the definition of comfort food. Taco chili *plus* macaroni and cheese? Umm . . . yes, please! A longtime fan favorite on the Skinnytaste blog, this recipe is perfect for feeding a crowd, and the leftovers make great lunches. If you'd like to spice it up, swap the cheddar for pepper Jack or habanero cheddar!

TACO SEASONING

1½ teaspoons garlic powder

1½ teaspoons ground cumin

1½ teaspoons chili powder*

1½ teaspoons sweet paprika

½ teaspoon dried oregano

1 teaspoon kosher salt

CHILI

Olive oil spray (I like my Misto or Bertolli)

1⅓ pounds 93% lean ground turkey

1 medium onion, chopped

3 garlic cloves, minced

1 red bell pepper, chopped

1 (10-ounce) can mild diced tomatoes with green chiles (I like Rotel)

1 (14.5-ounce) can small red beans,* rinsed and drained

1 (8-ounce) can tomato sauce

1 cup (8 ounces) fat-free refried beans*

1 (15-ounce) can reduced-sodium chicken broth*

8 ounces pasta shells, wheat or gluten-free (I like DeLallo)

¾ cup shredded reduced-fat sharp cheddar cheese*

2 tablespoons chopped fresh cilantro

2 tablespoons chopped fresh scallions

*Read the label to be sure this product is gluten-free.

PER SERVING	1 generous cup
CALORIES	359
FAT	8 g
SATURATED FAT	3.5 g
CHOLESTEROL	63 mg
CARBOHYDRATE	40 g
FIBER	8 g
PROTEIN	23 g
SUGARS	6 g
SODIUM	1,033 mg

For the taco seasoning: In a small bowl, combine the garlic powder, cumin, chili powder, paprika, oregano, and salt.

For the chili: Heat a Dutch oven or large pot with a fitted lid over medium-high heat. Spray it with oil. Add the turkey and brown the meat, using a wooden spoon to break it into small pieces as it cooks, 4 to 5 minutes. Add the onion, garlic, bell pepper, and taco seasoning. Cook, stirring, until fragrant, 2 to 3 minutes. Add the tomatoes, red beans, tomato sauce, refried beans, chicken broth, and 1½ cups water. Bring to a boil, reduce the heat to medium-low, cover, and simmer for 15 minutes to meld the flavors.

Stir in the pasta and simmer, uncovered, over medium heat until al dente, about 6 minutes or according to the package directions.

Remove the pot from the heat. Sprinkle the cheddar over the top of the chili, cover the pot, and let it sit until the cheese melts, 2 to 3 minutes. Serve immediately, garnished with the cilantro and scallions.

Shepherd's Pie Stew SERVES 6

This recipe has all the flavors of a traditional shepherd's pie, but lightened up and made into a stew. Fast and easy, this one-pot dish is loaded with vegetables and features fluffy gnocchi instead of the typical mashed potatoes. You can use lamb or beef instead of turkey, if you like, and diced potatoes can be substituted for gnocchi.

½ tablespoon olive oil

1 cup chopped onion

2 carrots, finely chopped

1 celery stalk, chopped

2 garlic cloves, minced

1½ pounds 93% lean ground turkey

1 teaspoon kosher salt

½ teaspoon freshly ground black pepper

¾ cup chopped mushrooms

2 tablespoons all-purpose flour, wheat or gluten-free

2 teaspoons tomato paste

5 cups reduced-sodium chicken broth*

1 teaspoon Worcestershire sauce*

1 teaspoon chopped fresh rosemary

1 teaspoon chopped fresh thyme

1 pound fresh or frozen potato gnocchi, gluten-free*

½ cup fresh or frozen corn kernels

½ cup fresh or frozen green peas

*Read the label to be sure this product is gluten-free.

PER SERVING	scant 1½ cups
CALORIES	376
FAT	11 g
SATURATED FAT	2.5 g
CHOLESTEROL	84 mg
CARBOHYDRATE	42 g
FIBER	4 g
PROTEIN	28 g
SUGARS	5 g
SODIUM	954 mg

In a Dutch oven or large pot, heat the oil over medium-high heat. Add the onion, carrots, and celery and cook, stirring, until beginning to soften, 4 to 5 minutes. Add the garlic and cook, stirring, until fragrant, about 30 seconds. Add the turkey, salt, and pepper and brown the meat, using a wooden spoon to break it into small pieces as it cooks, about 3 minutes. Add the mushrooms and cook, stirring, until softened, about 3 minutes. Sprinkle the flour over the mixture and cook, stirring, for 1 minute to cook the flour. Add the tomato paste, chicken broth, Worcestershire, rosemary, and thyme, and stir well. Bring to a boil. Reduce the heat to medium, cover, and simmer until the flavors meld, 10 to 12 minutes.

Stir in the gnocchi, corn, and peas. Increase the heat to high and cook, uncovered, according to the gnocchi package directions, 3 to 4 minutes. Divide among 6 bowls and serve.

Kielbasa and Cabbage SERVES 4

This dish feels like comfort food to me, perhaps because I grew up eating plenty of cabbage and Polish and Czech sausage, thanks to my dad, who was Czech. In this recipe, I cook the onions in olive oil with a bit of garlic to give the cabbage delicious flavor. Cabbage is such a low-calorie, low-carb food that you can enjoy a large bowl of this dish without overindulging. Bonus: It's super filling.

¾ pound uncured turkey kielbasa

Olive oil spray (I like my Misto or Bertolli)

1 tablespoon olive oil

1 medium onion, chopped

3 garlic cloves, minced

1 medium head (about 2 pounds) cabbage, cored and roughly chopped

¾ teaspoon plus ⅛ teaspoon kosher salt

Freshly ground black pepper

1 teaspoon red wine vinegar

PER SERVING	2 cups
CALORIES	209
FAT	10.5 g
SATURATED FAT	3 g
CHOLESTEROL	60 mg
CARBOHYDRATE	11 g
FIBER	3 g
PROTEIN	17 g
SUGARS	5 g
SODIUM	1,159 mg

Halve the kielbasa lengthwise and then cut it crosswise into ½-inch pieces.

Heat a Dutch oven or large pot over medium heat. Spray it with oil. Add the kielbasa and cook until heated through and browned, about 3 minutes per side. Transfer to a plate.

Reduce the heat to medium-low. Add the olive oil and onion and cook, stirring occasionally, until softened, 3 to 5 minutes. Add the garlic and cook until fragrant, about 1 minute. Add the cabbage, ¾ teaspoon of the salt, and pepper to taste. Cover and cook, stirring every 5 minutes, until the cabbage is wilted, about 15 minutes. Stir in the vinegar, return the kielbasa to the pot, cover, and cook until the kielbasa is hot and the cabbage is tender, 5 more minutes. Stir in the remaining ⅛ teaspoon salt and serve.

FOOD FACTS: COOKIN' WITH CABBAGE

Cabbage, a leafy vegetable of the Brassica family (which includes Brussels sprouts, cauliflower, bok choy, kale, and broccoli), is rich in vitamin C (an antioxidant) and fiber. People who frequently eat cabbage may reduce their risk of certain cancers.

Caramelized Onion Soup with Cauliflower and Melted Gruyère SERVES 6

Soups are often on the menu in my house during the winter and fall, and French onion is one of our absolute favorites. Fortunately, a big bowl of my slimmed-down version won't leave you feeling guilty because I gave the classic a healthy makeover. I swapped out the bread for cauliflower florets, which make for a tasty, carb-free raft for the golden, gooey cheese on top. Save this dish for the weekend because the onions need lots of time to caramelize—cook them low and slow to get that rich, golden color and intense flavor. You just can't rush perfection!

1 tablespoon unsalted butter

1 tablespoon olive oil

2 pounds Vidalia onions, halved lengthwise and thinly sliced

1 teaspoon kosher salt

Freshly ground black pepper

1/3 cup white wine

2 teaspoons dry sherry

2 tablespoons all-purpose flour, wheat or gluten-free

6 cups beef stock*

3 sprigs of fresh thyme

1 bay leaf

5 cups small cauliflower florets (about 1 pound, from 3/4 large head)

2 cups (5½ ounces) coarsely shredded Gruyère or Swiss cheese*

*Read the label to be sure this product is gluten-free.

PER SERVING	1½ cups
CALORIES	250
FAT	13 g
SATURATED FAT	6.5 g
CHOLESTEROL	34 mg
CARBOHYDRATE	18 g
FIBER	3.5 g
PROTEIN	11 g
SUGARS	11 g
SODIUM	812 mg

In a Dutch oven or large pot, melt the butter with the oil over medium-low heat. Add the onions and cook, stirring occasionally, until the onions are soft, about 15 minutes. Add ¼ teaspoon of the salt and pepper to taste and continue cooking, stirring occasionally, until the onions are golden brown and caramelized, 30 to 35 minutes.

Add the wine and sherry, increase the heat to high, and cook until the liquid evaporates, about 3 minutes. Add the flour and cook, stirring, for 2 to 3 minutes to cook the flour. Add the beef stock, thyme, bay leaf, and remaining ¾ teaspoon salt. Bring to a boil. Cover, reduce the heat to low, and simmer for 20 minutes to meld the flavors. Discard the thyme and bay leaf. Add the cauliflower florets and simmer until crisp-tender, 12 to 15 minutes.

When ready to serve, adjust an oven rack about 6 inches from the heating element. Ladle 1½ cups of soup into each of 6 ovenproof bowls. Top each with ⅓ cup of the cheese, place on a sheet pan, and broil until golden and bubbling, 3 to 4 minutes. Serve hot.

SKINNY SCOOP

Yellow onions or a mix of yellow, Vidalia, and red onions can be used in this soup.

Bacalao (Salt Cod) and Potato Stew SERVES 4

Bacalao, salted dried codfish, is the defining ingredient in this traditional Puerto Rican fish stew, which also has roots in Spain and Portugal. My mom always made *bacalao* on Fridays during Lent. Why would we eat salt cod when we have access to fresh fish? Because it tastes soooooo great! In fact, salt cod has been referred to as "prosciutto of the sea." Once it's soaked in repeated baths of cool water for about 24 hours, it's actually not salty at all, and the taste of desalinated salt cod is very mild.

1 pound bacalao (salted boneless cod or pollock)

1 (8-ounce) can tomato sauce

¼ cup white wine

2 tablespoons extra-virgin olive oil

Olive oil spray (I like my Misto or Bertolli)

3 medium Yukon Gold potatoes, peeled and cut into ¼-inch-thick slices

1 large white onion, thinly sliced lengthwise

4 hard-boiled eggs, cut into ¼-inch-thick slices

1 (4-ounce) jar pimientos or roasted red peppers, drained

2 teaspoons capers, drained

2 large garlic cloves, minced

3 tablespoons sliced (into rounds) pitted green olives

2 bay leaves

PER SERVING	2 cups
CALORIES	635
FAT	15.5 g
SATURATED FAT	3 g
CHOLESTEROL	358 mg
CARBOHYDRATE	36 g
FIBER	7 g
PROTEIN	82 g
SUGARS	7 g
SODIUM	Number varies due to soaking

SKINNY SCOOP

You can buy salt cod at most fishmongers and supermarket fish departments.

At least 24 hours before cooking, rinse the salt cod in a colander under running water for 5 minutes, then place it in a large bowl in the sink. Fill the bowl with cool water, covering the fish entirely, about 2 quarts. Let soak for about 1 hour. Pour out the water and refill the bowl again with fresh water. Repeat this process for the next 24 hours, leaving the fish to soak for increasingly longer periods of time and making sure you've changed the water at least four times. Drain, remove any bones that remain, and flake the fish into bite-size pieces.

In a medium bowl, combine 1 cup water, the tomato sauce, white wine, and olive oil.

Spray the bottom of a Dutch oven or large heavy pot with oil. Layer half of each ingredient in the following order: potatoes, cod, onion, hard-boiled eggs, pimientos, capers, garlic, olives, and bay leaf. Pour half of the tomato sauce mixture over the layers. Repeat with the remaining ingredients with the exception of the egg. Finish by arranging the remaining eggs on the top.

Cover and cook over medium heat for 10 minutes. Reduce the heat to low and simmer until the potatoes are tender when pierced with a fork, about 30 minutes. Discard the bay leaves, ladle into 4 bowls, and serve immediately.

Mussel Chowder with Bacon SERVES 2

This chowder is inspired by one that I had at the Claremont Hotel in Berkeley, California. It was out-of-this-world-good—loaded with mussels, simmered in cream, and so filling that I couldn't even touch my main course. My lighter version is just as good, but with a fraction of the calories. Rather than simmering everything in heavy cream, I add a bit at the very end—just enough to make it creamy. And instead of using flour to thicken it, I puree half of the soup and leave the rest chunky. The results are perfect. Don't be afraid of the fennel. It's wonderful when simmered in the soup. Don't believe me? Trust my husband, who isn't a fan of the stuff. He didn't even know it was in there.

3 slices center-cut bacon, chopped

½ small onion, chopped

2 garlic cloves, minced

1 small (4-ounce) Yukon Gold potato, peeled and cut into ¼-inch pieces

1 cup finely chopped fennel (from ½ bulb)

1 (8-ounce) bottle clam juice (I like Bar Harbor)

1 cup reduced-sodium vegetable broth*

2 bay leaves

¼ teaspoon kosher salt

Freshly ground black pepper

2 tablespoons heavy cream

20 medium mussels (12.5 ounces), scrubbed and debearded

Chopped fresh parsley, for garnish

*Read the label to be sure this product is gluten-free.

PER SERVING	1¼ cups chowder + 10 mussels
CALORIES	285
FAT	10.5 g
SATURATED FAT	5 g
CHOLESTEROL	69 mg
CARBOHYDRATE	23 g
FIBER	3 g
PROTEIN	24 g
SUGARS	3 g
SODIUM	1,005 mg

SKINNY SCOOP

To clean the mussels, rinse under running water and pull off the stringy beards. Discard any shells that are broken.

Heat a Dutch oven or large saucepan over medium heat. Add the bacon and cook, stirring occasionally, until crisped up a bit, 6 to 7 minutes. Using a slotted spoon, transfer the bacon to paper towels to drain.

Reduce the heat to low. Add the onion to the pot and cook, stirring, until softened, 4 to 5 minutes. Add the garlic and cook, stirring, until fragrant, about 1 minute. Add the potato, fennel, clam juice, broth, and bay leaves. Bring to a boil, then reduce the heat to medium-low. Simmer until the potato and fennel are soft, about 20 minutes. Add the salt and pepper to taste. Remove the bay leaf. Transfer half of the soup to a blender, blend until smooth, then return the puree to the pot.

Reduce the heat to low. Stir in the heavy cream (do not boil) and add the mussels, stirring well. Cover and cook until the mussels open, 4 to 5 minutes. Discard any mussels that do not open. Ladle the chowder into 2 bowls, garnish with the crispy bacon and chopped parsley, and serve.

Mussels in Garlicky White Wine Sauce SERVES 4

Not only are mussels delicious and inexpensive, they take about 5 minutes to cook, which makes them a weeknight winner! A crusty baguette or Italian bread is a must to soak up all the delicious, garlicky juice. Add a green salad and dinner is ready in under 15 minutes.

64 mussels (2½ pounds), scrubbed and debearded

½ tablespoon extra-virgin olive oil

3 garlic cloves, thinly sliced

¾ cup dry white wine

2 tablespoons seasoned bread crumbs

2 tablespoons chopped fresh parsley

8 ounces crusty bread, cut into 4 pieces

PER SERVING	16 mussels + 2 ounces bread
CALORIES	473
FAT	9 g
SATURATED FAT	2 g
CHOLESTEROL	79 mg
CARBOHYDRATE	46 g
FIBER	1.5 g
PROTEIN	41 g
SUGARS	2 g
SODIUM	1,165 mg

Discard any mussels with broken shells.

In a Dutch oven or large heavy pot, heat the oil over medium heat. Add the garlic and cook, stirring, until golden, 2 to 3 minutes. Add the wine and bring to a boil over high heat. Quickly add the mussels, cover, and cook, shaking the pot occasionally, until the mussels open, about 5 minutes. Discard any mussels that don't open. Stir in the bread crumbs and parsley.

Serve immediately with the bread on the side for dipping in the sauce.

Milda's Caldeirada (Portuguese Seafood Stew) SERVES 4

Potatoes and chorizo combine with fish and shellfish in a light tomato-saffron sauce to make the most delicious seafood stew ever! My aunt Milda, who once lived and worked in a predominantly Portuguese community, shared this recipe with me, and it has become one of my favorites. Any combination of fish and shellfish will work well in this dish. My aunt typically uses two different varieties of whole fish with the bones, but because I don't care for bones in my fish, I prefer to use fillets.

1 (12-ounce) halibut or Pacific cod fillet, cut into 2-inch pieces

1 (12-ounce) red snapper or sea bass fillet, cut into 2-inch pieces

½ teaspoon Old Bay Seasoning

⅛ teaspoon cayenne pepper

½ teaspoon kosher salt

⅛ teaspoon freshly ground black pepper

1 tablespoon extra-virgin olive oil

½ onion, halved and sliced

2 leeks, white parts only, halved lengthwise, sliced crosswise, and rinsed well

2 garlic cloves, chopped

3 tablespoons finely chopped fresh parsley, plus more for garnish

¾ pound Yukon Gold potatoes (2 medium), peeled and cut into ½-inch-thick slices

1 red bell pepper, cut into ¼-inch-wide slices

2 bay leaves

5 or 6 saffron threads

½ pound cleaned squid, halved and sliced

16 medium mussels (10 ounces), scrubbed and debearded

2 ounces dried chorizo, thinly sliced

1 (14.5-ounce) can petite diced tomatoes

½ cup low-sodium vegetable broth*

½ cup dry white wine

½ tablespoon tomato paste

½ teaspoon apple cider vinegar

*Read the label to be sure this product is gluten-free.

PER SERVING	1½ cups
CALORIES	483
FAT	13.5 g
SATURATED FAT	3.5 g
CHOLESTEROL	232 mg
CARBOHYDRATE	30 g
FIBER	4.5 g
PROTEIN	52 g
SUGARS	7 g
SODIUM	852 mg

Season the fish with the Old Bay, cayenne, salt, and black pepper. Set aside.

In a 6-quart Dutch oven, layer the ingredients in this order: the olive oil, onion, leeks, garlic, parsley, potatoes, bell pepper, 1 bay leaf, half of the saffron, half of the fish, half of the squid, half of the mussels, and half of the chorizo. Repeat the layering in this order: the remaining bay leaf, saffron, fish, squid, mussels, and chorizo.

In a medium bowl, combine the tomatoes, broth, wine, tomato paste, and vinegar. Gently pour the mixture over all the ingredients in the pot.

Preheat the oven to 375°F.

Set the pot over medium-high heat and bring to a boil. Reduce the heat to low and simmer for 10 minutes. Cover the pot and transfer it to the oven.

Bake until the potatoes are tender, 50 to 60 minutes. Discard the bay leaves, divide among 4 bowls, garnish with the parsley, and serve hot.

SKINNY SCOOP

You can substitute clams and shrimp (or whatever fresh local seafood is available in your area) for the squid and mussels, if you like.

Chinese Shrimp and Pork Dumpling Meatball Soup SERVES 4

If you're a fan of Chinese dumplings, you're going to flip for this umami-rich soup! We love going to eat in Flushing, Queens (a borough of New York City), where you can find the best authentic Chinese food, including the most delicious dumplings filled with everything from pork to shrimp and more. My favorite dumplings are filled with both shrimp and pork, which is the inspiration behind this soup. Instead of going through the effort of making the dumplings, I simply simmer the meat directly in the broth and add some vegetables. The meatballs are so tender, with so much depth of flavor, that my craving for dumplings is satisfied right in my own kitchen!

6 ounces peeled and deveined shrimp

6 ounces ground pork

1½ teaspoons grated fresh ginger

1 tablespoon reduced-sodium soy sauce*

1 tablespoon Shaoxing (Chinese rice wine) or dry sherry

½ teaspoon plus 2 pinches of kosher salt

8 ounces napa cabbage

2 medium scallions, finely chopped

½ tablespoon toasted sesame oil

4 cups low-sodium chicken broth*

6 ounces baby bok choy, quartered lengthwise

3 ounces shiitake mushrooms, thinly sliced

*Read the label to be sure this product is gluten-free.

PER SERVING	1¾ cups
CALORIES	213
FAT	11.5 g
SATURATED FAT	3.5 g
CHOLESTEROL	81 mg
CARBOHYDRATE	7 g
FIBER	2 g
PROTEIN	18 g
SUGARS	2 g
SODIUM	620 mg

In a small food processor, finely chop the shrimp. In a large bowl, combine the shrimp, pork, ginger, soy sauce, rice wine, and ½ teaspoon of the salt. Stir with a spatula until it is well combined and becomes a sticky paste. Cover with plastic wrap and refrigerate for 20 minutes.

In the same food processor, finely chop half of the cabbage. Transfer it to a medium bowl, sprinkle with the remaining 2 pinches of salt, and mix well with your hands. Let it sit for 15 minutes to release its liquid. Put the cabbage on a few layers of paper towels or cheesecloth, and twist tightly around the cabbage to squeeze out all the excess water. Roughly chop the remaining cabbage into 2-inch pieces and set aside.

Add the salted cabbage, scallions, and sesame oil to the shrimp-pork mixture. Stir well, then roll into 20 balls that are about ¾ ounce each.

In a large pot, bring the chicken broth to a boil over high heat. When boiling gently, add the meatballs, chopped cabbage, bok choy, and mushrooms. Reduce the heat to medium-low, cover, and cook until the meat is cooked and the vegetables are tender, about 10 minutes. Divide among 4 bowls and serve.

Shrimp Jambalaya SERVES 5

Thanks to fast-cooking parboiled (converted) brown rice, this healthy jambalaya comes together in a snap. Featuring the aromatic trinity of onion, celery, and pepper, plus smoked andouille chicken sausage, this easy dish will make your whole house smell delicious! If you can't find andouille chicken sausage, you can use turkey kielbasa in its place.

½ tablespoon olive oil

1 medium onion, chopped

1 celery stalk, chopped

1 green bell pepper, chopped

1 red bell pepper, chopped

3 garlic cloves, minced

8 ounces smoked andouille chicken sausage,* sliced into rounds

2 cups reduced-sodium chicken broth*

½ cup canned tomato sauce

1 (14.5-ounce) can petite diced tomatoes

3 sprigs of fresh thyme

1 teaspoon sweet paprika

¾ teaspoon dried oregano

¼ teaspoon cayenne pepper

1 teaspoon kosher salt

1 cup parboiled 20-minute brown rice (I like Uncle Ben's Whole Grain Brown Rice)

¾ pound peeled and deveined large shrimp

Chopped scallions, for garnish

*Read the label to be sure this product is gluten-free.

PER SERVING	1¾ cups
CALORIES	246
FAT	7 g
SATURATED FAT	5 g
CHOLESTEROL	114 mg
CARBOHYDRATE	23 g
FIBER	4 g
PROTEIN	22 g
SUGARS	7 g
SODIUM	1,572 mg

In a Dutch oven or heavy large pot, heat the oil over medium-low heat. Add the onion, celery, bell peppers, and garlic and cook, stirring occasionally, until softened, 5 to 7 minutes. Add the sausage and cook, stirring, until browned, about 5 minutes. Add the chicken broth, tomato sauce, tomatoes, thyme, paprika, oregano, cayenne, and salt. Bring to a boil over high heat. Add the rice, reduce the heat to low, cover, and simmer until the rice is cooked through, 20 to 22 minutes (cooking time will depend on your brand of rice). Increase the heat to high and stir in the shrimp. Cover and cook, stirring occasionally, until the shrimp are cooked through, 4 to 5 minutes. Serve hot, topped with the scallions.

Creamy Cheddar-Broccoli Soup SERVES 6

As a kid, I wouldn't touch broccoli . . . until I tried it with melted cheese. That was a real game changer, and the beginning of my love affair with the green veggie. The pairing inspired this soup, which is pure comfort in a bowl. Visitors to my blog agree, as it's a fan favorite. Kids love it, adults love it—I really haven't met anyone who doesn't slurp up every last drop. To make the soup thick and creamy *without* using cream, I put a few cups in the blender once it's cooked, then stir the puree back in.

1 tablespoon unsalted butter

1 small onion, chopped

1 medium carrot, chopped

1 celery stalk, chopped

2 garlic cloves, minced

2 tablespoons all-purpose flour, wheat or gluten-free

¼ teaspoon kosher salt

Freshly ground black pepper

2½ cups reduced-sodium chicken or vegetable broth*

1 cup fat-free milk

10 ounces russet or all-purpose potatoes (2 medium), peeled and chopped into small pieces

4 cups chopped (into small pieces) broccoli florets (about 2 heads)

1 tablespoon freshly grated Parmesan cheese

1¾ cups shredded reduced-fat sharp cheddar cheese*

*Read the label to be sure this product is gluten-free.

PER SERVING	1 generous cup
CALORIES	210
FAT	8.5 g
SATURATED FAT	5.5 g
CHOLESTEROL	25 mg
CARBOHYDRATE	20 g
FIBER	3.5 g
PROTEIN	15 g
SUGARS	6 g
SODIUM	542 mg

In a Dutch oven or large pot, melt the butter over medium-low heat. Add the onion, carrot, celery, and garlic and cook, stirring, until softened, 5 to 7 minutes. Add the flour, salt, and pepper to taste and stir until smooth. Add the chicken broth, milk, and potatoes. Increase the heat to high and bring to a boil. Reduce the heat to low, cover, and cook until the potatoes are soft, 10 to 15 minutes.

Stir in the broccoli florets and Parmesan. Cook, stirring occasionally, until the broccoli is tender, about 8 minutes. Remove from the heat, add the cheddar, and stir well until melted.

Using an immersion blender, blend the soup for a few seconds, leaving some chunks (or transfer about 3 cups of the soup to a regular blender, puree, and add it back to the soup). Ladle 1 generous cup into each of 6 bowls and serve hot.

Slow
Cooker

Loaded Buffalo Chicken Stuffed Sweet Potatoes SERVES 4

If you're a Buffalo chicken fan, you'll love this easy loaded sweet potato dish. The combination of spicy Buffalo sauce with sweet potatoes is surprisingly addictive. And if you haven't made sweet potatoes in the slow cooker yet, you'll never make them any other way again—it's my favorite way to cook them. They come out so tender and delicious.

4 medium sweet potatoes (about 7 ounces each)

1 pound boneless, skinless chicken breasts

¾ teaspoon garlic powder

½ cup Frank's RedHot sauce

½ cup Chive Ranch Dressing (page 31) or store-bought ranch-style dressing

1 tablespoon chopped scallions, for garnish

PER SERVING	1 loaded potato
CALORIES	806
FAT	11.5 g
SATURATED FAT	2.5 g
CHOLESTEROL	77 mg
CARBOHYDRATE	42 g
FIBER	6.5 g
PROTEIN	29 g
SUGARS	14 g
SODIUM	1,530 mg

Wash and dry the sweet potatoes. Wrap each potato in foil.

Season the chicken with the garlic powder and place it in one end of a slow cooker. Cover the chicken with ¼ cup of the hot sauce. Place the potatoes in the other end, stacking 2 on top of 2.

Cover and cook on low for 6 hours, until the chicken is cooked and the potatoes are tender when pierced with a fork. Remove the potatoes. Using two forks, roughly shred the chicken right in the pot. Add the remaining ¼ cup hot sauce and stir well.

When cool enough to handle, cut each sweet potato in half lengthwise, then divide among 4 plates. Top each half with ⅓ cup of the buffalo chicken and drizzle with 1 tablespoon of the dressing. Top with the scallions and serve.

SKINNY SCOOP

Most brands of ranch-style dressing sold in supermarkets are highly processed; they contain corn syrup and MSG, among other such ingredients. Making your own from scratch is simple. With the leftover buttermilk, you can make the Buffalo Drumsticks with Creamy Cabbage and Kale Slaw on page 171 or Spicy Fried Chicken Sandwiches on page 175, or you can use powdered buttermilk instead.

Complete BBQ Chicken Dinner SERVES 4

Summer in the slow cooker! Yes! This easy BBQ chicken dinner is made with bone-in, skinless chicken thighs (legs or breasts work great, too!), corn on the cob, and a quick slaw so you can have a taste of summer year-round. The corn is added to the slow cooker during the last 2 hours of cook time, but if you get home too late and can't get to your slow cooker in time, you can pop them in the microwave for 3 to 4 minutes.

8 bone-in chicken thighs
(5 ounces each), skin removed
and fat trimmed

1 teaspoon smoked paprika

1 teaspoon garlic powder

1 teaspoon kosher salt

½ cup of your favorite BBQ
sauce*

4 medium ears corn, husks on

SLAW

3 cups shredded green cabbage

1½ tablespoons olive oil

1½ tablespoons apple cider
vinegar

¼ teaspoon kosher salt

*Read the label to be sure this
product is gluten-free.

PER SERVING	2 thighs + 1 ear of corn + ½ cup slaw
CALORIES	548
FAT	18 g
SATURATED FAT	4 g
CHOLESTEROL	269 mg
CARBOHYDRATE	39 g
FIBER	4 g
PROTEIN	58 g
SUGARS	21 g
SODIUM	916 mg

Season both sides of the chicken with the paprika, garlic powder, and salt. Transfer to a slow cooker, bone side down, and pour ¼ cup of the BBQ sauce over the chicken.

Cover and cook on low for 6 hours, until the chicken is tender and cooked through, placing the corn over the chicken for the last 2 hours of cooking.

Transfer the corn to a cutting board. Brush the remaining ¼ cup BBQ sauce over the chicken and cover to keep warm.

For the slaw: In a medium bowl, toss the cabbage with the olive oil, vinegar, and salt.

When the corn is cool enough to handle, discard the husks. Serve alongside the chicken and slaw.

Fall-off-the-Bone Whole Rosemary Chicken SERVES 4

Making a whole chicken in the slow cooker is definitely a technique you need to keep in your back pocket. It's foolproof, and the chicken comes out so incredibly juicy and delicious it literally falls off the bones. Plus, there's always plenty of jus leftover to pour over everything. To make it a meal, I added carrots and potatoes to the pot, but any root vegetable or winter squash would work. And leftover chicken is perfect for salads, soups, sandwiches, and more. To keep it skinny, I take the skin off before eating . . . but I won't tell if you don't!

8 sprigs of fresh rosemary

2 teaspoons kosher salt

2 teaspoons sweet paprika

1 teaspoon garlic powder

1 teaspoon onion powder

1 teaspoon dried thyme

¼ teaspoon freshly ground black pepper

1 pound baby Yukon Gold potatoes, quartered

24 baby heirloom carrots (about 1 pound)

1 whole chicken (4 pounds), giblets removed, chicken rinsed and patted dry with paper towels

PER SERVING	one-quarter skinless chicken + ¾ cup potatoes + 6 carrots + gravy
CALORIES	398
FAT	11 g
SATURATED FAT	3 g
CHOLESTEROL	127 mg
CARBOHYDRATE	29 g
FIBER	7 g
PROTEIN	44 g
SUGARS	7 g
SODIUM	790 mg

SKINNY SCOOP

This dish fits best in a 6-quart oval slow cooker.

Finely chop enough rosemary leaves to get 1 tablespoon. Set the remaining sprigs aside. In a small bowl, combine the chopped rosemary, 1½ teaspoons of the salt, the paprika, garlic powder, onion powder, dried thyme, and pepper.

Place the potatoes in one side of a 6-quart oval slow cooker and put the carrots in the other side. Season with the remaining ½ teaspoon salt. Top with 2 rosemary sprigs.

Rub the spice mixture all over the chicken and stuff the cavity with the remaining 4 rosemary sprigs. Transfer the chicken to the slow cooker, putting it on top of the vegetables, breast side up.

Cover and cook on low for 8 hours, until the chicken is cooked through and falls off the bone and the vegetables are tender. Using a wide spatula, carefully transfer the chicken to a dish or platter. Transfer the vegetables to a separate platter. Discard the skin and rosemary sprigs and carve the chicken. Place the jus in a gravy separator and serve with the chicken and vegetables.

Chipotle Chicken Tostadas SERVES 4

This easy shredded chicken dish is delicious, smoky, and mildly spicy—and so versatile! We love it piled high on crisp tostada shells, which are messy and fun to eat with your hands, but the chicken would also be fantastic in tacos or over brown rice or quinoa. Lime wedges on the side are a must!

CHICKEN

1 pound boneless, skinless chicken breasts

¾ teaspoon kosher salt

Freshly ground black pepper

¾ cup canned tomato sauce

¼ cup low-sodium chicken broth*

2 tablespoons adobo sauce (from canned chipotle peppers in adobo sauce)

2 garlic cloves, minced

1 teaspoon ground cumin

Juice of ¼ lime

TOSTADAS

1 cup canned fat-free refried beans* (I like Trader Joe's)

1 teaspoon ground cumin

½ teaspoon kosher salt

2 cups shredded green cabbage

1 teaspoon olive oil

Juice of ½ lime

8 (5-inch) corn tostadas (I like Charras)

FOR SERVING

4 ounces thinly sliced avocado (from 1 small Hass)

¼ cup light sour cream

1 radish, thinly sliced

2 tablespoons chopped fresh cilantro

Lime wedges

*Read the label to be sure this product is gluten-free.

PER SERVING	2 tostadas
CALORIES	428
FAT	17.5 g
SATURATED FAT	4 g
CHOLESTEROL	78 mg
CARBOHYDRATE	43 g
FIBER	9 g
PROTEIN	32 g
SUGARS	4 g
SODIUM	903 mg

For the chicken: Sprinkle the chicken breasts with ¼ teaspoon of the salt and black pepper to taste. Transfer them to a slow cooker.

In a small bowl, combine the tomato sauce, chicken broth, adobo sauce, garlic, cumin, and remaining ½ teaspoon salt. Pour the mixture over the chicken.

Cover and cook on low for 4 to 6 hours, until the chicken can be easily shredded with two forks. Pour half of the sauce out of the slow cooker and reserve. Shred the chicken using two forks (do this in the pot) and stir in the lime juice. Add some of the reserved sauce to moisten as needed.

For the tostadas: In a medium bowl, combine the refried beans, cumin, and ¼ teaspoon of the salt. Stir well.

In a large bowl, toss together the cabbage, olive oil, lime juice, and remaining ¼ teaspoon salt.

To serve, place 2 tostadas on each of 4 plates. Spread 2 tablespoons of the refried beans over each tostada. Drain the chicken and evenly mound about ¼ cup over the beans on each tostada. Divide the cabbage, avocado slices, and sour cream among the tostadas. Garnish with the radish and cilantro and serve immediately with lime wedges on the side.

Italian Stuffed Cubanelle Peppers SERVES 6

Cubanelle peppers, also known as Italian frying peppers, are perfect for stuffing because they are sweet with a mild flavor and have a thin skin. I love them filled as they are here, then slowly cooked in marinara sauce. No precooking the meat required—it cooks right in the peppers, which allows all the flavors to meld together into the most delicious dish. It's one of my favorite ways to eat them, swimming in sauce, topped with melted mozzarella cheese. A crisp green salad is perfect on the side.

6 sweet cubanelle peppers

½ pound 93% lean ground beef

2 sweet Italian chicken sausage links* (5½ ounces each), casings removed

¾ cup cooked brown rice (I like Trader Joe's frozen brown rice)

1¼ cups plus 6 tablespoons store-bought or homemade marinara sauce

2 teaspoons tomato paste

¼ cup freshly grated Parmesan cheese

1 large egg, beaten

¼ cup finely chopped onion

2 tablespoons chopped fresh parsley, plus more for garnish

1 garlic clove, minced

¾ teaspoon kosher salt

Freshly ground black pepper

6 tablespoons shredded part-skim mozzarella cheese* (I like Polly-O)

*Read the label to be sure this product is gluten-free.

PER SERVING	1 stuffed pepper
CALORIES	266
FAT	12.5 g
SATURATED FAT	4 g
CHOLESTEROL	89 mg
CARBOHYDRATE	18 g
FIBER	4 g
PROTEIN	22 g
SUGARS	6 g
SODIUM	644 mg

SKINNY SCOOP

This dish works best in a 6-quart oval slow cooker, since the larger surface area allows you to put the peppers in a single layer. If your slow cooker is too small, you can stack them. Any leftovers will keep in the freezer for at least 3 months.

Cut the tops off the peppers. Open up each pepper lengthwise by cutting down through the center of the pepper on one side, being careful not to cut it in half. Remove and discard the seeds. Finely chop the tops of the peppers and put them in a large bowl. Add the ground beef, sausage, brown rice, 6 tablespoons of the marinara sauce, the tomato paste, Parmesan, egg, onion, parsley, garlic, salt, and pepper to taste. Mix thoroughly. Stuff a generous ½ cup of the ground meat mixture into each pepper.

Pour ½ cup of the marinara sauce into the bottom of a slow cooker. Lay the peppers cut side up in the sauce. Cover with the remaining marinara sauce.

Cover and cook on low heat for 8 hours, until tender and cooked through. Top with the mozzarella, cover, and heat until melted, about 10 minutes. Place a stuffed pepper on each of 6 plates, garnish with the parsley, and serve.

Asian Chicken Lettuce Wraps SERVES 6

Shredded chicken from the slow cooker serves as an excellent foundation for so many dishes. From tacos to buffalo chicken wraps, chicken's versatility can't be beat, and it couldn't be any easier to prepare. Simply set it and forget it. Here, I toss the chicken with hoisin and other Asian seasonings to make a delicious filling for lettuce wraps. If you prefer, you can turn this into a big chopped salad instead of serving it as wraps.

CHICKEN

2 boneless, skinless chicken breasts (8 ounces each)

6 tablespoons hoisin sauce*

2 teaspoons Sriracha sauce

2 tablespoons reduced-sodium soy sauce*

1 tablespoon unseasoned rice vinegar

2 teaspoons grated fresh ginger

1 (8-ounce) can water chestnuts, drained and chopped

2 tablespoons chopped unsalted cashews

CARROTS

1 cup shredded carrots

2 tablespoons unseasoned rice vinegar

1 teaspoon toasted sesame oil

FOR SERVING

24 Boston or baby romaine lettuce leaves (from 2 heads)

2 scallions, greens only, thinly sliced

*Read the label to be sure this product is gluten-free.

PER SERVING	4 wraps
CALORIES	187
FAT	5 g
SATURATED FAT	1 g
CHOLESTEROL	49 mg
CARBOHYDRATE	17 g
FIBER	2.5 g
PROTEIN	18 g
SUGARS	8 g
SODIUM	616 mg

For the chicken: Place the chicken in a slow cooker and add enough water to cover by 1 inch. Cover and cook on low for 4 to 5 hours, until it can be easily shredded. Drain, transfer to a cutting board, and shred the meat with two forks.

In a large bowl, whisk together the hoisin, Sriracha, soy sauce, rice vinegar, and ginger. Add the chicken, water chestnuts, and cashews and toss well.

For the carrots: In a medium bowl, combine the carrots, rice vinegar, and sesame oil.

To serve, arrange 4 lettuce leaves on each of 6 serving plates. Divide the chicken among the lettuce cups, top with the carrots and scallions, and serve.

Ham and White Bean Soup   SERVES 6

My favorite part about making a ham for the holidays is the leftovers! There are countless ways to use the meat (sandwiches, soups, casseroles, etc.) *and* the ham bone. Here, I use the bone to create a wonderful broth that gives this soup fantastic flavor. At the end of cooking, I use my favorite, easy method of "lite"-ly thickening the soup: I puree some of the soup, including the beans and ham, and stir it right back into the rest. The creamy, spoon-clinging texture is just delicious.

1 leftover ham bone

2 cups chopped leftover ham (11 ounces)

2 (15-ounce) cans white beans,* rinsed and drained

10 ounces Yukon Gold potatoes (2 medium), peeled and finely chopped

2 medium carrots, chopped

1 celery stalk, chopped

½ cup frozen green peas

2 garlic cloves, minced

1 bay leaf

*Read the label to be sure this product is gluten-free.

PER SERVING	1⅓ cups
CALORIES	256
FAT	2.5 g
SATURATED FAT	1 g
CHOLESTEROL	24 mg
CARBOHYDRATE	39 g
FIBER	11 g
PROTEIN	21 g
SUGARS	4 g
SODIUM	886 mg

In a slow cooker, combine 3 cups water, the ham bone, chopped ham, beans, potatoes, carrots, celery, peas, garlic, and bay leaf.

Cover and cook on low for 8 hours, until the potatoes are tender. Discard the bone and bay leaf. Transfer 1½ cups of the soup to a blender and puree until smooth. Stir the puree back into the soup. Ladle 1⅓ cups into each of 6 bowls and serve hot.

SKINNY SCOOP

If you don't have a leftover ham, you can also purchase a ham steak and use a ham hock in place of the bone.

Split Pea Soup with Smoked Turkey SERVES 8

Split pea soup is the perfect cold-weather soup, as it's filling, flavorful, and made mostly from staple ingredients. The smoked turkey leg adds great depth of flavor, while the cilantro is a fresh addition that brings brightness to the soup. And I love that this slow cooker dish couldn't be any easier to make—there's no precooking needed at all. Simply throw the ingredients into the slow cooker, turn it on, and dinner is done when you get home! Simple and satisfying.

1 pound (2¼ cups) dried green split peas

2 large carrots, chopped

1 medium onion, chopped

¼ cup chopped celery

2 garlic cloves, minced

1 tablespoon chicken bouillon*
(I like Better Than Bouillon)

¼ cup chopped fresh cilantro

1 bay leaf

1 (16-ounce) smoked turkey leg, skin removed

*Read the label to be sure this product is gluten-free.

PER SERVING	1¼ cups
CALORIES	298
FAT	3 g
SATURATED FAT	1 g
CHOLESTEROL	68 mg
CARBOHYDRATE	38 g
FIBER	15.5 g
PROTEIN	31 g
SUGARS	6 g
SODIUM	333 mg

Rinse the peas under cold water. Transfer them to a slow cooker and add 6 cups water, the carrots, onion, celery, garlic, bouillon, cilantro, and bay leaf. Stir well. Nestle the turkey leg into the mixture.

Cover and cook on low for 8 hours. Remove the turkey leg and shred the meat off the bone. Discard the bone and bay leaf and stir the meat back into the soup. Serve hot. (The soup will thicken as it stands.)

SKINNY SCOOP

This makes enough taco filling for two
family meals, so I usually serve it one night
and freeze the other half for another time.
You can also prep several individual meals
in glass or plastic bowls, putting the taco
filling over rice, since leftovers will keep in
the refrigerator for 3 to 4 days.

Tex-Mex Turkey Tacos SERVES 8

These are the easiest turkey and black bean tacos on the planet! There's no need to brown the ground meat first, and it easily breaks apart after it's cooked. In creating a book of one-pot recipes, I've encountered quite a few challenges, especially when working on the slow cooker chapter. I was from the camp that believed that browning meat before adding it to the slow cooker enhances the flavor of your final dish. Plus, I thought that if I didn't, I would end up with a giant meatloaf. But this recipe proved me wrong. To my surprise, after slow cooking all day, the meat was tender and easily broke apart with a spoon. And the best part was just how delicious it turned out. I use the turkey bean filling for tacos, but it would also be great over brown rice for burrito bowls.

TACO FILLING

1 teaspoon ground cumin

1 teaspoon chili powder*

1 teaspoon sweet paprika

1 teaspoon dried oregano

1 teaspoon kosher salt

1 pound 93% lean ground turkey

1 (15-ounce) can black beans,* rinsed and drained

1½ cups jarred mild chunky salsa

GUACAMOLE

6 ounces avocado (from 1 large Hass), mashed with a fork

⅓ cup finely chopped tomato

2 tablespoons chopped red onion

1 tablespoon fresh lime juice

1 tablespoon chopped fresh cilantro

½ teaspoon kosher salt

TACOS

16 (6-inch) corn tortillas

2 cups shredded romaine lettuce

1 cup shredded cheddar cheese*

Light sour cream or Greek yogurt, for drizzling (optional)

*Read the label to be sure this product is gluten-free.

PER SERVING	2 tacos
CALORIES	349
FAT	14.5 g
SATURATED FAT	5 g
CHOLESTEROL	57 mg
CARBOHYDRATE	36 g
FIBER	9 g
PROTEIN	21 g
SUGARS	3 g
SODIUM	723 mg

For the taco filling: In a small bowl, combine the cumin, chili powder, paprika, oregano, and salt.

Place the ground turkey in the slow cooker, breaking it up loosely with your hands. Add the beans, top with the spice mixture, and pour the salsa over everything.

Cover and cook on low for 8 hours, until the meat is tender. Using a wooden spoon, break up the ground turkey and stir until everything is well combined.

For the guacamole: In a medium bowl, combine the avocado, tomato, red onion, lime juice, cilantro, and salt.

For the tacos: Warm the tortillas directly over a medium flame on the stove, about 20 seconds per side. Place 2 on each of 8 plates. Assemble each taco by placing ¼ cup of the taco filling on each tortilla, then divide the guacamole and lettuce among the tacos. Top each with 1 tablespoon of the cheddar and sour cream (if using) and serve.

Pot Roast with Potatoes and Vegetables SERVES 8

This cozy stew—loaded with potatoes, carrots, and mushrooms—is sure to please on a chilly night. The secret to making the most flavorful, tender pot roast in the slow cooker is using chuck roast, which is known for its rich, beefy flavor. I slice it during the last hour of cooking so the flavor of the delicious gravy seeps into every bite. To keep this recipe to one pot, I microwave the onions, but to take it to another level, I highly recommend caramelizing the onions in a separate skillet for the best flavor (or use the sauté function on a multicooker).

3 pounds trimmed beef chuck roast

1¾ teaspoons kosher salt

Freshly ground black pepper

3 tablespoons all-purpose flour, wheat or gluten-free

1½ cups reduced-sodium beef broth*

1 tablespoon Worcestershire sauce*

2 tablespoons tomato paste

2 large onions, cut into ¼-inch-thick slices

2 teaspoons olive oil

1 pound Yukon Gold potatoes, peeled and cut into 1-inch pieces

3 medium carrots, cut into 1-inch pieces

3 garlic cloves, chopped

4 sprigs of fresh thyme

16 ounces white mushrooms, quartered

1 tablespoon chopped fresh parsley, for garnish

*Read the label to be sure this product is gluten-free.

PER SERVING	1½ cups
CALORIES	362
FAT	13 g
SATURATED FAT	4.5 g
CHOLESTEROL	104 mg
CARBOHYDRATE	22 g
FIBER	3 g
PROTEIN	38 g
SUGARS	5 g
SODIUM	611 mg

SKINNY SCOOP

If you have a multicooker or don't mind dirtying a skillet, sear the flour-dusted beef in 1 teaspoon of oil over medium-high heat until browned on both sides. Transfer to the slow cooker and add 1 teaspoon oil to the skillet. Sauté the onions, stirring often, until soft and golden, about 15 minutes. Add to the slow cooker and proceed with step 4.

Season the beef with 1 teaspoon of the salt and pepper to taste, then dust with 1 tablespoon of the flour.

In a medium bowl, whisk together the broth, Worcestershire sauce, tomato paste, and remaining 2 tablespoons flour.

Place the onions in a bowl with the oil and mix. Microwave, covered, on high for 10 minutes, until soft, then stir. Cook, uncovered, an additional 3 to 5 minutes, until golden.

Place the beef in a slow cooker and cover with the onions. Sprinkle with ¼ teaspoon of the salt and pepper to taste. Add the beef broth mixture, the potatoes, carrots, garlic, and thyme. Cover and cook on low for 8 hours, until the meat is very tender.

Transfer the beef to a cutting board. Let it cool for at least 10 minutes so it doesn't fall apart when slicing. Using a sharp knife, slice the meat across the grain into slices that are about ⅛ inch thick. Return the sliced meat to the slow cooker, submerging it in the gravy. Add the mushrooms and remaining ½ teaspoon salt.

Cover and cook on high for 1 hour, until the mushrooms are tender. Keep warm until ready to serve. Garnish with the parsley just before serving, then ladle 1½ cups into each of 8 bowls.

Southwestern Beef and Black Bean Soup SERVES 8

This easy, dump-and-go slow cooker soup requires no cooking or browning beforehand—just throw it in and walk away! Loaded with beans, ground beef, tomatoes, and three types of peppers, it's got a bit of a kick, but you can adjust the spice to your taste. If you want it spicier, leave the seeds in the jalapeño, or for a milder soup, omit them, and swap the poblano for a sweeter green bell pepper, too.

SOUP

1 pound 95% lean ground beef

1 poblano pepper, chopped

1 red bell pepper, chopped

1 fresh jalapeño pepper, seeded and finely chopped

½ cup chopped onion

3 garlic cloves, chopped

2 (10-ounce) cans diced tomatoes with green chiles (I like Rotel)

1 (15-ounce) can low-sodium black beans,* rinsed and drained

1 (8-ounce) can tomato sauce

2 cups frozen corn kernels

2 cups reduced-sodium chicken broth*

¼ cup chopped fresh cilantro, plus more for garnish

1 teaspoon ground cumin

1 teaspoon dried oregano

¾ teaspoon kosher salt

FOR SERVING

Chopped scallions

8 ounces sliced avocado (from 2 small Hass)

Shredded cheddar cheese* (optional)

Sour cream (optional)

*Read the label to be sure this product is gluten-free.

PER SERVING	1¼ cups soup + 1 ounce avocado
CALORIES	247
FAT	7.5 g
SATURATED FAT	2 g
CHOLESTEROL	35 mg
CARBOHYDRATE	25 g
FIBER	7.5 g
PROTEIN	18 g
SUGARS	5 g
SODIUM	725 mg

For the soup: Place the ground beef in a slow cooker, breaking up the beef loosely with your hands. Add the remaining ingredients and stir well. Cover and cook on low for 8 hours, until the meat is tender. When done, break up the ground meat with a wooden spoon.

To serve, ladle the soup into 8 bowls topped with the cilantro, scallions, avocado, and, if desired, the cheddar and sour cream.

Chunky Brisket and Cabbage Soup SERVES 6

This is such a delicious, hearty soup, especially in the colder months when it's a great winter warmer. Brisket is the perfect cut of beef to cook in the slow cooker because of its fat and marbling, which gives this soup a rich flavor and texture. To balance out the richness, I loaded up the whole thing with cabbage and other vegetables. Because this book is focused on one-pot cooking, I had to get creative with sweating the onions, and I found that microwaving them until they softened did the trick. If you don't have a microwave, sauté them over medium heat for a few minutes before adding them to the slow cooker.

¼ cup chopped onion

2 garlic cloves, minced

1 pound beef brisket, trimmed and cut into 4 pieces

5 cups chopped green cabbage

1 celery stalk with leaves, sliced

1 medium carrot, sliced

1 (14.5-ounce) can petite diced tomatoes

2½ cups reduced-sodium beef broth*

1 tablespoon Worcestershire sauce*

1 tablespoon reduced-sodium soy sauce*

½ tablespoon tomato paste

½ teaspoon mustard powder

½ teaspoon celery seeds

½ teaspoon sweet paprika

½ teaspoon kosher salt

Freshly ground black pepper

*Read the label to be sure this product is gluten-free.

PER SERVING	1⅓ cups
CALORIES	167
FAT	4.5 g
SATURATED FAT	1.5 g
CHOLESTEROL	51 mg
CARBOHYDRATE	13 g
FIBER	3 g
PROTEIN	18.5 g
SUGARS	6 g
SODIUM	847 mg

Place the onion and garlic in a microwave-safe dish and microwave on high for 2 minutes to soften.

Transfer the onion and garlic to a slow cooker. Add the beef and top with the cabbage, celery, carrot, tomatoes, broth, Worcestershire sauce, soy sauce, tomato paste, mustard powder, celery seeds, paprika, salt, and pepper to taste.

Cover and cook on low for 10 hours, until the beef is tender. Shred the beef using two forks (do this in the pot). Stir together and serve.

Ropa Vieja SERVES 8

A dish of shredded beef and vegetables that resembles a heap of colorful rags, *ropa vieja*—Spanish for "old clothes"—is one of Cuba's most popular dishes. It's so popular, in fact, that it's one of the country's national dishes. I grew up eating this favorite meal, made with a recipe that was handed down from my surrogate Cuban grandmother. At home, we always enjoyed it over rice with plantains on the side, but you can also serve it with tortillas.

1 small onion, cut into ¼-inch-thick slices

2 pounds beef flank steak, cut into 3 pieces

1 teaspoon kosher salt

3 teaspoons ground cumin

Freshly ground black pepper

1 red bell pepper, cut into ¼-inch-thick slices

1 green bell pepper, cut into ¼-inch-thick slices

½ cup green olives with pimientos, drained, rinsed, and quartered, plus 2 tablespoons of brine

4 garlic cloves, chopped

⅓ cup reduced-sodium beef broth*

1 (8-ounce) can tomato sauce

2 tablespoons tomato paste

1 tablespoon apple cider vinegar

2 bay leaves

6 cups cooked warm brown rice, for serving

Chopped fresh cilantro, for garnish

*Read the label to be sure this product is gluten-free.

PER SERVING	¾ cup stew + ¾ cup brown rice
CALORIES	728
FAT	12.5 g
SATURATED FAT	4 g
CHOLESTEROL	78 mg
CARBOHYDRATE	115 g
FIBER	6.5 g
PROTEIN	37 g
SUGARS	3 g
SODIUM	526 mg

SKINNY SCOOP

Ropa vieja tastes even better the next day because the flavors have more time to meld. This is a perfect dish to make in large batches for leftovers or meal prep.

Place the onion in a small microwave-safe bowl and microwave on high for 1½ to 2 minutes to soften.

Season the meat with the salt, 2 teaspoons of the cumin, and black pepper to taste. Transfer to a slow cooker and add the softened onion, the bell peppers, olives, and garlic.

In a small bowl, combine the olive brine, beef broth, tomato sauce, tomato paste, and vinegar. Pour the mixture over the meat. Add the bay leaves.

Cover and cook on high for 6 hours or on low for up to 10 hours, until the meat is tender. When ready to serve, discard the bay leaves, shred the meat in the pot with two forks, and stir in the remaining 1 teaspoon cumin. Scoop ¾ cup rice onto each of 8 plates, top with ¾ cup stew, and garnish with cilantro to serve.

Spicy Lamb Korma SERVES 4

There are many different versions of lamb korma, since the dish varies from region to region in India. Some are made with cashews, others with almonds, and some are mildly spiced while others are fiery. In my take on the classic dish, simplified for the slow cooker, I use lean lamb leg, yogurt, tomatoes, aromatics, and spices, and I serve it with extra chilled yogurt, which helps combat the spiciness of the dish. The meat is tender and flavorful, but if lamb is not your thing, you can certainly make this with beef, chicken, or even venison.

1½ pounds lean trimmed lamb stew meat (leg), cut into 1-inch chunks

1¼ teaspoons kosher salt

1 cup 2% Greek yogurt

½ tablespoon grated fresh ginger

1 teaspoon ground turmeric

1 yellow onion, finely chopped

2 fresh jalapeño peppers, 1 minced and 1 thinly sliced for garnish

4 garlic cloves, minced

1 teaspoon olive oil

1 (14.5-ounce) can petite diced tomatoes

1 teaspoon ground coriander

1 teaspoon ground cumin

1 teaspoon garam masala*

½ teaspoon ground cardamom

½ teaspoon cayenne pepper

Chopped fresh cilantro, for garnish (optional)

Naan or brown rice, for serving (optional)

*Read the label to be sure this product is gluten-free.

PER SERVING	1 cup
CALORIES	327
FAT	11.5 g
SATURATED FAT	4 g
CHOLESTEROL	116 mg
CARBOHYDRATE	12 g
FIBER	2 g
PROTEIN	42 g
SUGARS	6.5 g
SODIUM	641 mg

Season the lamb with the salt. In a medium bowl, combine ½ cup of the yogurt, the ginger, and turmeric. Add the lamb and stir to coat.

In a microwave-safe bowl, combine the onion, minced jalapeño, garlic, and oil and microwave on high for 2 minutes to soften.

Transfer the onion mixture to a slow cooker with the lamb, tomatoes, coriander, cumin, garam masala, cardamom, and cayenne. Cover and cook on low for 8 hours, until the meat is tender.

Spoon the meat onto serving plates and garnish with the sliced jalapeño and cilantro (if using). Top with the remaining ½ cup yogurt and serve with naan or brown rice, if desired.

Spinach and Cheese Manicotti SERVES 7

One of my biggest challenges when cooking dinner is finding meals that please my husband *and* my kids. There's nothing that kills my motivation mojo more than spending an hour in the kitchen after a hard day's work, only to end up with complaints and half-eaten dishes. That's why I love this recipe. It's a total crowd-pleaser.

It's also easy to prep ahead, and you skip the hassle of boiling the noodles first, because they cook right in the sauce. And the best part: There's plenty of leftovers, which makes this a good freezable meal to add to your repertoire. Serve it with a crisp salad, and dinner is done!

1 (15-ounce) container part-skim ricotta cheese (I like Polly-O)

2 cups shredded part-skim mozzarella cheese

¼ cup freshly grated Pecorino Romano cheese (I like Locatelli)

1 (10-ounce) package frozen chopped spinach, thawed and squeezed of excess moisture

2 tablespoons minced fresh parsley, plus more for garnish

1 large egg, lightly beaten

¼ teaspoon kosher salt

Freshly ground black pepper

14 manicotti shells (8 ounces) (I like Barilla)

4 cups store-bought marinara sauce

PER SERVING	2 shells
CALORIES	414
FAT	14.5 g
SATURATED FAT	8 g
CHOLESTEROL	66 mg
CARBOHYDRATE	43 g
FIBER	5 g
PROTEIN	27 g
SUGARS	3 g
SODIUM	960 mg

In a medium bowl, combine the ricotta, 1 cup of the mozzarella, the pecorino, spinach, parsley, egg, salt, and pepper to taste. Transfer to a piping bag (or gallon-size zip-top plastic bag), cut a ½-inch piece off the end of the bag (or the corner of the plastic bag), and pipe the filling into the uncooked manicotti shells (about ¼ cup per shell).

Spread ¾ cup of the marinara sauce over the bottom of a 6-quart oval slow cooker. Arrange 7 stuffed manicotti shells in the sauce, and then stack the remaining 7 shells on top in a second layer. Cover with enough sauce to fully submerge all the pasta.

Cover and cook on low for 4 hours, until the pasta is tender. Add the remaining 1 cup mozzarella, cover, and cook until the cheese is melted, about 15 minutes. Divide among 7 plates, garnish with the parsley, and serve hot.

SKINNY SCOOP

This dish fits best in a 6-quart oval slow cooker.

NO SLOW COOKER? NO PROBLEM!

To make this in the oven, spread 1 cup of the sauce in a greased 9 x 13-inch baking dish. Arrange the stuffed manicotti shells in a single layer over the sauce. Top with the remaining sauce. Cover and bake at 375°F until the pasta is tender, 55 to 60 minutes. Uncover the dish and sprinkle the remaining mozzarella over the top. Cover and bake until the cheese is melted, 5 more minutes.

Vegetarian Butternut Chili SERVES 6

This simple, chunky vegetarian chili calls for basic pantry ingredients, spices, and either fresh or frozen butternut squash, which makes it the perfect meal to whip up when you have no time to hit the grocery store. Chipotles in adobo sauce are jalapeño peppers that have been dried and smoked, then canned in a tangy tomato-based sauce. They're smoky and spicy, though in small amounts (like what's in this recipe), you just get great flavor and not very much heat.

1 (14.5-ounce) can petite diced tomatoes

1½ cups canned tomato sauce

1 cup vegetable broth*

4 garlic cloves, minced

2 tablespoons chopped chipotle peppers in adobo sauce or paste

1 teaspoon ancho chile powder

1 tablespoon ground cumin

½ teaspoon kosher salt

Freshly ground black pepper

4 cups cubed (½-inch) fresh or frozen butternut squash

1½ cups canned black beans,* rinsed and drained

1½ cups fresh or frozen corn kernels

⅓ cup chopped scallions, plus more for garnish

1 tablespoon fresh lime juice

TOPPINGS

6 ounces sliced avocado (from 1 large Hass)

Chopped fresh cilantro

Reduced-fat sour cream or 2% Greek yogurt (optional)

*Read the label to be sure this product is gluten-free.

PER SERVING	1⅓ cups + 1 ounce avocado
CALORIES	354
FAT	5.5 g
SATURATED FAT	1 g
CHOLESTEROL	0 mg
CARBOHYDRATE	73 g
FIBER	13 g
PROTEIN	14 g
SUGARS	8 g
SODIUM	801 mg

In a slow cooker, combine the tomatoes, tomato sauce, vegetable broth, garlic, chipotle peppers, ancho powder, cumin, salt, and black pepper to taste. Stir well. Add the butternut squash, beans, corn, scallions, and lime juice, and stir well.

Cover and cook on low for 6 to 8 hours, until the butternut is tender. Divide among 6 bowls and serve topped with the scallions, avocado, cilantro, and sour cream (if using).

Indian Butter Chickpeas SERVES 6

This mildly spiced chickpea curry is a vegetarian take on butter chicken, one of my favorite Indian dishes. It simmers low and slow in the most fragrant, mild tomato-based sauce, and totally satisfies my craving for Indian food. You can serve it in a bowl with mini naan bread on the side or over basmati rice, if you prefer. Made with pantry staples and spices, it's both economical and easy to make.

4 (15-ounce) cans chickpeas,* rinsed and drained

2 (14.5-ounce) cans diced tomatoes

5 garlic cloves, minced

2 teaspoons grated fresh ginger

1 teaspoon ground coriander

1 teaspoon ground cumin

1 teaspoon ground turmeric

1 teaspoon garam masala*

1/4 teaspoon cayenne pepper

1/2 cup canned full-fat coconut milk, plus more (optional) for drizzling

1 tablespoon ghee or butter

1/2 teaspoon kosher salt

1/4 cup chopped fresh cilantro, for garnish

6 mini (1.76 ounces each) naan (optional; I like Stonefire)

*Read the label to make sure this product is gluten-free.

PER SERVING	1 generous cup (not including coconut drizzle)
CALORIES	325
FAT	10.5 g
SATURATED FAT	5.5 g
CHOLESTEROL	5 mg
CARBOHYDRATE	46 g
FIBER	1.5 g
PROTEIN	14 g
SUGARS	3 g
SODIUM	653 mg

Put the chickpeas in a slow cooker.

In a blender, combine the tomatoes, garlic, ginger, coriander, cumin, turmeric, garam masala, and cayenne. Blend until smooth. Pour the puree into the slow cooker over the chickpeas. Fill the blender with 3 cups water, swoosh the water around, then pour it into the slow cooker.

Cover and cook on low for 6 to 8 hours, until the flavors meld. Stir in the coconut milk, ghee, and salt.

Garnish with the cilantro. Drizzle with a bit more coconut milk, if desired, and serve the naan on the side, if desired.

Grill Pan
& Grill

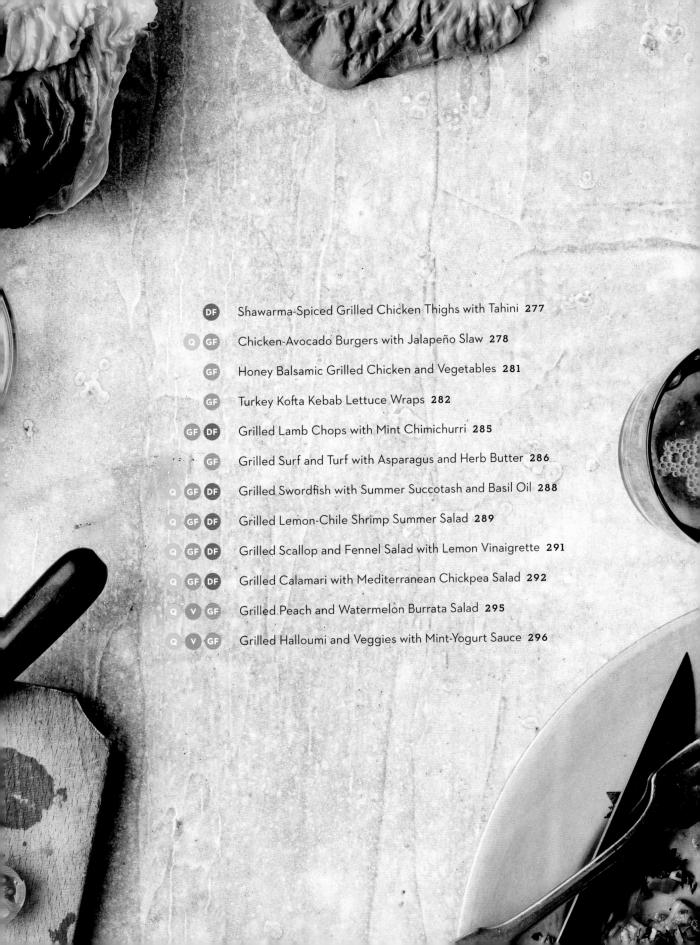

Shawarma-Spiced Grilled Chicken Thighs with Tahini SERVES 4

I love this easy version of the classic Turkish street food *shawarma*, which is traditionally cooked on a rotating spit. Though it's usually served wrapped in a pita or over couscous, it can be enjoyed at home for a fuss-free dinner on a platter with tons of fresh garden vegetables and tahini sauce drizzled over the top. If you prefer white meat, you can use chicken breasts instead of the thighs.

CHICKEN

½ tablespoon extra-virgin olive oil

Juice of 1 lemon

3 garlic cloves, minced

1 teaspoon ground cumin

1 teaspoon smoked paprika

¼ teaspoon curry powder

¼ teaspoon ground turmeric

⅛ teaspoon ground cinnamon

Pinch of crushed red pepper flakes

1¼ teaspoons kosher salt

Freshly ground black pepper

1 pound boneless, skinless chicken thighs, trimmed of fat

TAHINI SAUCE

¼ cup tahini paste

½ tablespoon extra-virgin olive oil

1 small garlic clove, minced

2 teaspoons fresh lemon juice

⅛ teaspoon kosher salt

FOR ASSEMBLY

1 head butter lettuce, leaves torn

2 Persian (mini) cucumbers, sliced on an angle

1 large heirloom tomato, sliced

¼ cup sliced pitted Kalamata olives

Oil, for the grill

1 medium red onion, cut into 8 wedges

2 pocketless pitas

Chopped fresh parsley, for garnish

4 lemon wedges

PER SERVING	1 thigh + ½ pita + 1½ tablespoons tahini sauce + vegetables
CALORIES	426
FAT	19 g
SATURATED FAT	3.5 g
CHOLESTEROL	108 mg
CARBOHYDRATE	36 g
FIBER	6.5 g
PROTEIN	32 g
SUGARS	5 g
SODIUM	751 mg

For the chicken: In a medium bowl, whisk together the olive oil and lemon juice. Whisk in the garlic, cumin, paprika, curry powder, turmeric, cinnamon, pepper flakes, salt, and black pepper to taste. Pour the marinade into a zip-top plastic bag and add the chicken, massaging it to evenly coat. Refrigerate for at least 1 hour or up to overnight.

For the tahini sauce: In a small bowl, combine 3 tablespoons water, the tahini, olive oil, garlic, lemon juice, and salt. The consistency should be smooth enough to pour; add more water to loosen if needed.

Arrange the lettuce, cucumbers, tomato, and olives on a platter.

Preheat a grill pan over medium-high heat (or preheat a grill to medium-high). Spray the pan with oil (or rub the grates with oil). Grill the chicken until cooked through, 5 to 6 minutes per side. Transfer to the open half of the platter and tent with foil.

Wipe the grill pan clean and spray it with more oil (or just rub the grates with oil again). Grill the onion wedges until they have grill marks, about 3 minutes per side. Grill the pitas until heated through, about 1 minute per side. Cut the pitas in half and transfer them to the platter. Garnish the tahini sauce with the parsley. Serve with the lemon wedges.

Chicken-Avocado Burgers with Jalapeño Slaw SERVES 6

These burgers—with unexpected pieces of tender avocado in every bite—are flavorful and delicious. Tommy thinks they would be a hit if they were on a burger joint's menu, which is his way of telling me he really likes them! The slaw is a must. It has just a slight kick and the perfect amount of crunch and texture. If you prefer to skip the buns, you can double the slaw or serve them wrapped in lettuce leaves.

BURGERS

1 pound 92% lean ground chicken

⅓ cup panko bread crumbs, regular or gluten-free

¼ cup chopped fresh cilantro

1 fresh jalapeño pepper, seeded and finely chopped

2 tablespoons grated red onion

1 garlic clove, grated

Juice of 1 lime

1 teaspoon kosher salt

⅛ teaspoon freshly ground black pepper

4 ounces diced avocado (from 1 small Hass)

JALAPEÑO SLAW

2 cups thinly sliced green cabbage

¼ small red onion, thinly sliced

1 fresh jalapeño pepper, seeded and thinly sliced

3 tablespoons chopped fresh cilantro

Juice of 1 lime

2 teaspoons olive oil

¼ teaspoon kosher salt

Oil, for the grill

6 slices reduced-fat pepper Jack cheese (I like Sargento)

6 whole wheat or gluten-free burger buns

PER SERVING	1 burger
CALORIES	354
FAT	16.5 g
SATURATED FAT	5 g
CHOLESTEROL	75 mg
CARBOHYDRATE	30 g
FIBER	6 g
PROTEIN	23 g
SUGARS	5 g
SODIUM	633 mg

For the burgers: In a large bowl, combine the chicken, panko, cilantro, jalapeño, red onion, garlic, lime juice, salt, and black pepper. Mix well. Gently fold in the avocado, then form into 6 patties.

For the jalapeño slaw: In a medium bowl, combine the cabbage, red onion, jalapeño, cilantro, lime juice, olive oil, and salt. Set aside.

Preheat a grill pan over medium heat (or preheat a grill to medium). Spray the pan with oil (or rub the grates with oil). Grill the patties until cooked through in the center, about 6 minutes per side, adding the cheese in the last 2 minutes of cooking.

Open the buns and grill cut side down until heated, 30 to 60 seconds.

On each of 6 plates, put a burger on the bottom of each bun and top with the jalapeño slaw. Top with the other bun half and serve immediately.

Honey Balsamic Grilled Chicken and Vegetables SERVES 6

 GF

Nothing beats an easy summer dish made entirely on the grill, so you don't have to heat up your kitchen! I use my gas grill all summer long for cooking meats and veggies—they taste deliciously smoky and the edges get nice and charred. The best way to grill veggies is to purchase some grill pans or baskets so the vegetables don't fall through the grates. Of course, if you don't have an outside grill, a grill pan will work, too!

1½ pounds thin-sliced chicken breast cutlets

3 tablespoons store-bought pesto

Juice of ½ lime

1 garlic clove, crushed through a garlic press

¼ teaspoon crushed red pepper flakes

1 teaspoon kosher salt

3 tablespoons balsamic vinegar

2 tablespoons extra-virgin olive oil

1 tablespoon raw honey

1 pound asparagus, tough ends trimmed

2 medium zucchini, cut into ¼-inch-thick slices

1 red bell pepper, cut into strips

Oil, for the grill

Freshly ground black pepper

PER SERVING	3 ounces chicken + 1 cup vegetables
CALORIES	258
FAT	11.5 g
SATURATED FAT	2 g
CHOLESTEROL	74 mg
CARBOHYDRATE	11 g
FIBER	3 g
PROTEIN	28 g
SUGARS	8 g
SODIUM	396 mg

In a large zip-top plastic bag, combine the chicken, pesto, lime juice, garlic, pepper flakes, and ½ teaspoon of the salt. Massage the marinade into the chicken, making sure all the chicken is coated evenly. Let it marinate in the refrigerator for at least 1 hour, or overnight for best results.

In a small bowl, whisk together the vinegar, oil, honey, and ¼ teaspoon of the salt.

Preheat a grill to medium-high (or preheat a grill pan over medium-high heat). Rub the grates with oil (or spray the pan with oil).

Put the asparagus, zucchini, and bell pepper on 1 large grill serving tray or 2 smaller trays (or cook in batches). Spray with oil and sprinkle with the remaining ¼ teaspoon salt and pepper to taste. Grill, turning constantly, until the edges are browned, 6 to 8 minutes. Transfer to a platter.

Grill the chicken until grill marks appear and the chicken is cooked though, 4 to 5 minutes per side. Transfer to the platter with the vegetables. Pour the balsamic dressing over everything and serve.

Turkey Kofta Kebab Lettuce Wraps SERVES 4

The word *kofta* (or *kefta*), which has Persian origins, means "grounded" or "pounded." They are essentially oval-shaped, spiced meatballs often made with lamb or beef, or sometimes even seafood—I've even seen kofta made with crab. I usually make them with ground turkey mixed with a blend of onions, garlic, spices, and fresh herbs. In the summer, they make a great appetizer served on a platter with grilled pita bread, sliced tomatoes, cucumbers, and tahini. In this recipe, I turn them into a handy lettuce wrap using baby romaine leaves (I've found them at Costco); they're the perfect size to hold the kofta.

4 garlic cloves

1¼ pounds 93% lean ground turkey

¼ cup finely grated red onion

3 tablespoons chopped fresh parsley

3 tablespoons chopped fresh mint

1 tablespoon ground coriander

1 teaspoon ground cumin

½ teaspoon ground allspice

½ teaspoon ground cinnamon

¼ teaspoon cayenne pepper

¼ teaspoon ground ginger

1½ teaspoons kosher salt

¼ teaspoon freshly ground black pepper

16 (6-inch) bamboo skewers, soaked in water for 30 minutes if grilling outdoors

Oil, for the grill

FOR ASSEMBLY

16 baby romaine lettuce leaves (from 1 large or 2 small heads) or butter lettuce leaves

½ cup 0% Greek yogurt

1 cup chopped Persian (mini) cucumber

¼ cup chopped red onion

Chopped fresh parsley and/or mint, for garnish

Freshly ground black pepper

PER SERVING	4 wraps
CALORIES	260
FAT	12.5 g
SATURATED FAT	3 g
CHOLESTEROL	107 mg
CARBOHYDRATE	8 g
FIBER	2 g
PROTEIN	31 g
SUGARS	3 g
SODIUM	537 mg

Crush the garlic through a garlic press or mash with a mortar and pestle or the side of a chef's knife.

In a large bowl, combine the turkey, garlic paste, onion, parsley, mint, coriander, cumin, allspice, cinnamon, cayenne, ginger, salt, and black pepper until well blended. Form the mixture into 16 balls (about 1½ ounces each) and wrap each around the tip of a skewer. Flatten each around the skewer into an oval about 4 inches long and ½ inch thick. Place the kebabs on a large tray or sheet pan, cover, and refrigerate for at least 30 minutes or up to 12 hours.

Preheat a grill pan over medium heat (or preheat a grill to medium). Lightly spray the pan with oil (or lightly rub the grates with oil).

Cook the skewers, turning occasionally, until the turkey is cooked through in the center, 3 to 4 minutes per side.

To assemble the wraps, remove the kofta from the skewers. Arrange 4 lettuce leaves on each of 4 plates. Top each leaf with 1 kofta, ½ tablespoon yogurt, and equal amounts of cucumber and red onion. Garnish with the chopped parsley and/or mint and season with the pepper to taste.

Grilled Lamb Chops with Mint Chimichurri SERVES 4

Lamb chops are my go-to for nights when I need a quick and easy meal that I know both Tommy and Madison will love. I make them year-round—on my grill pan when it's cold outside, or on the outdoor grill when the weather is warm. The fresh, zingy mint chimichurri—a play on an Argentinian staple—brightens up the whole dish, and mint pairs so perfectly with lamb. This dish is especially great in the summer when mint and tomatoes grow out of control in my garden.

8 bone-in lamb loin chops (3½ ounces each), trimmed

1 teaspoon kosher salt

Freshly ground black pepper

4 garlic cloves, minced or crushed through a garlic press

MINT CHIMICHURRI

2 tablespoons finely chopped red onion

2 tablespoons apple cider vinegar

2 tablespoons extra-virgin olive oil

¼ teaspoon kosher salt

3 tablespoons finely chopped fresh mint

2 tablespoons finely chopped fresh parsley

1 garlic clove, minced

⅛ teaspoon crushed red pepper flakes, or more to taste

⅛ teaspoon freshly ground black pepper

FOR SERVING

Oil, for the grill

1 small head red or green leaf lettuce, leaves torn

1⅓ cups halved heirloom cherry tomatoes

PER SERVING	2 lamb chops + salad
CALORIES	370
FAT	17 g
SATURATED FAT	5 g
CHOLESTEROL	127 mg
CARBOHYDRATE	10 g
FIBER	4.5 g
PROTEIN	43 g
SUGARS	4 g
SODIUM	495 mg

FOOD FACTS: FALL IN LOVE WITH LAMB

Lamb is a tasty and nutrient-rich protein that's loaded with vitamin B12, niacin, zinc, and selenium. The leanest cuts of lamb include the loin (such as loin chops), shank, and leg— all of which are comparable to beef or pork in terms of calories and fat.

Place the lamb chops in a large bowl, sprinkle with the salt and pepper to taste, then rub them with the garlic. Cover with plastic wrap and marinate at room temperature for at least 30 minutes or as long as overnight refrigerated.

For the mint chimichurri: In a medium bowl, combine the red onion, vinegar, olive oil, and salt and let it sit for about 5 minutes. Stir in 1 tablespoon water, the mint, parsley, garlic, pepper flakes, and black pepper. Refrigerate until ready to use (it can be made a few hours ahead).

Preheat a grill pan over medium-high heat (or preheat a grill to medium-high). Spray the pan with oil (or rub the grates with oil). Grill the chops until a thermometer inserted in the side of each chop registers 145°F for medium-rare, 4 to 6 minutes per side, or longer to your preferred doneness.

To serve, place 2 chops on each of 4 plates. Divide the torn lettuce leaves among the plates and top each with ⅓ cup cherry tomatoes. Drizzle each serving of salad and lamb with 2 tablespoons mint chimichurri and serve.

Grilled Surf and Turf with Asparagus and Herb Butter SERVES 4

If you've got a serious craving for both steak *and* seafood, this dish—made with a combo of grilled filet mignon and succulent shrimp and scallops, all topped with a garlicky herb butter—is the answer. It's a beloved dinner classic that's easy enough to make any night of the week, yet worthy enough to save for special occasions.

4 filet mignon steaks (5 ounces each)

1 teaspoon plus a pinch of kosher salt

Freshly ground black pepper

20 peeled and deveined jumbo shrimp (¾ pound)

10 ounces (8 to 10) dry-packed jumbo sea scallops

2 tablespoons unsalted butter, at room temperature

2 garlic cloves, minced

2 teaspoons chopped fresh thyme

Oil, for the grill

32 thin asparagus spears (1 pound), tough ends trimmed

PER SERVING	1 steak + 2 scallops + 5 shrimp + 8 asparagus spears
CALORIES	399
FAT	13 g
SATURATED FAT	5.5 g
CHOLESTEROL	237 mg
CARBOHYDRATE	8 g
FIBER	2.5 g
PROTEIN	62 g
SUGARS	2 g
SODIUM	717 mg

Season the steak on both sides with ¾ teaspoon of the salt and pepper to taste. Let it come to room temperature, about 30 minutes.

Meanwhile, season the shrimp and scallops with the remaining ¼ teaspoon salt and pepper to taste.

In a small bowl, combine the butter, garlic, and thyme.

Preheat a grill pan over medium heat (or preheat a grill to medium). Spray the pan with oil (or lightly rub the grates with oil). Add the asparagus, season with a pinch each of salt and pepper, and cook until slightly charred on the bottom, about 5 minutes. Turn and cook until crisp-tender, 4 to 5 more minutes. Transfer to a serving platter and tent with foil to keep warm.

Spray the grill pan with more oil (or rub the grates with more oil) and increase the heat to medium-high. Grill the steaks until the bottom is browned, about 5 minutes. Flip and cook for about 5 more minutes for medium to medium-rare, or longer to your desired doneness. Transfer the steak to the platter of asparagus and tent with foil.

Using a paper towel, wipe the grill pan clean and spray it with more oil (or just rub the grates with oil again). Add the shrimp and scallops and cook until opaque, 2 to 3 minutes per side. Transfer to the platter of steak and asparagus.

Top the steaks, shrimp, scallops, and asparagus with the herb butter. Toss to coat and melt the butter. Serve immediately.

Grilled Swordfish with Summer Succotash and Basil Oil SERVES 4

My daughter Madison isn't a huge fan of fish, but she doesn't mind swordfish because the taste and texture are similar to chicken. Swordfish is also great for grilling because it's isn't flaky (like most other fish), and it has a firmer, meat-like texture. Served over a summer salad inspired by the Southern favorite succotash—made with a fresh-tasting combination of sweet summer corn, tomatoes, and lima beans tossed in basil oil—this is a fish dish your whole family will devour.

SALAD

2 tablespoons extra-virgin olive oil

¼ cup packed fresh basil leaves

1 garlic clove, peeled

½ teaspoon kosher salt

Pinch of crushed red pepper flakes

4 medium ears corn, husked

Olive oil spray (I like my Misto or Bertolli)

Freshly ground black pepper

1½ cups halved heirloom cherry tomatoes

1 cup frozen baby lima beans, thawed

FISH

4 wild-caught swordfish steaks (6 ounces each), 1 inch thick

½ teaspoon kosher salt

Freshly ground black pepper

Olive oil spray (I like my Misto or Bertolli)

PER SERVING	1 fish steak + 1¹⁄₃ cups salad
CALORIES	448
FAT	19.5 g
SATURATED FAT	4 g
CHOLESTEROL	112 mg
CARBOHYDRATE	30 g
FIBER	5.5 g
PROTEIN	40 g
SUGARS	4 g
SODIUM	456 mg

For the salad: To make basil oil, in a small blender or food processor, combine 1 tablespoon water, the olive oil, basil, garlic, ¼ teaspoon of the salt, and the pepper flakes. Blend until smooth.

Preheat a grill pan over medium heat (or preheat a grill to medium). Spray the corn with oil and season it with the remaining ¼ teaspoon salt and black pepper to taste. Grill, turning, until charred and cooked through, about 12 minutes. Let cool, then cut off the kernels and put them in a large bowl. Add the tomatoes, lima beans, and basil oil and toss well.

For the fish: Sprinkle the swordfish with the salt and black pepper to taste. Spray both sides of the fish with oil.

Spray the pan or grill with oil, then grill the swordfish steaks until opaque throughout, 3 to 4 minutes per side.

To serve, divide the salad among 4 serving plates and top each with a piece of fish.

Grilled Lemon-Chile Shrimp Summer Salad SERVES 4

This is the salad I crave all summer long, as it's loaded with the season's bounty of fresh garden tomatoes, cucumbers, and corn. To add protein to make this a complete meal, I love to grill up some shrimp. My favorite way to season shrimp for the grill is simple: lemon juice, garlic, oregano, and pepper flakes. It's a little spicy but incredibly flavorful, and it pairs wonderfully with the salad.

Oil, for the grill

2 medium ears corn, husked

1 tablespoon olive oil

Grated zest and juice of ½ lemon

1 tablespoon fresh oregano leaves

1 tablespoon chopped fresh parsley

2 garlic cloves, minced

¼ teaspoon crushed red pepper flakes

⅛ teaspoon kosher salt

Freshly ground black pepper

24 peeled and deveined tail-on colossal shrimp (about 1¼ pounds)

SALAD

5 cups chopped romaine lettuce (1 medium head)

½ English cucumber, peeled and chopped

1 medium tomato, sliced into wedges

¼ small red onion, thinly sliced

Grated zest and juice of ½ lemon

2 tablespoons extra-virgin olive oil

1 tablespoon red wine vinegar

¼ teaspoon kosher salt

Freshly ground black pepper

8 ounces sliced avocado (from 2 small Hass)

PER SERVING	2 cups salad + 6 shrimp
CALORIES	374
FAT	20 g
SATURATED FAT	2.5 g
CHOLESTEROL	169 mg
CARBOHYDRATE	21 g
FIBER	7.5
PROTEIN	29 g
SUGARS	4 g
SODIUM	476 mg

Preheat a grill pan over medium-high heat (or preheat a grill to medium-high). Spray the pan with oil (or rub the grates with oil).

Put the corn on the grill and cook, turning to cook all sides, until slightly charred, about 10 minutes. When cool enough to handle, cut the kernels off the cobs.

Meanwhile, in a small bowl, combine the olive oil, lemon zest, lemon juice, oregano, parsley, garlic, pepper flakes, salt, and black pepper to taste. Stir well. Add the shrimp and toss until coated. (If cooking on a grill, thread the shrimp on metal skewers.)

Respray the pan or re-oil the grill, then grill the shrimp until opaque and cooked through, 1½ to 2 minutes per side.

For the salad: In a large bowl, combine the lettuce, cucumber, tomato, and red onion. In a small bowl, whisk together the lemon zest, lemon juice, olive oil, vinegar, salt, and pepper to taste. Drizzle the vinaigrette over the salad and toss well to coat.

Divide the salad among 4 shallow bowls. Top equally with the corn, avocado, and grilled shrimp.

Grilled Scallop and Fennel Salad with Lemon Vinaigrette SERVES 4

Scallops are so meaty and delicious, and they take just minutes to cook, which makes this salad a perfectly light and fast weeknight dish. The grilled fennel, which has a gentle anise flavor, is such a nice match for the scallops, too. When grilled, the flavor of the fennel becomes pleasantly sweet and mellow.

¼ cup fresh lemon juice

3 tablespoons extra-virgin olive oil

1 tablespoon chopped fresh parsley

¾ teaspoon plus ⅛ teaspoon kosher salt

Freshly ground black pepper

16 dry-packed jumbo sea scallops (1½ pounds total)

8 (12-inch) bamboo skewers, soaked in water for 30 minutes if grilling outdoors

2 large fennel bulbs (12 ounces each), stalks and fronds removed

Oil, for the grill

4 cups arugula

2 radishes, thinly sliced

PER SERVING	1 salad
CALORIES	277
FAT	12 g
SATURATED FAT	1.5 g
CHOLESTEROL	53 mg
CARBOHYDRATE	12 g
FIBER	3 g
PROTEIN	30 g
SUGARS	4 g
SODIUM	659 mg

SKINNY SCOOP

Buy the largest scallops you can find, and be sure to pat them dry and season them just before grilling to get a good sear. Cook them on a very hot grill or grill pan without flipping them until you get some good grill marks.

In a small bowl, whisk together the lemon juice, 2½ tablespoons of the olive oil, the parsley, ¼ teaspoon of the salt, and pepper to taste.

Remove the crescent-shaped tendon from the side of each scallop. Use a paper towel to pat each scallop dry, then thread them in groups of 4 onto two parallel skewers to keep the scallops in place while grilling. Keep refrigerated until ready to grill.

Leaving the core of the fennel bulbs intact, stand each bulb up on one end and cut the fennel in half from top to bottom. Cut each half into four ¼-inch-thick slices for a total of 8 slices. Drizzle with the remaining ½ tablespoon olive oil and sprinkle with ½ teaspoon of the salt and pepper to taste.

Preheat a grill pan over high heat (or preheat a grill to high). Spray the pan with oil (or rub the grates with oil).

Remove the scallops from the refrigerator and season with the remaining ⅛ teaspoon salt and pepper to taste.

Working in batches, grill the fennel until tender and grill marks form, about 4 minutes on one side and 2 minutes on the other. Set aside.

Spray the pan with more oil (or rub the grill grates generously with oil to prevent the scallops from sticking). Grill the scallop skewers for 4 minutes on one side, then turn them over and cook until the scallops are just cooked through and barely opaque in the middle, about 2 more minutes.

Arrange 1 cup of arugula on each of 4 plates. Top each with 2 slices grilled fennel, 4 scallops, and radish slices. Drizzle about 1½ tablespoons of the lemon vinaigrette over the top of each plate. Serve warm.

Grilled Calamari with Mediterranean Chickpea Salad SERVES 4

While traveling through the Mediterranean last year with my family, I had the opportunity to see so many amazing places, but Greece was my favorite by far. Walking through the stone streets of Old Town of Rhodes, I fell in love not only with the delicious food, but also with the warm people, who made us feel so welcome. In this fresh and easy salad, I re-created a little taste of the Mediterranean.

SALAD

1 large (14-ounce) English cucumber, cut into 1-inch cubes

1 medium green bell pepper, cut into 1/2-inch squares

1 cup grape tomatoes, quartered

1 (15-ounce) can chickpeas,* rinsed and drained

16 Kalamata olives, pitted and halved

1/4 cup chopped red onion

2 tablespoons extra-virgin olive oil

Juice of 1 lemon

1/2 teaspoon kosher salt

Freshly ground black pepper

CALAMARI

Oil, for the grill

1 1/2 pounds cleaned calamari, tubes only

1 tablespoon extra-virgin olive oil

1 garlic clove, minced

1 teaspoon dried oregano

3/4 teaspoon kosher salt

Freshly ground black pepper

8 (8-inch) bamboo skewers, soaked in water for 30 minutes if grilling outdoors

2 lemons, 1 cut into 8 wedges and 1 halved

1 tablespoon chopped fresh parsley, for garnish

*Read the label to be sure this product is gluten-free.

PER SERVING	2 skewers + 1 3/4 cups salad
CALORIES	396
FAT	16 g
SATURATED FAT	2.5 g
CHOLESTEROL	396 mg
CARBOHYDRATE	32 g
FIBER	3 g
PROTEIN	33 g
SUGARS	5 g
SODIUM	707 mg

For the salad: In a large bowl, combine the cucumber, bell pepper, tomatoes, chickpeas, olives, and red onion. Drizzle with the olive oil and lemon juice, season with the salt and pepper to taste, and toss well. Divide among 4 plates.

For the calamari: Preheat a grill pan over high heat.

Wash the squid and pat dry with paper towels. Cut it into 1/2-inch rings. Toss the squid in a bowl with the olive oil, garlic, and oregano. Season all sides with the salt and pepper to taste. Thread the squid evenly onto 8 bamboo skewers with a lemon wedge in the middle of each skewer.

When the pan is very hot, spray it with oil. Cook the calamari skewers, in batches as needed, until the edges are slightly charred and browned, 2 to 3 minutes per side. Remove from the pan (or grill). Grill the lemon halves cut side down until charred, about 2 minutes.

To serve, place 2 calamari skewers over each salad, squeeze the grilled lemons over the tops, and garnish with the parsley.

SKINNY SCOOP

Cut the calamari into rings that are the same size so they cook evenly. Lay them flat on a grill pan, which should be very hot before grilling, to make sure all of them cook. Take care not to overcook the calamari.

Grilled Peach and Watermelon Burrata Salad SERVES 4

  GF

Although burrata—a fresh cheese made with mozzarella and cream—is undeniably the star of this light summer salad, the juicy grilled peaches and refreshing watermelon are pretty hard to resist. This salad also happens to be gorgeous, and it comes together fast. Heck, you don't even have to grill the peaches if you want to enjoy it even faster!

4 peaches, cut into ½-inch-thick wedges

Olive oil spray (I like my Misto or Bertolli)

4 small balls burrata cheese (1 pound total)

4 cups cubed seedless watermelon

½ cup loosely packed watercress

2 tablespoons balsamic glaze (I like DeLallo)

PER SERVING	1 salad
CALORIES	408
FAT	25 g
SATURATED FAT	16.5 g
CHOLESTEROL	81 mg
CARBOHYDRATE	31 g
FIBER	3 g
PROTEIN	23 g
SUGARS	27 g
SODIUM	348 mg

Preheat a grill pan over medium-high heat (or preheat a grill to medium-high). Spray the peaches with oil, then grill them cut sides down, just long enough to make marks, about 2 minutes per side.

To serve, place a ball of burrata in the center of each of 4 plates and arrange the grilled peaches, watermelon cubes, and watercress around it. Drizzle everything with the balsamic glaze.

Grilled Halloumi and Veggies with Mint-Yogurt Sauce SERVES 4

Dining al fresco with lots of grilled veggies, dips, cheese, olives, and a glass of rosé is how I like to eat all summer long. Halloumi—a salty firm, white, low-fat cheese from Cyprus that is also popular in Greece and other places in the Mediterranean—is perfect for grilling. It sears and colors quickly when it hits a hot grill, and while the interior softens, the cheese doesn't melt; it just warms up nicely for a pleasant, chewy, squeaky bite. If you can't find Halloumi, you can make this with feta instead.

1 cup 2% Greek yogurt

1 garlic clove, minced

4 tablespoons chopped fresh mint

¾ teaspoon kosher salt

Freshly ground black pepper

8 ounces Halloumi, sliced into 8 pieces

1 red onion, cut into ⅛-inch-thick rounds

2 Japanese eggplants, cut on an angle into ¼-inch-thick slices

3 red, green, or yellow bell peppers, cut into ½-inch-wide strips

Olive oil spray (I like my Misto or Bertolli

1 English cucumber, cut on an angle into ¼-inch-thick slices

9 ounces cherry tomatoes on the vine

20 Kalamata olives, pitted

PER SERVING	2 ounces cheese + ¼ cup sauce + 5 olives + ¼ of the veggies
CALORIES	372
FAT	20 g
SATURATED FAT	11.5 g
CHOLESTEROL	46 mg
CARBOHYDRATE	33 g
FIBER	13 g
PROTEIN	23 g
SUGARS	15 g
SODIUM	995 mg

In a small bowl, combine the yogurt, garlic, 2 tablespoons of the mint, ¼ teaspoon of the salt, and black pepper to taste. Set aside.

Preheat a grill pan over medium-high heat (or preheat a grill to medium-high).

Spray the Halloumi, onion rounds, eggplant, and bell peppers all over with oil. Sprinkle with the remaining ½ teaspoon salt and black pepper to taste. Grill the vegetables, turning occasionally, until nicely charred, about 10 minutes. Arrange on a serving platter with the cucumber, tomatoes, and olives.

Grill the cheese, turning occasionally, until grill marks appear, 5 to 6 minutes. Transfer the cheese to the platter of vegetables and sprinkle with the remaining 2 tablespoons mint. Serve with the yogurt sauce on the side.

ACKNOWLEDGMENTS

It's hard to believe I have a third cookbook—it feels like yesterday I was dreaming of writing my first! I am filled with so much gratitude that I get to do what I love every single day! A heartfelt thank-you to all of you who made it possible.

So first and foremost, a massive thank-you to every single person who has been part of the Skinnytaste family, especially to my dedicated fans—without you this would not be possible.

To my mom, it's been a rough year losing my dad. You're one of the strongest women I know! Thank you to both you and Dad for together sharing your passion and love of cooking with me and my brother, Ivan, and getting us involved in the kitchen at a very young age. I find comfort in cooking the dishes Dad used to make, and those memories will last a lifetime. To Ivan, you are always my rock, and I am beyond grateful to have you in my life. To my husband, Tommy, for being my biggest cheerleader, best food critic, and for always inspiring so many new winning recipe ideas. And to my children: Karina, thank you for keeping me updated on the latest food trends; and Madison, I love that you're turning into a little foodie yourself!

A big thank-you once again to Heather K. Jones, R.D. Working with you on this third cookbook, it is starting to feel almost effortless! And to her team: Danielle Hazard, whose culinary background makes her extra special at noticing all the little details, and Donna Fennessy, for polishing all my words.

To my recipe tester and right-hand woman, aka Aunt Ligia Caldas, thank you for keeping me organized and making sure I eat my fruit every morning—I would be lost without you! And to my uncle Rene and cousins Nina and Camila, for the final thumbs-up on my creations.

To my fearless agent, Janis Donnaud—you're the best, and I am grateful to have you in my corner. Thank you for always having my back!

Thank you to the Clarkson Potter team, for continually believing in me and Skinnytaste: Doris Cooper, Ashley Meyer, Jenn Sit, Carly Gorga, and Erica Gelbard, I am lucky to work with such an incredible group of ladies. And to all the folks at Potter, especially Mia Johnson, who designed the book and cover and also gave me a tour of the Bay Area in California.

To the photography team—I was blown away with every photo. Thank you for making my book look gorgeous! Eva Kolenko, you're an amazing photographer; Ryan Reineck, you have many talents—thank you for making every dish look stunning; and Claire Mack, thank you for all your beautiful propping!

To my friends Pete and Nicole Dolan, thank you for letting me shoot in your gorgeous kitchen! And to Jacqueline Shepherd and Marci Balken, for doing makeup up and hair.

To my cousin Kat and Aunt Milda, you came to my rescue after the loss of my dad, the hardest time in my life. I am forever grateful.

And last but not least, to all my girlfriends. Thank you for keeping me laughing: Gabbie, Kim, Denise H, Raquel, Doreen, Denise P, Tara, Nalini, Roseanne, and Julia. I love you all!

INDEX

GINA HOMOLKA is the #1 *New York Times* bestselling author of *The Skinnytaste Cookbook* and *Skinnytaste Fast and Slow* and the founder of *Skinnytaste*, the award-winning blog that's been featured in *Cooking Light*; *O, The Oprah Magazine*; and *Better Homes & Gardens* and on Glamour.com and FineCooking.com, among other media outlets. She lives on Long Island with her husband and their two children.

HEATHER K. JONES, R.D., is a registered dietitian, the author of several nutrition books, and the founder of heatherkjones.com, a weight-loss site about healing and hope instead of diets and deprivation.

Copyright © 2018 by Gina Homolka
Photographs copyright © 2018 by Eva Kolenko
Selected recipes first appeared on Skinnytaste.com

All rights reserved.
Published in the United States by Clarkson Potter/Publishers, an imprint of the Crown Publishing Group, a division of Penguin Random House LLC, New York.
crownpublishing.com
clarksonpotter.com

CLARKSON POTTER is a trademark and **POTTER** with colophon is a registered trademark of Penguin Random House LLC.

Skinnytaste® is a registered trademark of Skinnytaste, Inc.

Library of Congress Cataloging-in-Publication Data
Names: Homolka, Gina, author. | Jones, Heather K., author.
Title: Skinnytaste one and done : 140 no-fuss dinners for your Instant Pot, slow cooker, air fryer, sheet pan, dutch oven, and more / Gina Homolka with Heather K. Jones.
Other titles: Skinny taste one and done | Skinnytaste.
Description: First edition. | New York : Clarkson Potter/Publishers, [2018] | includes index.

Identifiers: LCCN 2018015876 | ISBN 9781524762155 (hardcover) | ISBN 9781524762162 (ebook)
Subjects: LCSH: Quick and easy cooking. | Electric cooking, Slow. | Dutch oven cooking | One-dish meals. | Low-calorie diet—Recipes. | Reducing diets—Recipes. | LCGFT: Cookbooks.
Classification: LCC YX714 .H6334 2018 | DDC 641.5/12—dc23 LC record available at https:lccn.loc.gov/2018-015876

Hardcover ISBN 978-1-5247-6215-5
Ebook ISBN 978-1-5247-6216-2
B&N edition 978-1-9848-2287-1
Target edition 978-1-9848-2288-8

Printed in China

Book and cover design by Mia Johnson
Photography by Eva Kolenko

10 9 8 7 6 5 4 3 2 1

First Edition

skinnytaste
ONE & DONE

Bonus Recipes

THERE'S ALWAYS ROOM FOR MORE!
Here are a few exclusive recipes—all made in a single vessel—that I'm so excited for you to try. You'll find dreamy fried avocado tacos that are lightened up in your air fryer; a luxurious king crab leg dinner that takes only 15 minutes to prepare; a big healthy salad that's perfect for meal prep; and a simple, hearty black bean and chorizo soup that simmers all day in the slow cooker.

Air-Fryer Crunchy-Creamy Avocado Tacos SERVES 4

The first time I tried fried avocado tacos was at Torchy's in Austin, Texas, a place where they know how to make a mean taco. As much as I love avocados, I have a hard time taking something so healthy and deep-frying it. No worries—air fryer to the rescue! These vegetarian tacos are truly special, filled with "fried" avocados that are crunchy on the outside yet cool and creamy within.

PICO DE GALLO

½ cup chopped tomato

¼ cup chopped onion

1 tablespoon finely chopped fresh jalapeño pepper

1 tablespoon chopped fresh cilantro

1 teaspoon fresh lime juice

¼ teaspoon kosher salt

POBLANO-LIME SAUCE

¼ of a poblano pepper, with seeds

Olive oil spray (I like my Misto or Bertolli)

⅓ cup light sour cream

1 tablespoon fresh lime juice

⅛ teaspoon kosher salt

Freshly ground black pepper

TACOS

Olive oil spray (I like my Misto or Bertolli)

2 tablespoons all-purpose flour, wheat or gluten-free

1 large egg, lightly beaten

¾ cup panko bread crumbs*

¼ teaspoon chili powder*

¾ teaspoon kosher salt

8 ounces avocado (from 2 small Hass), cut into a total of 16 wedges

8 corn tortillas, warmed

½ cup shredded romaine lettuce

½ cup (2½ ounces) crumbled queso fresco

Chopped fresh cilantro, for garnish

*Read the label to make sure the product is gluten-free.

PER SERVING	2 tacos
CALORIES	358
FAT	17 g
SATURATED FAT	5 g
CHOLESTEROL	64 mg
CARBOHYDRATE	44 g
FIBER	8 g
PROTEIN	11 g
SUGARS	3 g
SODIUM	517 mg

SKINNY SCOOP

To warm the tortillas, heat them directly over the flame of a gas stove until lightly charred, about 30 seconds per side.

For the pico de gallo: In a small bowl, combine the tomato, onion, jalapeño, cilantro, lime juice, and salt.

For the poblano-lime sauce: Preheat an air fryer to 325°F. Spray the poblano with oil, place it in the air fryer basket, and cook for 15 minutes, until blistered and tender. Transfer to a small food processor or blender and add the sour cream, lime juice, salt, and black pepper to taste. Blend until smooth.

For the tacos: Preheat the air fryer to 390°F.

Place the flour on a plate. Place the egg in a shallow bowl. On a second plate, combine the panko, chili powder, and ¼ teaspoon of the salt.

Season the avocado with the remaining ½ teaspoon salt. Dredge each wedge first in the flour, then in the egg, and finally in the panko, shaking off any excess. Spray both sides with oil and set on a plate.

Working in batches, add the avocado wedges to the air fryer basket in a single layer. Cook for 8 minutes, turning halfway, until golden and crisp. Repeat with the remaining avocado wedges.

To serve, top each tortilla with 2 pieces of fried avocado. Top the avocado with 1 tablespoon each of shredded lettuce, pico de gallo, queso fresco, and poblano-lime sauce. Garnish with the cilantro.

Steamed King Crab Legs with Corn, Asparagus, and Lemon-Butter Sauce SERVES 2

We love splurging on king crab legs once in a while for a treat. It's ridiculously easy to cook—it takes only about 15 minutes from start to finish, sides included! Making them at home is also a lot cheaper than ordering them out, so for us, this is the way to go for a date night at home. My favorite trick to lighten up the butter sauce is to add lots of lemon juice to it once melted. It's delicious!

1½ pounds frozen king crab legs (about 4 large), rinsed

½ pound asparagus, tough ends trimmed

2 medium ears corn, husked

2 tablespoons unsalted butter

2 tablespoons fresh lemon juice

⅛ teaspoon kosher salt

Freshly ground black pepper

PER SERVING	2 crab legs + ¼ pound asparagus + 1 ear of corn
CALORIES	494
FAT	15 g
SATURATED FAT	8 g
CHOLESTEROL	173 mg
CARBOHYDRATE	24 g
FIBER	5 g
PROTEIN	68 g
SUGARS	6 g
SODIUM	n/a

Cut the crab legs at the joints so they will fit in the pot.

Pour 1 inch of water into a large pot and bring to a boil over high heat. Add the asparagus and corn, cover, and cook until the asparagus is crisp-tender, about 2 minutes. Transfer the asparagus to a plate and tent with foil. Continue cooking until the corn is cooked through, about 3 more minutes. Transfer to the plate of asparagus and tent with foil.

Add more water to maintain 1 inch, bring to a boil, and add the crab legs to the pot. Cover and cook until heated through, about 10 minutes.

Meanwhile, melt the butter in the microwave in a small microwave-safe bowl and stir in the lemon juice.

To serve, divide the corn and asparagus between 2 plates and sprinkle with the salt and pepper to taste. Using kitchen shears, cut a slit along the shells of the crab legs to easily remove the meat. Divide the crab between the plates and serve each with 2 tablespoons of the lemon-butter sauce for dipping.

SKINNY SCOOP

Look for crab legs that are bright in color and relatively free of clumps of ice crystals or freezer burn. You can also use snow crabs in place of the king crab.

Pressure Cooker Ultimate Reset Salad SERVES 2

This is the dish I crave after long trips away at conferences, retreats, or vacation. A big healthy salad full of my favorites: chickpeas, eggs, avocado, and crisp romaine. It just so happens that most of these ingredients are staples in my pantry and fridge. To switch it up, I sometimes add canned Italian tuna or swap the chickpeas for white beans.

2 large eggs

1 (15-ounce) can chickpeas,* rinsed and drained

2 tablespoons chopped red onion

5 teaspoons extra-virgin olive oil

5 teaspoons red wine vinegar

3 cups chopped lettuce, such as romaine

1½ cups chopped English cucumber

1 small tomato, sliced into wedges

2 ounces sliced avocado (from ½ small Hass)

¼ teaspoon kosher salt

Freshly ground black pepper

*Read the label to be sure this product is gluten-free.

PER SERVING	1 salad
CALORIES	548
FAT	26 g
SATURATED FAT	4 g
CHOLESTEROL	186 mg
CARBOHYDRATE	59 g
FIBER	5 g
PROTEIN	24 g
SUGARS	4 g
SODIUM	675 mg

Place the steaming rack/trivet in the bottom of an electric pressure cooker. Pour 1 cup water into the pot. Place the eggs on the rack. Cover and cook on high pressure for 5 minutes, until hard-boiled. Natural release for 5 minutes, then quick release until the pressure subsides. Quickly run the eggs under cold running water until they are cool enough to hold. Peel right away, discard the shells, and slice into quarters.

Meanwhile, in a medium bowl, combine the chickpeas, red onion, 1 teaspoon of the olive oil, and 1 teaspoon of the vinegar.

Divide the lettuce between 2 plates. Divide the chickpeas, cucumber, tomato, avocado, and eggs between the plates. Drizzle 2 teaspoons olive oil and 2 teaspoons vinegar over each salad and sprinkle with the salt and pepper to taste.

SKINNY SCOOP

You can double the recipe and make salads in jars for lunch for the week. To do so, make the dressing separately by whisking together the oil, vinegar, salt, and pepper. Into the bottom of the jars, first pour in the dressing. Then layer in the ingredients, starting with the chickpeas and finishing with the lettuce at the top. To eat, shake well and pour onto a plate.

NO PRESSURE COOKER? NO PROBLEM!

To make this in a medium pot, add the eggs and enough water to cover the eggs by 2 inches. Bring to a boil over medium heat, then remove the pot from the heat. Cover the pot and let it sit for 20 minutes. Quickly run the eggs under cold running water until they are cool enough to hold. Peel and slice into quarters, then proceed with the rest of the recipe.

Slow Cooker Black Bean and Chorizo Soup with Queso Fresco SERVES 8

Making this soup from scratch using dried beans takes about 10 hours to simmer in the slow cooker, but if you prep it at night and let it cook while you sleep, it will feel like it took no time at all!

1 pound dried black beans

1 cup chopped onion

3 garlic cloves, minced

4 large poblano peppers

3¾ cups low-sodium chicken broth*

3 small links dry chorizo (9 ounces total), sliced

1 fresh jalapeño pepper, halved lengthwise and seeded

1 tablespoon plus ½ teaspoon ground cumin

1 teaspoon smoked paprika

2 bay leaves

¾ teaspoon kosher salt

TOPPINGS

8 ounces sliced avocado (from 2 small Hass)

¼ cup chopped fresh cilantro

1 fresh jalapeño pepper, sliced into thin rings

¾ cup (4 ounces) crumbled queso fresco

1 lime, cut into 8 wedges

*Read the label to be sure this product is gluten-free.

PER SERVING	1⅓ cups + toppings
CALORIES	364
FAT	13 g
SATURATED FAT	4 g
CHOLESTEROL	19 mg
CARBOHYDRATE	45 g
FIBER	12 g
PROTEIN	19 g
SUGARS	4 g
SODIUM	406 mg

SKINNY SCOOP

Remember to soak the beans for at least 8 hours or use the quick-soak method on the package directions. Always buy dried beans from stores with a high turnover; old beans can take twice as long to cook as a fresh batch.

Rinse the beans and put them in a medium bowl. Cover with water by 2 inches and let soak for at least 8 hours or as long as overnight. Drain and discard the water.

Place the onion and garlic in a microwave-safe bowl and microwave on high for 1 minute to soften. Transfer to a slow cooker.

Working with 1 or 2 at a time, put the poblanos directly on the burner of a gas range set to medium heat or under the broiler. Using kitchen tongs, turn the poblanos as each side blisters until the skin is toasted and blackened, but do not blacken so much that it starts to peel or turn into ash, 4 to 5 minutes per side. Transfer the poblanos to a zip-top plastic bag. Once they are all in the bag, seal it and let the peppers "sweat" for about 15 minutes. Open the bag and see if they are ready by pinching part of the skin of each; if it tears and peels off easily, they're ready. Discard the skins and seeds from each poblano. Chop and transfer to the slow cooker.

To the slow cooker, add the broth, chorizo, jalapeño, 1 tablespoon of the cumin, the smoked paprika, and bay leaves. Cover and cook on low for 10 hours, until the beans are tender. Discard the bay leaves and stir in the remaining ½ teaspoon cumin and the salt. Place 2 cups of the beans and the jalapeño halves in a blender and puree until smooth. Stir the puree back into the slow cooker.

To serve, ladle the soup into 8 serving bowls. Top each with equal amounts of the avocado, cilantro, jalapeño rings, and queso fresco. Serve each with the lime wedge on the side.